OXFORD WORLD'S CLASSICS

ON THE NATURE OF THE UNIVERSE

LUCRETIUS (T. LUCRETIUS CARUS) lived in the terrible times of the collapse of the Roman republic into chaos and civil war, and this is reflected in his writing. Nothing is known for certain about his life, but scholars agree that he was born shortly after 100 BC and died between 55 and 50 BC. The *gens Lucretia* was aristocratic, and he was probably a member of it. His poem shows familiarity with the luxurious life-style of great houses in Rome, and his deep feeling for the countryside and its people and animals invites one to imagine that his family owned country estates. Certainly he was expensively educated, and apart from being a master of Latin he acquired a deep knowledge of the Greek language, its literature and philosophy.

There is a famous story told by St Jerome that he died of madness caused by a love-philtre, and composed his poem during lucid intervals. This is unlikely.

RONALD MELVILLE studied Classics at Magdalene College, Cambridge, and was a civil servant until his retirement in 1973. He was brother to the late A. D. Melville, who initiated this translation and who translated Ovid and Statius for Oxford World's Classics. Ronald Melville died in 2001.

DON FOWLER was Fellow and Tutor in Classics at Jesus College, Oxford.

PETA FOWLER is Lecturer in Classics at St Hugh's College, Oxford.

OXFORD WORLD'S CLASSICS

For over 100 years Oxford World's Classics have brought readers closer to the world's great literature. Now with over 700 titles—from the 4,000-year-old myths of Mesopotamia to the twentieth century's greatest novels—the series makes available lesser-known as well as celebrated writing.

The pocket-sized hardbacks of the early years contained introductions by Virginia Woolf, T. S. Eliot, Graham Greene, and other literary figures which enriched the experience of reading. Today the series is recognized for its fine scholarship and reliability in texts that span world literature, drama and poetry, religion, philosophy and politics. Each edition includes perceptive commentary and essential background information to meet the changing needs of readers.

OXFORD WORLD'S CLASSICS

▬▬

LUCRETIUS

On the Nature of the Universe

▬▬

Translated by
RONALD MELVILLE

With an Introduction and Notes by
DON AND PETA FOWLER

OXFORD
UNIVERSITY PRESS

OXFORD
UNIVERSITY PRESS

Great Clarendon Street, Oxford OX2 6DP

Oxford University Press is a department of the University of Oxford.
It furthers the University's objective of excellence in research, scholarship,
and education by publishing worldwide in

Oxford New York

Athens Auckland Bangkok Bogotá Buenos Aires Cape Town
Chennai Dar es Salaam Delhi Florence Hong Kong Istanbul Karachi
Kolkata Kuala Lumpur Madrid Melbourne Mexico City Mumbai Nairobi
Paris São Paulo Shanghai Singapore Taipei Tokyo Toronto Warsaw

with associated companies in Berlin Ibadan

Oxford is a registered trade mark of Oxford University Press
in the UK and in certain other countries

Published in the United States
by Oxford University Press Inc., New York

Translation © Sir Ronald Melville 1997
Editorial matter © Don and Peta Fowler 1997

British Library Cataloguing in Publication Data

Data available

Library of Congress Cataloging in Publication Data

Data available

ISBN 0-19-281761-2

3 5 7 9 10 8 6 4

Typeset by Hope Services (Abingdon) Ltd.
Printed in Great Britain by
Cox & Wyman Ltd.
Reading, Berkshire

TRANSLATOR'S PREFACE

I made this translation between May 1994 and November 1995, working for a couple of hours in the evening after dinner, with a glass of port at hand in case I got stuck. My brother Alan had completed a first draft of Book 1 and most of Book 2 when he died, and I started on it to help him. It is to him that I owe the joy and privilege of living for eighteen months in mind and spirit in the company of one of the world's greatest poets.

There are some admirable prose translations of Lucretius, by Munro, Bailey, Rouse, and Latham. I have been particularly helped by the last two in the elucidation of difficult passages, and I owe to them numerous happy turns of phrase. I am especially indebted to Professor E. J. Kenney of Cambridge University for his criticism and encouragement.

Above all I am indebted to Charterhouse, to those great teachers Frank Fletcher and A. L. Irvine, who laid in me the enduring foundations of classical scholarship and of a love of English poetry.

R.H.M.

CONTENTS

INTRODUCTION

'All nature, as it is in itself, consists of two things: there are bodies and there is void in which these bodies are and through which they move.' This statement could have come from the opening of any textbook of natural science before the modern elaboration of subatomic physics: in fact it is a translation of two lines by a Latin poet writing over 2,000 years ago, who based his account of the world on the theories of a Greek philosopher living over 200 years earlier still. Lucretius' *On the Nature of the Universe*, as its title suggests, gives an account of the world, the universe, and everything in terms of atomic physics. (The Latin title *De rerum natura* is even more general: it means literally 'On the Nature of Things'.) As the only detailed account of ancient atomism to come down to us more or less intact, it has been enormously influential on the development of both science and philosophy: and the account of the development of human civilization in Book 5 of the work has been of similar importance, through Rousseau and others, in the development of modern social science. In the light of this, it is easy simply to marvel at the poem's anticipations of modern ideas. But the work invites many other readings: as the product of first-century BC Rome and a key text in our constructions of the end of the Roman Republic, as a philosophical meditation on human happiness, and as perhaps the greatest didactic poem ever written in any language. The power of the work resides above all in the intersection of the reading practices which these different classifications invite.

We know less about the life of T. Lucretius Carus, the author of *On the Nature of the Universe*, than about almost any other Latin poet. His full name is given only in the manuscripts of his work, and nothing is known of his place of birth or social status, though both have been the subject of much speculation. The only secure date is a reference in a letter of Cicero (*To his Brother Quintus* 2. 10(9) 3) written in February 54 BC. In this Cicero praises Lucretius' *poemata* as possessing both flashes of genius (*ingenium*) and great artistry (*ars*)—that is, as combining the qualities of an inspired and a craftsmanlike poet. This is certainly a reference to *On the Nature of the Universe*, and, although *poemata* could refer to just selections, the easiest hypothesis is that Lucretius' poem was published by this time. The poem has often been thought to be unfinished: if so, Lucretius may have been dead by the time of the letter. But textual corruption rather than incompleteness may be responsible for the problems in the text. St Jerome (fourth–fifth century AD, but basing himself on the first–second-century AD writer Suetonius) reports the story (later made famous by Tennyson and others) that Lucretius wrote the poem in brief intervals of sanity after having been driven mad by a love-potion given him by his wife, and eventually committed suicide. If this story were true, it would be surprising that it was not used by Ovid half a century later in defending his *Art of Love* or by the fathers of the church attacking paganism and Epicureanism: it may be the result of a biographical reading of parts of Books 3 and 4, or of confusion with Lucretius' contemporary the politician C. Licinius Lucullus, of whom a similar story is told. Nor is there any reason to believe Jerome's statement that Cicero edited *On the Nature of the Universe* after its author's death. The tale to tell of Lucretius' life may be one of madness and premature death: equally, it may well be that the author was perfectly sane, and gave his poem to the world well before he died in his bed.

The addressee of the poem is one Memmius, who must be C. Memmius, a prominent politician associated also with Lucretius' poetic contemporary Catullus. Memmius was praetor in 58, and a candidate in 54 for the consulship of 53: but, after a complicated electoral pact that went wrong, he was found guilty of corruption in 52 and went into exile in Athens. In the summer of 51, Cicero wrote to him on behalf of the Epicurean group in Athens, asking him not to demolish what was left of Epicurus' house (*Letters to Friends* 13. 1. 3–4), and suggesting that Memmius was not on good terms with the Epicureans. It is not impossible that he had been annoyed by the dedication of *On the Nature of the Universe*: despite its warm praise of him in the prologue, the poem is orthodox in its Epicurean condemnation of political life (3. 59–84, 995–1002, 5. 117–35: see below). But in any case, the poem does not imply that Memmius was a convinced Epicurean (cf. 1. 102–3). There can be no clear distinction between Memmius as the didactic addressee and the more generalized second person of the reader, but Memmius' public persona will not have been irrelevant: *On the Nature of the Universe* is not unpolitical.

The times of its production were difficult ones for the Roman

Republic. *How* difficult can be seen from a remark of the historian Michael Crawford, justifying the tone of his book *The Roman Republic*:

> Some parts of this story may perhaps seem unduly dramatic; I can only say that a century like that between 133 BC and 31 BC, which killed perhaps 200,000 men in 91–82 and perhaps 100,000 men in 49–42, in both cases out of a free population of Rome and Italy of 4,500,000 and which destroyed a system of government after 450 years *was* a cataclysm.[1]

The events he singles out are the terrible 'Social War' between Rome and the other Italian cities, with the civil war between Marius and Sulla which took place more or less simultaneously, and the civil wars between Pompey and Caesar and in the aftermath of Caesar's death. But to the people living through them, the events between the death of Sulla in 78 BC and Caesar's crossing the Rubicon in 49 would hardly have seemed like the eye of the storm. The 60s and 50s BC saw increasing political violence at Rome, but the gangs on the streets were only a secondary weapon in the political struggle of the élite: the main battleground was the law courts. The easiest way to rid oneself of an opponent was to prosecute him on some charge, genuine or trumped-up: so Lucretius' addressee Memmius began his career as a Tribune of the People in 66 by unsuccessfully prosecuting Lucullus' brother Marcus, and as praetor in 58 he joined forces with the orator and poet Gaius Licinius Calvus in an attack on Caesar's tool Publius Vatinius. The trials which called forth Cicero's great speeches (and many lost ones) were mostly political; he himself had not bothered with a trial when he executed the leaders of the so-called 'Catilinarian Conspiracy' in 63, but it was the threat of prosecution by Clodius for that in 58 which forced him into exile for a year. And behind the street-fighting and the political trials was the real contest between the dynasts Caesar, Pompey, and Crassus; temporarily united in 60 by the pact we know as the 'First Triumvirate' (renewed in 56 at Lucca), each was in reality waiting for the chance to achieve domination. Men such as Clodius and Memmius were their tools, as they themselves arguably were in turn of the social and economic forces beginning to concentrate on the omega point that was to be the establishment of autocratic rule at Rome.

We know that within a decade of the publication of *On the Nature of the Universe* the Republic would be at an end: in the 50s, in this 'time of trouble' (I. 41) the disorder and corruption doubtless looked more like the normal state of political life at Rome. The perspective of *On the Nature of the Universe* is exactly that, a 'seeing through' and a 'looking down', as

[1] (London, 1978), 13.

Lucretius makes plain at the beginning of Book 2, where he contrasts the serene security of the wise with what has been called 'a picture of the typical life-style of a Roman aristocrat':[2]

> O wretched minds of men! O hearts so blind!
> How dark the life, how great the perils are
> In which whatever time is given is passed!
>
> (2. 14–16)

The condemnation at the beginning of Book 3 is even more trenchant (59 ff.), while later in the same book Lucretius offers a famous version of the myth of Sisyphus as an allegory for the political life that was the almost inevitable destiny of each and every member of the Roman élite:

> Sisyphus also in this life appears
> Before our eyes. He seeks the people's votes
> Athirst to get the Lictor's rods and axes,
> And always loses and retires defeated.
> For to seek power that's empty and never got
> And always vainly toil and sweat for it
> This is to strain to push up the steep hill
> The rock that always from the very top
> Rolls headlong down again to the plain below.
>
> (3. 995–1002)

The solution that Lucretius offers to this human misery is a simple one: conversion to the doctrines of the Greek philosopher Epicurus, who over 200 years earlier had seen

>   that deep in every home
> Were aching hearts and torments of the mind
> All hapless, self-inflicted without pause,
> And sorrows breeding furious laments.
>
> (6. 14–16)

The Master himself was born in 341 BC, six years after Plato's death in 347 and six years before Aristotle, at the height of his powers, was to set up his school in the Lyceum. He was born on Samos, but he was an Athenian citizen, his father having gone to the island as a colonist in 352; accordingly, when Epicurus was 18 he went to Athens as an 'ephebe'— that is, to undergo the newly reorganized two-year period of 'national service' which was the prerequisite to becoming a full citizen. The years

---

[2] E. Wistrand, *Caesar and Contemporary Roman Society* (Gothenburg, 1979), 58.

of his ephebate saw the death of Alexander the Great and Athens's brief revolt against Macedonian power; one consequence of its defeat was the loss of Samos. Epicurus joined his parents at Colophon in Asia Minor. His movements for the next fifteen years are not completely certain, but he was at some stage active as a philosopher and teacher at Mytilene on Lesbos and at Lampsacus on the Hellespont. By the time he returned to Athens in 306 he already had a reputation and devoted disciples; he bought the 'Garden' which was to remain the headquarters of the school until its disappearance in late antiquity and established a small philosophical community. He presided over this community until his death in 270 BC, by which time it was the centre of a philosophical network expanding beyond its original bases in Asia Minor and Athens to the whole of the Greek world. From his last days, we have a will leaving the Garden to his successors, and a letter of farewell to a young Epicurean, Idomeneus:

On this truly happy day of my life, as I am at the point of death, I write this to you. The disease in my bladder and stomach are pursuing their course, lacking nothing of their natural severity: but against all this is the joy in my heart at the recollection of my conversations with you. Do you, as I might expect from your devotion from boyhood to me and to philosophy, take good care of the children of Metrodorus.   (Diogenes Laertius 10. 22, trans. C. Bailey)

It was this inner calm that attracted men to Epicurus and what he offered to give them with his philosophy. It was a calm which was achieved in spite of the events of history which were taking place outside the Garden. Like Lucretius, Epicurus lived in 'interesting times': the half-century between his ephebate and death saw the bitter aftermath of Macedonian hegemony as the successors of Alexander fought to divide the Greek world between them. The warlords battled over Athens, perhaps less for military than for prestige reasons: in defending Epicurus' character against ancient criticisms, one of the points Diogenes Laertius makes is that 'although Greece was at that time in great straits he continued to live there, and only once or twice made a voyage to Ionia and the neighbourhood to see his friends' (10. 10, trans. C. Bailey). The worst moment of all came in 294, when the city was attacked by Demetrius Poliorcetes: in describing the horrors of that siege, Plutarch tells us that starvation was so acute that a father and a son fought over a dead mouse, but 'Epicurus kept his companions alive by counting out and distributing beans amongst them' (*Life of Demetrius* 34. 2). It was spiritual rather than material sustenance, however, which Epicurus offered to the inhabitants of the Garden in those troubled times. The atmosphere in the community must have been a little like that in the ashram of a modern-day guru. The disciples—who included both men and women—were united not only by strong communal affection and a shared philosophy but also by devotion to their master. This devotion to the person of Epicurus was a striking feature of the school, as it still is centuries later for Lucretius, who praises his master in the prologues to Books, 1, 3, 5, and 6. The praise may seem at times excessive, and unpleasantly redolent of that offered to modern-day charlatans (Plutarch is scandalized at an account by Epicurus of how his young disciple Colotes embraced his knees: *Against Colotes* 1117b). But in a turbulent world Epicurus gave men the peace they wanted and could not find outside the Garden.

The original context of Epicurus' teaching was in the communities he established, and he lays great stress on the practice of philosophical discussion and on the oral apprehension and memorization of his doctrines. This stance puts Epicurus in the line of moral educators whose archetype was Socrates and whose most conspicuous representatives in the generation before Epicurus had been Diogenes and Pyrrho, the effective founders of Cynicism and Scepticism respectively. Unlike these men, however, Epicurus wrote books, and a large number of them, on a variety of topics in physics and ethics (over forty titles are known). The most important work was the immensely long *On Nature* in thirty-seven books, whose title is recalled in Lucretius' own title. This somewhat discursive work was written over a period of years, and because of its very length it must have been used mostly as a reference work by later Epicureans; luckily there were epitomes which gave the essentials of the philosophy in a shorter compass. Epicurus seems to have regarded it as highly important that such summaries should be available, and the only works of his that have come down to us whole rather than in fragmentary quotations or papyrus remains belong to this class. These works, preserved in the *Lives of the Philosophers* of Diogenes Laertius (?third century AD), are the *Letter to Herodotus* (a general epitome of the philosophy), the *Letter to Pythocles* (on the 'phenomena of the sky'), the *Letter to Menoeceus* (on ethics), and the *Master Sayings* (a collection of forty maxims for living). Another collection of maxims, put together by a later Epicurean, was discovered in the nineteenth century, the so-called *Vatican Sayings*.

Later Epicureans also wrote extensively, from the time of the Master himself to the later Roman Empire, though in most cases we only have fragments. Lucretius' contemporary Philodemus, active at Rome from the 80s BC, wrote a large number of works, extensive fragments of which were found in the so-called 'Villa of the Papyri' in Herculaneum (Ercolano), near Naples, at the end of the eighteenth century (a fragment of Lucretius has recently been identified amongst the same collection). The most eloquent memorial of all, however, is perhaps a huge inscription put up in the second century AD in the centre of Oenoanda (in Lycia, now southern Turkey) by one Diogenes. One of the largest Greek inscriptions known, it gives a full exposition of Epicureanism in several separate treatises. A passage near its beginning eloquently attests to the continuing attraction of the Epicurean way, and why figures such as Diogenes and Lucretius felt it important to try to save their fellow human beings:

Having already reached the sunset of my life (being almost on the verge of departure from the world on account of old age), I wanted, before being overtaken by death, to compose a [fine] anthem [to celebrate the] fullness [of pleasure] and to help those who are well-constituted. Now if only one person or two or three or four or five or six or any larger number you choose, sir, provided that it is not very large, were in a bad predicament, I should address them individually and do all in my power to give them the best advice. But, as I have said before, the majority of people suffer from a common disease, as in a plague, with their false notions about things, and their number is increasing (for in mutual emulation they catch the disease from one another, like sheep); moreover, [it is] right to help [also] generations to come (for they belong to us, though they are still unborn); and, besides, love of humanity prompts us to aid also the foreigners who come here. Now, since the remedies of the inscription reach a larger number of people, I wished to use this stoa to advertise publicly the [medicines] that bring salvation. These medicines we have put [fully] to the test; for we have dispelled the fears [that grip] us without justification, and, as for pains, those that are groundless we have completely excised, while those that are natural we have reduced to an absolute minimum, making their magnitude minute. (fr. 3, trans. M. F. Smith)

In setting out the Master's philosophy, then, Lucretius places himself in a long line of Epicureans, though he is unique in doing so extensively in verse. Much of the poem is concerned with what we would call physical science, but the reason for this focus is that the Epicureans believed that it was vital to understand the basic principles of the universe if one was not to have 'false opinions' about the world which would wreck one's happiness. Epicurus aimed to give men peace of mind, what he called *ataraxia*, 'being undisturbed'; the metaphysics, the physics, the epistemology, the psychology, the theology were all designed to provide this peace. There was no room for the high Platonic or Stoic ideal of Tennyson's *Ulysses*, 'to follow knowledge like a sinking star | beyond the utmost reach of human thought'; for Epicurus, we need knowledge only because without it we are unhappy:

If doubts about celestial phenomena did not cause us disturbance, nor those about death, that it might really concern us, nor the failure to realize the limits of pains and desires, then we would have no need of scientific reasoning. (*Master Sayings* 11)

First of all then do not think that there is any other end to the knowledge of celestial phenomena . . . than peace of mind (*ataraxia*) and sure confidence. (*Letter to Pythocles* 85)

Epicureanism has been called the philosophy of certainty, and Pythocles is offered not just *ataraxia* but also 'sure confidence'. Anxieties are caused by doubts; the explanations which remove these doubts must themselves be securely based or the doubts will return. There is no room for scepticism, and the Epicurean watchword was 'All sensations are true'. If I see a cow, my perception of that cow is occasioned by something real, an image emanating from the cow which represents to me the way the cow really is. When I learned the word 'cow', a real cow was pointed out to me; every time I say or think the word, that original clear image should be present so long as I have not let my mind be distorted by mischievous misdefinitions of 'cowness'. If I look at the world and think along with it in its terms, I cannot go wrong; as Epicurus says in the *Letter to Herodotus* (50), 'falsehood and error always lie in the addition of opinion'. Scientific reasoning—*physiologia*—is a continual recall to look at the world the way it really is, and because of this it needs the assurance provided by Epicurean epistemology. Epicurus called this branch of his philosophy *kanonikon*, from the Greek *kanon*, a rule, and Lucretius develops the metaphor in his own way in Book 4:

> Lastly, in a building, if the ruler is crooked
> And the square is faulty and misses the straight line
> And the level is even slightly unbalanced,
> The whole house then will of necessity
> Be wrongly constructed and be falling over,
> Warped, sloping, leaning forward, leaning back,
> All out of proportion, so that some parts seem
> Ready to collapse, and the whole destined to fall,
> A victim to the first false measurements.
> So your reasoning about things must be false and warped
> Whenever it is based upon false senses.

(4. 513–21)

There is an apparent paradox here, however. The senses are the way in which we discover reality; but the reality they reveal is one of an infinite number of atoms blindly moving in an infinite void, now coming together to form compounds, indeed whole worlds, now coming apart as these worlds and the compounds in them are dissolved. This revelation is very different from the phenomenal world; and Epicurus' predecessor Democritus (fifth century BC), who offered a very similar vision, encapsulated the contrast in a famous dictum that 'colour is by convention, sweet by convention, a compound by convention . . . what is real are the void and the atoms' (fr. B125). Epicurus reacted strongly against this because he thought that it devalued the world of the senses as a guarantee of reality, but some form of the duality is essential to his philosophy also. Understanding involves both 'the face of nature and her laws' (*On the Nature of the Universe* 1. 148 = 2. 61, 3. 39, 6. 41), both the world of colour, light, and sound and the blind dance of the atoms in the void. This duality is not an unbridgeable gulf; our experience of the world can lead us to an apprehension of its secrets. In the first place, we can use the concepts derived from the world about us as models for thought about the inaccessible world of the atoms. If we wish to think about atomic movement, for instance, Lucretius suggests we picture the motion of dust particles in a ray of light:

> You will see a multitude of tiny bodies
> All mingling in a multitude of ways
> Inside the sunbeam, moving in the void,
> Seeming to be engaged in endless strife,
> Battle, and warfare, troop attacking troop,
> And never a respite, harried constantly,
> With meetings and with partings everywhere.
> From this you can imagine what it is
> For atoms to be tossed perpetually
> In endless motion through the mighty void.

> (2. 116–24)

But more importantly the visible world can signify, can be a sign of the visible. It cannot do so directly; to use Epicurus' legal metaphor, the phenomenal world cannot 'witness to' the unseen. But it can 'witness against'; we can show that certain hypotheses about reality are ruled out by the world around us. The hypothesis that the atoms are at rest in compounds is ruled out by the constant motion of the dust particles: as Lucretius puts it, 'their dancing shows that within matter | Secret and

hidden motions also lie' (2. 127–8). In this way we can move from the
phenomenal world to the level of the atoms and grasp the reality of
things:

> The terrors of the mind flee all away,
> The walls of heaven open, and through the void
> Immeasurable, the truth of things I see.

> (3. 16–17)

It is on this epistemological basis that Epicurus erects his metaphysics
and physics; the void and the atoms, their eternal motion, the infinite
universe with its infinite worlds. To grasp this construction is to see that
there is no place in it for a providential god binding the elements together
or controlling the seasons for our good. To see how compounds come to
be and fall apart is to appreciate how the life of a human being is but a
special case of this process and how there is nothing still in existence to
be troubled by death once it has taken place. Gods there are indeed, for
we see them in our dreams; death is indeed all about us; but they are not
the gods of popular belief, interfering in our lives, and it is not the death
of mythology, the prelude to purgatory, hell, or just the unknown.
Epicureanism offers at once novelty—a new version of reality—and a
comforting reassurance that things are, after all, as they are; no hell
beneath us, above us only sky.

This double aspect of the philosophy, at once novel and familiar,
continues into its most famous doctrine, the exaltation of pleasure as the
end of life and the flight from pain as the only evil. To pursue pleasure
and avoid pain is natural, and no argument is needed to sustain the doctrine, as Cicero makes the Epicurean Torquatus remark:

Every animal, as soon as it is born, seeks for pleasure and delights in it as the
Chief Good, while it recoils from pain as the Chief Evil and so far as possible
avoids it. This it does as long as it remains unperverted, at the prompting of
Nature's own unbiased and honest verdict. Hence Epicurus refuses to admit any
necessity for argument or discussion to *prove* that pleasure is desirable and pain
to be avoided. These facts, he thinks, are perceived by the sense, as that fire is hot,
snow white, honey sweet, none of which things need to be proved by elaborate
argument: it is enough merely to draw attention to them.   (*On the Final Terms
of Good and Evil* 1. 30, trans. H. Rackham)

We have only to listen to our bodies, uncorrupted by false ideas: 'the voice
of the flesh is: not to be hungry, not to be thirsty, not to be cold' (*Vatican
Sayings* 33), a voice Lucretius turns into the bark of nature:

> Do you not see that Nature cries for this,
> And only this, that pain from out the body
> Shall be removed away, and mind enjoy
> Sweet sense of pleasure, freed from care and fear?

> (2. 16–19)

But this simple and natural truth was expressed in a complex theory of pleasure and pain whose details are still controversial, which to many in both ancient and modern times has seemed bizarre and unconvincing, and which to Lucretius seemed a great and new discovery of his Master:

> Therefore with words of truth he purged men's hearts
> And set a limit to desire and fear.
> He showed the nature of that highest good
> For which all mankind strives, and showed the way,
> The strait and narrow path which leads to it
> If we go forward with unswerving steps.

> (6. 24–8)

As with the physics and epistemology, Epicurean moral theory offers simultaneously a recall to the way we have always really known the world to be and a new understanding of it.

The basis of this understanding is a double division of the notion of pleasure. The one division, between pleasure of the body and pleasure of the mind, is obvious and is shared with other ancient philosophies. But the second division is more important and more unusual. Epicurus distinguished between what he called *katastematic* pleasures, pleasures of the 'steady state' (*katastema*), and *kinetic* pleasures, pleasures of motion (*kinesis*). The latter are what we most obviously think of as pleasures: the pleasures of the senses, of pleasant-tasting food and drink, of pleasant sights and sounds, of sex (i.e. the pleasures of touch). These are the result of stimulation or 'variation' of the sense organs, and when the stimulation ceases, they cease. When stimulation is absent, we have no feeling of pleasure or pain in the sense organs. These pleasures are essential to our notion of pleasure; in a famous dictum which succeeded in shocking many, Epicurus said that he could not conceive of the good if one removed the pleasures of taste and sex and of pleasant sounds and sights (fr. 67). Whereas for others the desire for these pleasures was a fatal chain which enslaved men's higher functions, for Epicurus they were perfectly harmless so long as they did not cause pain later on as a side effect and so long as one had the correct attitude to them. What that correct attitude was was spelled out in the distinction between 'natural' and 'necessary' desires:

Of desires, some are necessary, some natural but not necessary, some neither necessary nor natural but the result of empty opinion. The desire for food and drink and for clothing is necessary; that for sex is natural but not necessary; but that for a certain kind of food or a certain kind of clothing or a certain kind of sex is neither natural nor necessary.   (fr. 496)

The desire for the pleasures of the senses is not necessary—one can live on gruel and water, one does not die without sex—but it is perfectly natural. As soon, however, as one starts to want not just something pleasant to drink but a particular vintage of a particular wine, and not just sexual pleasure but sexual pleasure with a particular person, one is no longer listening to the body, but to the mind; an obsession is developing whose inevitable consequence is displeasure that the desired object is missing or anxiety that it might be.

It is the first group in the Epicurean division of desires, the desires which are both natural and necessary, whose satisfaction provides *katastematic* pleasure, the pleasure of the 'steady state'. Without food, drink, and warmth we die; when we are hungry, thirsty, or cold, our body has a physical lack, a gap in its constitution which must be filled, which causes us pain, and which, if not dealt with, will lead to death. Lucretius uses the image of a building in danger of collapse:

> So food is taken, to prop up the body,
> And working inside renews the strength and stops
> Through veins and limbs the gaping desire to eat.

> (4. 867–9)

The desire for food, drink, and warmth is thus urgent and implacable; unlike the desire for *kinetic* pleasure, it demands satisfaction. But also unlike the desire for *kinetic* pleasure, it is finite in this demand. As the holes in the body are filled, the parts which were deficient cease to cause us pain and attain the pleasure of the steady state, of painless satisfaction; and the limit to this process is the filling of all the holes. Once the deficiency is completely remedied, further ingestion of food can bring no more *katastematic* pleasure, though we may enjoy the taste of the food as a *kinetic*, sensual, pleasure. As Epicurus puts it in the third *Master Saying*, 'The boundary to the size of pleasures is the removal of all that is painful', and more explicitly in the eighteenth saying, 'The pleasure in the flesh is not increased, when once that which causes pain is removed, but only varied.' So the desire for these pleasures also, though demanding satisfaction, is no tyrannical monster, dragging our rational minds in wayward directions, but is easily satisfied. If one is hungry, all the body needs is for its deficiency to be remedied; as far as it is concerned, anything will do, even battery chickens and soya mince.

This fact, that the real needs of the body are easily satisfied, is the key to the understanding of the links between Epicurus' theory of pleasure and pain and the rest of his philosophy. Just as there are *katastematic* and *kinetic* pleasures of the body (*aponia*, 'lack of distress', and *euphrosyne*, 'enjoyment', respectively), so there are of the mind. The *kinetic* pleasure of the mind, *chara* or 'joy', occurs when the mind reflects upon *kinetic* pleasure of the body and concentrates on its sensations. The term for *katastematic* pleasure of the mind, however, we have met before; it is *ataraxia*, 'freedom from disturbance'. We saw that a man who is disturbed by fear of the gods and of death cannot be happy; and he cannot even enjoy the everyday pleasures of the body, *katastematic* and *kinetic*. Lucretius uses the image of a murky pool:

> headlong out of doors
> The fear of Hell be thrown, which from its depths
> Disquiets the life of man, suffusing all
> With the blackness of death, and leaving no delights
> Pure and unsullied.

(3. 37-40)

But nor can a man possess *ataraxia* if he is continually worried that he will lose all that is worth living for. By reminding him how small his needs really are, and how easily satisfied, that anxiety is removed. In fact the fear of deprivation, whether of things the person really needs, like food, or of things which he only thinks he needs, things like wealth and power which are the object of desires neither necessary nor natural: this fear participates in a complex syndrome with the fears of the gods and of death. We fear the gods partly because of what they may take from us; we fear death similarly as a deprivation of the things we think we need. But because we are so terrified of the gods and death, we cling to the objects of our desire as if to life itself. As Lucretius remarks in the prologue to Book 3, 'Greed and blind lust for fame . . . These wounds of life in no small part are fed | By fear of death' (3. 59-64). There is thus a syndrome of fears and desires which intensify each other in turn and which constitute for the Epicurean the normal state of humanity before the saving message of Epicurus.

To deal with this syndrome, Epicurus must attack on a broad front; he must not only oppose directly the erroneous ideas about the world which lead to a belief in interfering gods and an irrational terror of death; he must also, with his philosophy of pleasure, remove that fear of want and pain which is increased by those fears and in turn increases them. Lucretius' poem concentrates on the direct attack on the fears of the gods and of death, but we are not allowed to forget the message about pleasure and pain. It is most obviously present in the prologue to Book 2, which refers to the third and fourth of the *Master Sayings* as the prologue to Book I referred to the first pair, but it is alluded to throughout the poem, in the anthropology of Book 5 as much as the physiology of Book 4, and the final test of our understanding of the doctrine, as of the rest of Lucretius' message, is the plague which closes the whole poem. There are many details about Epicureanism about which Lucretius is silent; as a rounded picture of the philosophy in all its aspects it cannot compete even with an epitome like the *Letter to Herodotus*, which itself omits much. But in its relentless reason assault on men's fears, of the gods, of death, of want, of pain, it gives the true essence of Epicureanism.

On the Nature of the Universe is an exposition of Epicureanism: it is also a poem, in the original some 7,400 lines of Latin hexameters. Whether or not it failed to receive the final corrections of its author, it is substantially complete: it opens with an elaborate prologue, and the prologue to Book 6 states explicitly that this is the final book (6. 92–5). The ending is abrupt, and textually corrupt, though we may well have the final lines displaced (see note on 6. 1247–51). There are a number of closural features at the end, most notably a recall of the funeral of Hector at the end of Homer's *Iliad*, and, although the ending on the plague at Athens and the many deaths it caused is in stark contrast to the opening description of the first day of spring and the appeal for help to Venus, the polarity can be made to have point. By the end of the poem the reader will have passed from birth to death, and in the process come to see like Lucretius that the angst-ridden activity of everyday life is pointless, and that true happiness must be sought elsewhere.

As well as the great initial prologue to Book 1, each of the other books also has a prologue, and the concluding section of each book in some way stands apart from the rest of the book: striking examples are the attack on love in Book 4, and the final plague. Each book is a unity in terms both of structure and of subject matter. *Book 1* deals with the basic metaphysical and physical premises of Epicureanism, beginning with the proposition that nothing comes to be out of nothing, and concluding with a description of the collapse of our world which is presented as a counterfactual consequence of the belief that all elements tend towards the centre of the earth but which anticipates the Epicurean accounts of the death of our world at the end of Book 2 and in Book 5. *Book 2* deals with the motion and shape of the atoms, and how these are relevant to the relationship between primary and secondary qualities: it concludes with the important Epicurean doctrine of the infinite number of worlds in the universe, and the connected proposition that our world has both a birth and a death (recalling the end of Book 1). *Book 3* gives an account of the nature of the human soul, and argues both that it is mortal and that, because of this, death is not to be feared. *Book 4* discusses a variety of psychological and physiological phenomena, especially perception, and argues against scepticism: as remarked above, it concludes with an attack on love, seen as a mental delusion. *Book 5* argues for the mortality of our world, and then gives a rationalist and anti-providentialist account of its creation and early history, concluding with the section on the development of human civilization which is perhaps the most famous part of the poem. *Book 6* then proceeds to account for those phenomena of our world which are most likely to lead to false belief in the gods—thunder and lightning, earthquakes, volcanoes, etc.—and ends with the aetiology of disease and the plague at Athens.

This clearly defined book structure is more typical of prose philosophical treatises than of hexameter poetry, and it is replicated at levels both above and below that of the individual book. The books form three pairs, in which Books 1 and 2 deal with atomic phenomena up to the level of the compound, Books 3 and 4 deal with human beings, and Books 5 and 6 deal with the world: there is thus a clear sense of expanding horizons, as we move from the atomic to the macroscopic level. The twin targets of the work as a whole are fear of the gods and of death: the first and last pairs deal more with the former fear, by explaining phenomena that would otherwise be felt to require divine intervention in the world, while the central books, and especially Book 3, tackle the fear of death head on. But the two motives are intermingled throughout the work. The six books may also be organized into two halves, with Books 1–3 dealing with basic premises, Books 4–6 with what follows from those basic premises: the problematic prologue to Book 4 (repeated almost verbatim from 1. 921–50: see notes), with its stress on Lucretius' twin roles as poet and philosopher, thus functions as a 'proem in the middle' for the second half. The existence of more than one possible structural analysis in this way is typical of *On the Nature of the Universe* as a whole (contrast 3. 31–40 with 5. 55–63).

Below the level of the book, the subject matter is carefully delineated and individual propositions within sections signposted with markers such as 'First', 'Next', and 'Finally': the verse is similarly often articulated into blocks of two or more verses, with careful arrangement of words within the block. This division of the text corresponds to the Epicurean stress on the intelligibility of phenomena: everything has a *ratio* or systematic explanation, the world can be analysed and understood. If we are to believe Cicero, however, this is in marked contrast to the formlessness of earlier Epicurean writing in Latin (Amafinius and Rabirius: cf. Cic. *Academica* 1. 5, *On Ends* 1. 22, 29, 2. 30, 3. 40, and see notes on 5. 337).

Every major proposition in *On the Nature of the Universe* can be paralleled in other Epicurean sources, and it is likely that the majority at least of the arguments for these propositions also existed in the Epicurean tradition. We do not know, however, to what extent the poem had a single main source, and if so, what that source was. The title (cf. 1. 25) recalls that of Epicurus' major treatise 'On Nature' mentioned above, but the structure of that work as we know it from papyrus fragments differs in significant respects from that of *On the Nature of the Universe* and that presumably also goes for any (lost) epitome. There is a much closer correspondence, however, with the extant *Letter to Herodotus* of Epicurus, passages of which are closely translated (see notes on 1. 159 etc.), although *On the Nature of the Universe* is longer and the order of topics is sometimes changed. One plausible hypothesis is that the *Letter to Herodotus* provided the basic core of the poem, but this was expanded from a variety of other sources. Other prose philosophical and scientific sources are also drawn on, including Plato and the medical writing ascribed to Hippocrates (see notes to 3. 526 , 3. 487, etc.), though we can never be certain that some of this had not already been assimilated into the atomist tradition. The final part of Book 3 in particular (with the prologues to Books 2 and 3 and the end of Book 4) contains material from the so-called 'diatribe' tradition of practical philosophical rhetoric, in which a direct assault is made on the false beliefs of common humanity. The poem also draws on a wide range of literary texts in both Greek and Latin, from Homer to Ennius and Latin drama (see notes). Particularly important is the lost philosophical didactic poetry of Empedocles (fifth century BC), which is known only in fragments whose reconstruction is controversial, but which, like *On the Nature of the Universe*, set out in verse an account of the workings of the universe. Empedocles' use of a theory of four elements is criticized (1. 705–829), and the religious content of his verses often perverted to Lucretius' own ends (see notes to

1. 1116, 5. 100 , 5. 226) but his two opposed principles of 'Love' and 'Strife' influence the prologue and elsewhere (see note to 1. 33), and his stance as a 'master of truth' offering an important secret to his audience is one that is enthusiastically taken up by Lucretius.

In its dense negotiation with a wide variety of texts in different genres, *On the Nature of the Universe* is typical of Latin poetry: an obvious comparison is with Virgil's *Aeneid*, written some thirty years after Lucretius' poem (and engaged in a constant dialogue with it). Philosophical themes are common in Latin poetry—the *Odes* of Horace, for instance, often deal with ethical topics—but what distinguishes *On the Nature of the Universe* is the centrality of its engagement with science and philosophy. Similarly, modern readers are likely to approach the text with a variety of interests, as simultaneously a first-century BC philosophical treatise, an account of ancient science, and one of the greatest of all Latin poems. Traditionally, the differing reading practices of the text's critics have been polarized around an opposition between 'philosophy'—perhaps more properly science—and poetry. The 'problem' of the text has been seen as that of reconciling these two opposed ways of reading, and the 'solution' of much modern criticism has been to show how much, in fact, the poetics of the poem are in harmony with its philosophical and scientific concerns. The text gives a central role, for instance, to a rich and dense use of the pre-eminent poetic trope of metaphor: it is no coincidence that the article which is credited with first stressing this in modern times (by H. Sykes Davies) was published in T. S. Eliot's journal *Criterion*.[3] Lucretius' revaluation this century parallels that of Donne and the Metaphysicals as recuperated by Pound and Eliot. Lucretius' metaphors, as David West showed in his brilliant little study *The Imagery and Poetry of Lucretius*,[4] are sharp and complex, though they have not always been well dealt with by his translators and commentators. But metaphors and models such as the atoms as 'seeds' have become in recent years a central concern of scientists and philosophers as well, and there are obvious parallels between a poet's concern with the concrete specifics of language and the Epicurean call to pay attention to the 'first image' associated with each word. This is one aspect of a general call to look at the world 'before our eyes' which again can be seen as simultaneously a poet's interest in evocative description and a scientist's concern with the empirical basis of hypotheses about the unseen. 'Look and think' is an injunction both can share. Another aspect of this is the extensive use, especially in the first

[3] H. Sykes Davies. 'Notes on Lucretius', *Criterion*, II (1931–2), 25–42.
[4] (Edinburgh, 1969).

part of the poem, of the argument-form known as *modus tollendo tollens* or 'denying the consequent', whose form is:

If P, then Q (e.g. 'If there is no void, there is no motion')
But not Q ('But (we can see that) it is not the case that there is no motion');
Therefore not P ('Therefore it is not the case that there is no void').

The process of refuting hypotheses about the unknown by reference to observed reality was known to the Epicureans as 'witnessing against': it is the basic argument form of science, which formulates hypotheses and attempts to refute them with empirical data. But the appeal to empirical reality often contained in the second premiss—'but you can *see* that this consequence cannot be true'—is also a key poetic feature of *On the Nature of the Universe*. On the one hand, the descriptions of the world as it is serve constantly to ground readers in lived reality, bring them back to the way things are, the ordinary and comprehensible life that we live before we begin to be assailed by philosophical doubts. On the other, the descriptions of the world as it is figured by the opponents play a major part in what has always been seen as a strong satirical element in the poem, mocking the delusions of the unphilosophic, as in the very first argument:

> For if things came out of nothing, all kinds of things
> Could be produced from all things. Nothing would need a seed.
> Men could arise from the sea, and scaly fish
> From earth, and birds hatch in the sky.
> Cattle and farm animals and wild beasts of every kind
> Would fill alike farmlands and wilderness,
> Breed all mixed up, all origins confused.
> Nor could the fruits stay constant on the trees,
> But all would change, all would bear everything.
>
> (1. 159–66)

The satirical edge to the poem goes deeper than this, however. Epicureanism is in one sense a negative philosophy, in that the emphasis falls on removing the confusions and delusions of unphilosophic humanity, all the false opinions that prevent human beings from being happy. Its central metaphors are of purging and liberating, freeing people from complex accretions of popular belief: its positive content is much simpler, to live a natural life listening to the voice of the body, 'not to be hungry, not to be thirsty, not to be cold . . .'. It shares this stance of heroic removal of superstition and nonsense with much of the rhetoric of modern science, with its implicit or explicit role of sweeping away humbug and recalling us to the plain and simple facts. This Baconian project was famously celebrated in the poem Abraham Cowley wrote 'To the Royal Society' on its foundation:

> Some few exalted Spirits this latter age has shown,
> That labour'd to assert the Liberty
> (From Guardians who were now Usurpers grown)
> Of this old Minor still, Captiv'd Philosophy;
> But 'twas rebellion call'd to fight
> For such a long-oppressed Right.
> Bacon at last, a mighty Man arose
> Whom a wise King and Nature chose
> Lord Chancellor of both their Lawes,
> And boldly undertook the injur'd pupils cause.
>
> Authority, which did a Body boast,
> Though 'twas but air condens'd and stalk'd about,
> Like some old Giant's more Gigantic Ghost,
> To terrifie the Learned Rout
> With the plain Magick of true Reason's Light,
> He chac'd out of our sight,
> Nor suffer'd Living men to be misled
> By the vain shadows of the Dead:
> To graves, from whence it rose, the conquer'd Phantome fled;
> He broke that Monstrous God which stood
> In midst of th'Orchard, and the whole did claim,
> Which with a useless Sith of Wood,
> And something else not worth a name,
> (Both vast for shew, yet neither fit
> Or to defend or to Beget;
> Ridiculous and Senceless Terrors!) made
> Children and superstitious Men afraid.
> The Orchard's open now, and free;
> Bacon has broke that Scar-crow Deitie.

Cowley's praise of Bacon is based on Lucretius' praise of Epicurus in 1. 62–79:

> When human life lay foul for all to see
> Upon the earth, crushed by the burden of religion,
> Religion which from heaven's firmament
> Displayed its face, its ghastly countenance,
> Lowering above mankind, the first who dared

> Raise mortal eyes against it, first to take
> His stand against it, was a man of Greece.
> He was not cowed by fables of the gods
> Or thunderbolts or heaven's threatening roar,
> But they the more spurred on his ardent soul
> Yearning to be the first to break apart
> The bolts of nature's gates and throw them open.

The heroism of this revolt in the name of earth and humanity against the empty tyranny of the gods goes closely in *On the Nature of the Universe* with Lucretius' poetic empiricism, which constantly recalls us from the mists and darkness of false belief to the plain light of scientific reasoning. Poet and philosopher/scientist unite in inviting us simply to use our eyes and see the world for what it is, to *see through* the 'words | Of terror from the priests' (I. 103). It is the enlightenment rhetoric of a Voltaire, echoed in modern times by scientists like Richard Dawkins: a recall from flights of fancy to what Epicurus called 'sober reckoning', to the *nature of things*.

And yet the very terms in which this revolt is celebrated so powerfully must give us pause for thought. What attracts us to the assault on myth in *On the Nature of the Universe*, the great Enlightenment project of freeing humanity from delusion, attracts because of its own mythical form: at its heart are those images of Nature unchained, of the hero Epicurus challenging heaven and bringing back victory over it.

> The loathsome mask has fallen, the man remains
> Sceptreless, free, uncircumscribed, but man
> Equal, unclassed, tribeless, and nationless,
> Exempt from awe, worship, degree, the king
> Over himself . . .

as the Platonist Shelley put it in a passage of *Prometheus Unbound* full of Lucretian echoes. This sort of rhetoric is not sober reckoning, but an inspiring call to liberation whose efficacy depends on means denied by the scientism it champions. Epicurus said that the only virtue of style was clarity, and the rhetoric of *On the Nature of the Universe* endorses this view of language as ideally a transparent window onto reality. If we can but drain language of its false accretions and get back to the plain sense of words, then we can have access to the way things are. But the poem does not just tell it as it is, but constructs a complex world of images and metaphors which refutes this naïve view of language as merely a window on truth. What we buy into when we endorse this grand vision of the triumph of reason is a construction in language whose appeal is entirely due to its linguistic richness—the linguistic richness that ironically the underlying theory cannot accommodate. *On the Nature of the Universe* is a complex statement of the simplicity of things, and the tension between those two drives is not—and cannot be—resolved within the poem.

One particular aspect of this contrast which has always seemed strange to readers is the presence in the poem of figures such as the personified Nature, Mother Earth, and especially Venus, as invoked at the opening of the poem:

> O mother of the Roman race, delight
> Of men and gods, Venus most bountiful,
> You who beneath the gliding signs of heaven
> Fill with yourself the sea bedecked with ships
> And earth great crop-bearer, since by your power
> Creatures of every kind are brought to birth
> And rising up behold the light of sun.

There is nothing unepicurean in the evocation of a god: despite their denial of divine interference in the world, the Epicureans believed the gods existed, and that our cultivation of them could bring us images of divine tranquillity on which we could model our lives. There is also a clear allegory, in that Venus is equated with pleasure, the chief good in the Epicurean ethical system, and it is through the pursuit of pleasure that animals and humans procreate and create. The prologue is 'set' at dawn on the first day of spring, 1 April, when Venus' major festival, the *Veneralia*, was celebrated at Rome, and there need be nothing doctrinally unorthodox about the way that the new year is described. Similarly, Lucretius takes pains to explain that his use of the notion of Mother Earth is just a trope, and should not lead to the idea that earth is sentient or deserves cult:

> Indeed the earth is now and has been always
> Devoid entirely of any kind of feeling.
> The reason why it brings forth many things
> In many ways into the light of sun
> Is that it holds a multitude of atoms.
> If anyone decides to call the sea Neptune,
> And corn Ceres, and misuse the name of Bacchus
> Rather than give grape juice its proper title,
> Let us agree that he can call the earth
> Mother of the Gods, on this condition—
> That he refuses to pollute his mind
> With the foul poison of religion.

(2. 652–60)

Although these usages by Lucretius have traditionally been seized upon by opponents wishing to find traces of a subversive religiosity within the text, as Hume pointed out in his *Dialogues Concerning Natural Religion*, the religious gain little by this move: to say that for the Epicureans Nature becomes a god is of little help to a theist if the notion of divinity is so redefined. Venus, Nature, and Mother Earth are place-markers who dramatize the conflict between providentialist and Epicurean views of the world but must eventually be discarded by the Epicurean. Ultimately, all that happens anywhere is that atoms move at random in the void:

> For certainly not by design or mind's keen grasp
> Did primal atoms place themselves in order,
> Nor did they make contracts, you may be sure,
> As to what movements each of them should make.
> But many primal atoms in many ways
> Throughout the universe from infinity
> Have changed positions, clashing among themselves,
> Tried every motion, every combination,
> And so at length they fall into that pattern
> On which this world of ours has been created.
>
> (1. 1021-8)

But the question remains why we ever needed these figures to help us make the move to Epicurean truth, and what we do with them when we have reached it. The attraction of *On the Nature of the Universe* consists, again, in the myths and stories that we tell about the world: but there is no room for the richness of those stories within the philosophy itself.

But that does not mean, of course, that we cannot take from the poem a message which may not be perfectly Epicurean but which is one of its great lessons. The world *is*, ultimately, atoms and void, blind motion in emptiness, and there is, as Epicurus and Lucretius insisted, no divine hand providentially ordering things for our benefit. What we can construct on that basis is, however, a world of infinite complexity and delight, of which the images, metaphors, and stories that make up *On the Nature of the Universe* are an essential part. And we can do so knowing that those complexities are no more than stories, and yet delighting in them. *On the Nature of the Universe* gives us both a glimpse into how the world is, and a sense of what we can make of it:

> And now from all these things delight and joy,
> As it were divine, takes hold of me, and awe
> That by your power nature so manifest
> Lies open and in every part displayed.
>
> (3. 28-30)

SELECT BIBLIOGRAPHY

Texts

W. H. D. Rouse revised M. F. Smith (with translation, Cambridge, Mass., 1975).
See also C. Bailey (Oxford, 1922), K. Müller (Zurich, 1975). There is a bibliography of editions by C. Gordon (2nd edn., London, 1985).

Commentaries

C. Bailey (with text and translation, 3 vols., Oxford, 1947). See also the older English commentaries of H. A. J. Munro (with text and translation, 4th edn., London, 1886), W. A. Merrill (New York, 1907), and W. E. Leonard and S. B. S. Smith (Madison, 1942), with those of C. Giussani (Italian; Turin, 1896–8), A. Ernout and L. Robin (French; Paris, 1925–8), and the Latin commentaries of G. Wakefield (Glasgow, 1796–7) and K. Lachmann (Berlin, 1850).

    Book 1: P. M. Brown (Bristol, 1985).

    Book 3: E. J. Kenney (Cambridge, 1971).

    Book 4: J. Godwin (Warminster, 1986), R. D. Brown, *Lucretius on Love and Sex* (Leiden, 1987).

    Book 5: C. D. N. Costa (Oxford, 1984).

    Book 6: J. Godwin (Warminster, 1991).

Bibliography

A. Dalzell, 'A Bibliography of Work on Lucretius 1945–1972', *Classical World*, 66 (1973), 389–427, 67 (1973), 65–112.

C. D. Giovine, 'Lucrezio', in *Syzetesis* (Festschrift for M. Gigante, Naples, 1983), ii. 649–77.

General discussions

J. Masson, *Lucretius, Epicurean and Poet* (2 vols., London, 1907–9).

D. West, *The Imagery and Poetry of Lucretius* (Edinburgh, 1969).

E. J. Kenney, *Lucretius* (Greece and Rome New Surveys in the Classics, 11; Oxford, 1977).

J. M. Snyder, *Puns and Poetry in Lucretius' De rerum natura* (Amsterdam, 1980).

D. Clay, *Lucretius and Epicurus* (Cornell, 1983).

J. D. Minyard, *Lucretius and the Late Republic* (Leiden, 1985).

P. R. Hardie, *Virgil's* Aeneid: *Cosmos and Imperium* (Oxford, 1986).

C. Segal, *Lucretius on Death and Anxiety* (Princeton, 1990).

M. R. Gale, *Myth and Poetry in Lucretius* (Cambridge, 1994).

P. Boyancé, *Lucrèce et l'Épicurisme* (Paris, 1963).

P. H. Schrijvers, *Horror ac divina voluptas: Études sur la poétique et la poésie de Lucrèce* (Amsterdam, 1970).

A. Schiesaro, *Simulacrum et Imago* (Pisa, 1990).

Collections of essays

Lucretius, ed. D. R. Dudley (London, 1965).

Lucrèce, ed. O. Gigon (Fondation Hardt *Entretiens*, 24; Geneva, 1978: includes articles in English).

Probleme der Lukrezforschung, ed. C. J. Classen (Hildesheim, 1986: includes articles in English) (cited hereafter as Classen).

Selected general articles

H. Sykes Davies, 'Notes on Lucretius', *Criterion*, 11 (1931–2), 25–42 (in Classen).

P. Friedländer, 'The Pattern of Sound and Atomic Theory in Lucretius', *American Journal of Philology*, 62 (1941), 16–34 (in Classen).

P. de Lacy, 'Process and Value, an Epicurean Dilemma', *Transactions of the American Philological Association*, 88 (1957), 114–26.

W. S. Anderson, 'Discontinuity in Lucretian Symbolism', *Transactions of the American Philological Association*, 91 (1960), 1–29.

C. J. Classen, 'Poetry and Rhetoric in Lucretius', *Transactions of the American Philological Association*, 99 (1968), 77–118 (in Classen).

E. J. Kenney, 'Doctus Lucretius', *Mnemosyne*, 23 (1970), 366–92 (in Classen).

D. West, 'Virgilian Multiple-Correspondence Similes and their Antecedents', *Philologus*, 114 (1970), 262–75.

R. D. Brown, 'Lucretius and Callimachus', *Illinois Classical Studies*, 7 (1982), 77–97.

A. Dalzell, 'Language and Atomic Theory in Lucretius', *Hermathena*, 143 (1987), 19–28.

E. M. Thury, 'Lucretius' Poem as a *Simulacrum* of the *De rerum natura*', *American Journal of Philology*, 108 (1987), 270–94.

R. Mayer, 'The Epic of Lucretius', *Papers of the Leeds International Latin Seminar*, 6 (1990), 35–43.

G. B. Conte, 'Instructions for a Sublime Reader: Form of the Text and Form of the Addressee in Lucretius' *De rerum natura*', in *Genres and Readers*, trans. G. W. Most (Baltimore, 1994), 1–34.

A. Schiesaro, 'The Palingenesis of the *De rerum natura*', *Proceedings of the Cambridge Philological Society*, 40 (1994), 81–107.

Epicureanism

H. Usener, *Epicurea* (Leipzig, 1887: still main collection of fragments).

G. Arrighetti, *Epicuro Opere* (2nd edn., Turin, 1973: includes some material not in Usener, with Italian translation and commentary).

C. Bailey, *Epicurus, the Extant Remains* (Oxford, 1926: incomplete, but with English translation and commentary).

A. A. Long and D. N. Sedley, *The Hellenistic Philosophers* (2 vols., Cambridge, 1987: most helpful thematic collection. Vol. i has translations, vol. ii the original texts with commentary).

C. Bailey, *The Greek Atomists and Epicurus* (Oxford, 1928).

J. M. Rist, *Epicurus: An Introduction* (Cambridge, 1972).

D. Konstan, *Some Aspects of Epicurean Psychology* (Leiden, 1973).

B. Frischer, *The Sculpted Word: Epicureanism and Philosophical Recruitment in Ancient Greece* (Berkeley and Los Angeles, 1982).

A. A. Long, *Hellenistic Philosophy* (London, 1984).

E. Asmis, *Epicurus' Scientific Methodology* (Ithaca, 1984).

P. Mitsis, *The Pleasures of Invulnerability* (Ithaca, 1988).

There is also much of interest in M. Nussbaum, *The Therapy of Desire* (Princeton, 1994, esp. 140–279), and J. Annas, *Hellenistic Philosophy of Mind* (Berkeley and Los Angeles, 1992) and *The Morality of Happiness* (Oxford, 1993).

Reception

G. D. Hadzits, *Lucretius and his Influence* (London, 1935).

W. B. Fleischmann, *Lucretius and English Literature 1680–1740* (Paris, 1964).

H. Jones, *The Epicurean Tradition* (London, 1989).

Other works referred to in the notes

H. Diels, *Doxographi Graeci* (Berlin, 1879). This gives the standard texts (in Greek) of the so-called 'doxographic' tradition of philosophical summaries (see notes on 3. 138, 6. 96), especially the reconstructed account of 'Aetius' (?first century AD), which gives the opinions of ancient philosophers and scientists on a variety of topics.

Theophrastus, *Meteorology*, edited and translated from the Syriac and Arabic by H. Daibler, 'The *Meteorology* of Theophrastus in Syriac and Arabic Translation', in W. W. Fortenbraugh and D. Gutas, *Theophrastus, His*

Psychological, Doxographical, and Scientific Writings (New Brunswick, 1992), 166–293. This is an important source for the 'meteorological' topics in Book 6.

Epicurean texts are cited where possible from the collection by Usener, whose numeration is usually given in other collections.

SYNOPSIS OF THE POEM

This poem is difficult, particularly Books 1 and 2. Lucretius translates into Latin a scientific/philosophical treatise written in Greek some 200 years earlier; and not only into Latin, but into verse. He does not always make himself clear. But Lucretius was a superb poet and even the most technical passages are usually poetical, and are frequently illustrated by wonderful imagery. The book is full of moral fervour, designed to rescue mankind from the fear of gods and the fear of death; and this leads Lucretius to write some of the greatest poetry ever written.

There are six 'books'. Each contains a prologue, 1. 1–149, 2. 1–61, 3. 1–93, 4. 1–25, 5. 1–90, and 6. 1–95, that is easy to read. Books 1 and 2 set out the atomic theory, invented by the Greeks, that the universe consists of nothing but atoms and void. Book 3 demonstrates that the soul consists of the same, and dies when the body dies. Book 4 explains the mechanism of our senses, and goes on to discuss dreams and sex. Book 5 deals with the origin of the world and the dawn of human civilization. Book 6 considers thunderstorms, lightning, earthquakes, volcanic eruptions, the Nile, the magnet, and diseases.

The argument in **Book 1** starts with two principles: that nothing ever came into being from nothing, and that nothing ever returns to nothing. Atoms are solid, indestructible, invisible, everlasting, and infinite in number, and there is void, in which they move. Discussion follows of various Greek philosophers who got it wrong, and the book ends with a demonstration that the universe is infinite.

Book 2 states that atoms are in continual motion, moving straight down through the void, except that sometimes they swerve (hence comes free will). By their collisions and combinations they make molecules, which make everything that exists. Atoms have many different shapes, but the number of elements is limited, though the quantity is infinite; and the number of possible combinations is limited, so that species can be preserved. Atoms have no colour, heat, sound, moisture, smell, or feeling. Death disperses atoms, which are then reunited. The universe contains many other worlds besides ours, and none are made by gods, all by random collisions of atoms. Our world has begun to decay and will collapse.

Book 3 discusses the nature of mind and spirit—the soul. They are part of man just as much as his body. They act together on the body. They are made of very small atoms. They live united with the body and if separated from it they die. Mind and spirit are mortal. Thirty different arguments prove this, many persuasive, many strange, some very amusing and some deeply moving. Finally, in line 830 there is a great cry of triumph 'Therefore death nothing is to us'. There follow some 250 lines of superb poetry.

Book 4 explains the nature of vision, hearing, taste, smell, and the way things enter the mind and how the mind works. Lucretius then discusses sleep and from sleep proceeds to dreams and from dreams to sex (lines 962–end). The passages on sex are remarkable, written with extraordinary intensity of feeling.

Book 5 begins by showing that the world is mortal and will one day be destroyed. It was not made by gods, or by design, but by random and accidental collisions of atoms. There follows a magnificent description of the creation which resulted. There is then a long discussion of sun and moon, day and night, and eclipses. At line 772 begins a famous description of the beginning of life on earth and the development of civilization.

Book 6 describes thunder, lightning, thunderbolts, waterspouts, clouds, earthquakes, the sea, the eruptions of Etna, the Nile, Avernian lakes and other places, wells and springs, the magnet, and diseases, and ends with a description (following Thucydides) of the great plague in Athens in 430 BC.

Line numbering in text and notes refers to the Latin text.

LUCRETIUS

On the Nature of the Universe

BOOK ONE

O mother of the Roman race, delight
Of men and gods, Venus most bountiful,
You who beneath the gliding signs of heaven
Fill with yourself the sea bedecked with ships
And earth great crop-bearer, since by your power
Creatures of every kind are brought to birth
And rising up behold the light of sun;   5
From you, sweet goddess, you, and at your coming
The winds and clouds of heaven flee all away;
For you the earth well skilled puts forth sweet flowers;
For you the seas' horizons smile, and sky,
All peaceful now, shines clear with light outpoured.
For soon as spring days show their lovely face,   10
And west wind blows creative, fresh, and free
From winter's grip, first birds of the air proclaim you,
Goddess divine, and herald your approach,
Pierced to the heart by your almighty power.
Next creatures of the wild and flocks and herds
Bound across joyful pastures, swim swift streams,
So captured by your charms they follow you,   15
Their hearts' desire, wherever you lead on.
And then through seas and mountains and tearing rivers
And leafy homes of birds and verdant plains,
Striking sweet love into the breasts of all
You make each in their hearts' desire beget
After their kind their breed and progeny.
Since you and only you are nature's guide   20
And nothing to the glorious shores of light
Rises without you, nor grows sweet and lovely,
You I desire as partner in my verses
Which I try to fashion on the Nature of Things,   25
For Memmius, my friend, whom you have willed

At all times to excel in every grace.
For his sake all the more endow my words,
Goddess divine, with everlasting charm.

        Make in the meantime brutal acts of war
30 In every land and sea be lulled to sleep.
For only you can succour humankind
With tranquil peace, since warfare's savage works
Are Mars' dominion, mighty lord of arms,
Who vanquished by the eternal wound of love
Throws himself oft upon your holy bosom
35 And pillowing his shapely neck, looks up
And, gazing at you, feeds his hungry eyes,
Goddess, with love and lolling back his breath
Hangs on your lips. As he lies resting there
Upon your sacred body, come, embrace him
And from your lips pour out sweet blandishments,
40 Great lady, and for your Romans crave the calm of peace.
Since neither I, in our country's time of trouble,
Can bring a mind untroubled to my task,
Nor in such straits can Memmius' famous line
Be found to fail our country in its need.
For perfect peace gods by their very nature
45 Must of necessity enjoy, and immortal life,
Far separate, far removed from our affairs.
For free from every sorrow, every danger,
Strong in their own powers, needing naught from us,
They are not won by gifts nor touched by anger.

50   And now, good Memmius, receptive ears
And keen intelligence detached from cares
I pray you bring to true philosophy;
Lest you should scorn and disregard my gifts
Set out for you with faithful diligence
Before their meaning has been understood.
The most high order of heaven and of the gods
55 I shall begin to explain to you, and disclose
The primal elements of things from which
Nature creates, increases, nourishes
All things that are, and into which again
Nature dissolves them when their time has come.

These in the language of philosophy
It is our custom to describe as matter
Or generative bodies, or seeds of things,
Or call them primal atoms, since from them, 60
Those first beginnings, everything is formed.

When human life lay foul for all to see
Upon the earth, crushed by the burden of religion,
Religion which from heaven's firmament
Displayed its face, its ghastly countenance,
Lowering above mankind, the first who dared 65
Raise mortal eyes against it, first to take
His stand against it, was a man of Greece.
He was not cowed by fables of the gods
Or thunderbolts or heaven's threatening roar,
But they the more spurred on his ardent soul 70
Yearning to be the first to break apart
The bolts of nature's gates and throw them open.
Therefore his lively intellect prevailed
And forth he marched, advancing onwards far
Beyond the flaming ramparts of the world,
And voyaged in mind throughout infinity,
Whence he victorious back in triumph brings 75
Report of what can be and what cannot
And in what manner each thing has a power
That's limited, and deep-set boundary stone.
Wherefore religion in its turn is cast
Beneath the feet of men and trampled down,
And us his victory has made peers of heaven.

One thing I fear now is that you may think 80
There's something impious in philosophy
And that you are entering on a path of sin.
Not so. More often has religion itself
Given birth to deeds both impious and criminal:
As once at Aulis the leaders of the Greeks,
Lords of the host, patterns of chivalry,
The altar of the virgin goddess stained 85
Most foully with the blood of Iphianassa.
The braiding band around her maiden locks
Dropped down in equal lengths on either cheek;

She saw her father by the altar stand
90 In sorrow, the priests beside him hiding knives,
And all the people weeping when they saw her;
Then dumb with fear she sank down on her knees.
Nor could it help, poor girl, at such a time
That she first gave the king the name of father.

95 For men's hands lifted her and led her on
Pale, trembling, to the altar, not indeed
That in fulfilment of the ancient rite
The brilliant wedding hymns should be her escort,
But that a stainless victim foully stained,
At the very age of wedlock, sorrowing,
She should be slaughtered by a father's blade,
100 So that a fleet might gain a favouring wind.
So great the power religion had for evil.

You yourself, overcome at times by words
Of terror from the priests, will seek to abandon us.
How many dreams indeed they even now
105 Invent, to upset the principles of life
And all your happiness confound with fear.
And rightly so. For if men could but see
A sure end to their woes, somehow they'ld find the strength
To defy the priests and all their dark religion.
110 But as it is, men have no way, no power
To stand against them, since they needs must fear
In death a never-ending punishment.
They do not know the nature of the soul,
Whether it is born, or on the contrary
Makes its way into us at birth, and whether
It perishes with us, when death dissolves it,
115 Or goes to Hades' glooms and desolate chasms,
Or into other creatures finds its way
By power divine, as our own Ennius sang,
Who first brought down from lovely Helicon
A garland evergreen destined to win
Renown among the nations of Italy.
120 Though none the less in his immortal verse
He has expounded that there does exist
A realm of Acheron, in which endure
Not souls of ours and bodies, but some kind

Of wraiths or phantoms, marvellously pale.
And thence the form of Homer, ever deathless,
Came forth, he tells, and pouring out salt tears   125
Began to unfold the nature of the world.

   Therefore we must lay down right principles
Concerning things celestial, what makes
The motions of the sun and moon, what force
Governs affairs on earth, and most of all
By keenest reasoning perceive whence comes   130
The spirit and the nature of the mind.
And we must ask ourselves what thing it is
That terrifies our minds, confronting us
When we are awake but sickened with disease,
Or buried in sleep, so that we seem to see
And hear in their very presence men who are dead,
Whose bones lie in the cold embrace of earth.   135

   Nor do I fail to see how hard it is
To bring to light in Latin verse the dark
Discoveries of the Greeks, especially
Because of the poverty of our native tongue,
And the novelty of the subjects of my theme.
But still your merit, and as I hope, the joy   140
Of our sweet friendship, urge me to any toil
And lead me on to watch through nights serene
In my long quest for words, for poetry,
By which to shine clear light before your mind
To let you see into the heart of hidden things.   145

   Therefore this terror and darkness of the mind
Not by the sun's rays, nor the bright shafts of day,
Must be dispersed, as is most necessary,
But by the face of nature and her laws.

   We start then from her first great principle
That nothing ever by divine power comes from nothing.
For sure fear holds so much the minds of men   150
Because they see many things happen in earth and sky
Of which they can by no means see the causes,
And think them to be done by power divine.
So when we have seen that nothing can be created
From nothing, we shall at once discern more clearly   155

The object of our search, both the source from which each thing
Can be created, and the manner in which
Things come into being without the aid of gods.

For if things came out of nothing, all kinds of things
160 Could be produced from all things. Nothing would need a seed.
Men could arise from the sea, and scaly fish
From earth, and birds hatch in the sky.
Cattle and farm animals and wild beasts of every kind
Would fill alike farmlands and wilderness,
Breed all mixed up, all origins confused.
165 Nor could the fruits stay constant on the trees,
But all would change, all could bear everything.
For lacking its own generative bodies
How could a thing have a mother, fixed and sure?
But as it is, since each thing is created
From fixed specific seeds, the source from which
It is born and comes forth into the shores of light
170 Is its material and its primal atoms.
That is why all things cannot be born of all things,
Because in each dwells its distinctive power.

And why do roses flourish in the spring
And corn in summer's heat, and grapes in autumn,
175 Unless because each thing that is created
Displays itself when at their own due time
Fixed seeds of things have flowed together, and the seasons
Attend, and safe and sound the quickened earth
Brings tender growth up to the shores of light?
180 But if they came from nothing, they'ld spring up
Quite suddenly, at uncertain intervals,
And wrong times of the year, since primal atoms
Would not be there for an unfavourable season
To restrain from generative union.
Nor would time be needed for the growth of things,
185 For seeds to collect, if they could grow from nothing.
For little babes would suddenly be young men
And in a trice a tree shoot up from earth.
None of this happens, it is plain, because
All things grow slowly, as is natural,
From a fixed seed, and growing keep their character.

So you may know that each thing gets its growth 190
And nourishment from its own material.

And add to this that without the year's fixed rains
The earth cannot put forth its gladdening fruits,
Nor deprived of food can any animal
Beget its kind and keep its life intact.
So you may sooner think that many bodies 195
Are common to many things, like letters in words,
Than that anything can exist without first beginnings.

Again, why could not nature fashion men so huge
That they could walk through the sea as across a ford 200
And tear apart great mountains with their hands,
And outlive many living generations
If not because each thing needs for its birth
A fixed material that governs what can arise?
So we must admit that nothing can come from nothing, 205
For seed is needed, from which all things created
Can spring, and burgeon into air's soft breezes.

Lastly, since we see tilled land is better
Than untilled, and the work of hands yields better fruits,
It is plain to see that in the ground there lie 210
First elements of things, which when we turn
The fertile clods with ploughshare and break up
The earth's good soil, we start to life and growth.
But if they were not there, then without our labour
You'ld see things grow much better by themselves.

The next great principle is this: that nature 215
Resolves all things back into their elements
And never reduces anything to nothing.
If anything were mortal in all its parts,
Anything might suddenly perish, snatched from sight.
For no force would be needed to effect
Disruptions of its parts and loose its bonds. 220
But as it is, since all things are composed
Of everlasting seeds, until some force
Has met it, able to shatter it with a blow,
Or penetrate its voids and break it up,
Nature forbids that anything should perish.

225   And all those things which time through age removes,
         If utterly by its consuming power
         All the material of them is destroyed,
         Whence then does Venus into the light of life
         Bring back the race of animals, each after its kind,
         Or, when brought back, whence has the well-skilled earth
         The power to nourish them and make them grow,
         Providing food for each after its kind?
230   Whence come the rivers flowing from afar
         That feed it? Whence does ether feed the stars?
         For all things mortal must have been consumed
         By time illimitable and ages past.
         But if through that length of time, those ages past,
         Things have existed from which this world of ours
235   Consists and is replenished, then certainly
         They must be endowed with nature imperishable.
         Therefore things cannot ever return to nothing.

         Again, all things alike would be destroyed
         By the same force and cause, were they not held fast
         By matter everlasting, fastened together
240   More or less tightly in its framing bonds.
         A touch would be enough to cause destruction,
         Since there would be no eternal elements
         Needing a special force to break them up.
         But as it is, since the bonds which bind the elements
245   Are various and their matter is everlasting
         They stay intact, until they meet a force
         Found strong enough to break their textures down.
         Therefore no single thing returns to nothing
         But at its dissolution everything
         Returns to matter's primal particles.

250   Lastly, showers perish when father ether
         Has cast them into the lap of mother earth.
         But bright crops rise, and branches in the trees
         Grow green, trees grow and ripe fruit burdens them.
         Hence food comes for our kind and for wild beasts,
255   Hence we see happy cities flower with children,
         And leafy woods all singing with young birds,
         Hence cattle wearied by their swollen weight

Lie down across rich pastures, and the white milky stream
Flows from their udders. Hence the young progeny
Frisk with weak limbs on the soft grass, their youthful minds   260
Intoxicated by the strong fresh milk.
Therefore all things we see do not utterly perish
Since nature makes good one thing from another,
And does not suffer anything to be born
Unless it is aided by another's death.

 Well now, since I have taught that things cannot be created   265
From nothing, nor, once born, be summoned back to nothing,
Lest you begin perchance to doubt my words,
Because our eyes can't see first elements,
Learn now of things you must yourself admit
Exist, and yet remain invisible.   270

 The wind, its might aroused, lashes the sea
And sinks great ships and tears the clouds apart.
With whirling tempest sweeping across the plains
It strews them with great trees, the mountain tops
It rocks amain with forest-felling blasts,
So fierce the howling fury of the gale,   275
So wild and menacing the wind's deep roar.
Therefore for sure there are unseen bodies of wind
Which sweep the seas, the lands, the clouds of heaven,
With sudden whirlwinds tossing, ravaging.
They stream and spread their havoc just as water   280
So soft by nature suddenly bursts out
In spate when heavy rains upon the mountains
With huge cascades have swollen a mighty flood,
Hurling together wreckage from the woods
And whole trees too; nor can strong bridges stand   285
The sudden force of water coming on,
So swirling with great rains the river rushes
With all its mighty strength against the piers.
It roars and wrecks and rolls huge rocks beneath its waves
And shatters all that stands in front of it.
So also must be the motion of the wind   290
When it blasts onward like a rushing river.
Wherever it goes it drives on all before it,
Sweeps all away with blow on blow, or else

In twisting eddy seizes things, and then
With rapid whirlwind carries them away.
295 Wherefore again and yet again I say
That winds have hidden bodies, since they rival
In character and action mighty rivers
Possessed of bodies plain for all to see.

Consider this too: we smell different odours
But never see them coming to our nostrils.
300 We can't see scorching heat, nor set our eyes
On cold, nor can we see the sound of voices.
Yet all these things must needs consist of bodies
Since they are able to act upon our senses.
For nothing can be touched or touch except body.

305 And clothes hung up beside a wave-tossed shore
Grow damp, but spread out in the sun they dry.
But how the moisture first pervaded them
And how it fled the heat, we do not see.
The moisture therefore is split up into tiny parts
310 That eyes cannot perceive in any way.

Then too, as the sun returns through many years,
A ring on a finger wears thin underneath,
And dripping water hollows out a stone,
And in the fields the curving iron ploughshare
Thins imperceptibly, and by men's feet
315 We see the highways' pavements worn away.
Again, bronze statues by the city gates
Show right hands polished thin by frequent touch
Of travellers who have greeted them in passing.
Thus all these things we see grow less by rubbing,
320 But at each time what particles drop off
The grudging nature of our vision stops us seeing.

Lastly, whatever time and nature add to things
Little by little, causing steady growth,
No eyes however keen or strained can see.
325 Nor again when things grow old and waste away,
Nor when cliffs overhanging the sea are worn
By salt-consuming spray, can you discern
What at each moment each of them is losing.
Therefore nature works by means of hidden bodies.

Yet all things everywhere are not held in packed tight
In a mass of body. There is void in things.
To grasp this fact will help you in many ways
And stop you wandering in doubt and uncertainty
About the universe, distrusting what I say.
By void I mean intangible empty space.
If there were none, in no way could things move.
For matter, whose function is to oppose and obstruct,
Would at all times be present in all things,
So nothing could move forward, because nothing
Could ever make a start by yielding to it.
But in fact through seas and lands and highest heaven
We see before our eyes that many things
In many different ways do move; which if there were no void,
Would not so much wholly lack their restless movement,
But rather could never have been produced at all,
Since matter everywhere would have been close-packed and still.

And however solid things are thought to be
Here is proof that you can see they are really porous.
In rocky caverns water oozes through,
The whole place weeping with a stream of drops.
Food spreads to every part of an animal's body.
Trees grow and in due time put forth their fruits,
Because all over them through trunks and branches
Right from the deepest roots food makes its way.
Sounds pass through walls, and fly into closed buildings,
And freezing cold can penetrate to the bones.
But if there were no void for bodies to pass through
You would not see this happen in any way.

Lastly, why do we see some things weigh heavier
Than others, though their volume is the same?
For if there is as much matter in a ball of wool
As there is in lead, the weight must be the same,
Since it is the function of matter to press downwards.
But void, by contrast, stays forever weightless.
Therefore a thing of equal size but lighter
Declares itself to have more void inside it,
But the heavier by contrast makes proclaim
That it has more matter in it and much less of void.

330

335

340

345

350

355

360

365

Therefore there is beyond doubt admixed with things
That which we seek with keen-scented reasoning,
That thing to which we give the name of void.

370   And here I must forestall what some imagine,
Lest led astray by it you miss the truth.
They say that water yields to scaly fish
Pressing against it, and opens liquid ways,
Because fish as they swim leave space behind them
Into which the yielding waves can flow together;
375 And that likewise other things can move about
And change their place, though every place is filled.
All this is based on reasoning wholly false.
For how, I ask you, shall the fish advance
Unless the water gives way? And how shall the water
380 Be able to move back when the fish cannot move?
Either then all bodies must be deprived of movement,
Or we must say that void is mixed with things,
So that each can take the initiative in moving.

My last point is this: if two moving bodies
385 Collide and then bounce far apart, all the space between them
Must be void until it is occupied by air.
And however quickly air flows in all round,
It cannot at once fill all the vacant space;
It must fill first one place and then the next
Until it gains possession of the whole.
390 If anyone thinks that when bodies have sprung apart
What happens is that the air becomes compressed,
He's wrong; for in this case a void is made
That was not there before, and likewise
A void is filled which previously existed.
395 Air cannot be compressed in such a way;
Nor if it could, could it, I think, without void
Shrink into itself and draw its parts together.
Wherefore whatever pleas you may advance
To prolong your argument, yet in the end
You must admit that there is void in things.

400   And many another proof I can adduce
To scrape up credit for my arguments.
But to a mind keen-scented these small traces

Suffice: from them you'll grasp the rest yourself.
As mountain-ranging hounds find by their scent
The lair of beast in leafy covert hid
Once they have got some traces of its track,   405
So one thing after another you by yourself
Will find that you can see, in these researches,
And penetrate all unseen hiding places
And draw the truth from them.
But if you are weary and find the going too hard   410
There's one thing, Memmius, I can safely promise you:
Such bounteous draughts from springs o'er-flowing drawn
With sweetest tongue my well-stored mind will pour
That first I fear slow-moving age will creep
Over our limbs and loose the bonds of life   415
Before the full store of my arguments
On any single thing has filled your ears.

   But now, to pick up the thread of my discourse,
All nature, as it is in itself, consists
Of two things: there are bodies and there is void   420
In which these bodies are and through which they move.
The senses which are common to men declare
That body has a separate existence.
Without faith firmly founded in our senses
There will be no standard to which we can refer
In hidden matters, giving us the power
To establish anything by reasoning.   425
If there were no place and space, which we call void,
Bodies could not be situated anywhere
And they would totally lack the power of movement,
As I explained a little time ago.

   Now here's a further point. Nothing exists   430
Which you could say is wholly distinct from body
And separate from void—a third nature of some kind.
For whatever exists must in itself be something;
If touch affects it however light and small
It will increase the amount of matter by much or little,   435
Provided it does exist, and swell its sum.
But if it is intangible, and cannot prevent
Anything anywhere from passing through it,

Doubtless it will be what we call empty void.
440   Besides, whatever exists will either act on things
Or else react to other things acting on it,
Or it will be such that things can happen in it.
But without body nothing can act or react
And nothing can give place save emptiness and void.
Therefore apart from void and matter no third substance
445   Can remain to be numbered in the sum of things,
Neither one that falls within the range of senses
Nor one that mind can grasp by reasoning.

For you will find that all things that can be named
Are either properties of these two things
Or else you can see that they are accidents of them.
450   A property is something that cannot be separated
Or removed from a thing without destroying it.
As weight to rocks, wetness to water, heat to fire,
Touch to all bodies, intangibility to void.
But slavery, by contrast, poverty and riches
455   Freedom, war, peace and all such things
As may come and go but leave things in their essence
Intact, these, as is right, we call accidents.

Time likewise does not exist by itself,
But a sense follows from things themselves
460   Of what has been done in the past, what now is present,
And what in addition is to follow after.
And no one has a sense of time distinct
From the movement of things or from their quiet rest.

Moreover, when they say that Helen's rape
And Troy's defeat in war are facts, we must be careful
465   To see that they do not drive us to admit
That these things have an independent existence,
Arguing that those ancient generations
Of whom these great events were accidents
By time irrevocable have all been borne away.
For whatever is done must be an accident
470   Either of the whole earth or of some place in it.
Moreover, if no matter had existed
Nor room or space for things to operate,

The flame of love would never have been fired
By Helen's beauty deep in Paris' heart
Nor kindled blazing battles of savage war.   475
No wooden horse unmarked by sons of Troy
Spawning the midnight Greeks from out its womb
Had set the towers of Ilium aflame.
So you may see that events never at all
Exist by themselves as matter does, nor can
Be said to exist in the same way as void.   480
But rightly you may call them accidents
Of matter and of place in which things happen.

Material objects are of two kinds, partly atoms
And partly also compounds formed from atoms.
The atoms themselves no force can ever quench,   485
For by their solidity in the end they win.
Though it is difficult to believe that anything
That is completely solid can exist.
For lightning passes through the walls of houses,
And likewise sound and voices; iron glows
White hot in fire, and boulders burst apart   490
In the fierce blaze of heat; the solidness
Of gold grows soft and melts, the ice of bronze
Is overcome by fire and liquefied;
And warmth and piercing cold both seep through silver
As when in solemn rite we hold the cup   495
We feel both when dewy water is poured in.
So nothing in the world seems really solid.
But yet, because true reason and nature itself
Compel, be with me, while I demonstrate
In a few verses that there do exist
Bodies that are both solid and everlasting,   500
Which we teach are seeds or primal atoms of things
From which now all creation has been made.

First, since we have found that nature is twofold,
Consisting of two widely different things—
Matter and the space in which things happen—   505
Each must exist by itself unmixed with the other.
For where there is empty space, which we call void,
There matter is not; and where matter takes its stand

There in no way can empty void exist.
510 Therefore primal atoms are solid and without void.

Again, since void exists in things created,
There must be solid matter surrounding it,
Nor could you prove by truthful argument
That anything hides void, and holds it within it,
Unless you accept that that which holds is solid.
515 And that again can be nothing but an assembly
Of matter, able to hold the void inside it.
Matter therefore, which is absolutely solid,
Can last for ever, though all else be dissolved.

520   Then further, if there were nothing void and empty,
The universe would be one solid mass.
On the other hand, unless there were definite bodies
Able to fill the space each occupies,
Then everything would be vacant space and void.
An alternation then of matter and void
Must clearly exist, the two quite separate,
525 Since the universe is not completely full
Nor yet completely empty. So definite bodies
Exist which distinguish empty space from full.
And, as I have just shown, these can neither be broken
By blows struck from outside, nor inwardly
Pierced and unravelled; neither can they be
530 Attacked and shaken in any other way.
For without void it is clear that nothing can
Be crushed or broken or split in two by cutting;
Nor can it let in moisture or seeping cold
535 Or penetrating fire, all forces of destruction.
And the more void a thing contains within it
The deeper strike the blows of those assailants.
Therefore if atoms are solid and without void,
As I have shown, they must be everlasting.

540   Besides, had matter not been everlasting,
All things by now would have returned to nothing,
And the things we see would have been born again from nothing.
But since I have shown that nothing can be created
From nothing, nor things made return to nothing,
545 The primal atoms must have immortal substance

Into which at their last hour all things can be resolved
And furnish matter to renew the world.
So atoms must be solid single wholes;
Nor can they be in any other way
Preserved intact from endless ages past
Throughout eternity to make things new.   550

    Consider this also: if nature had set
No limit to the breaking of things, the atoms of matter
Would have been ground so small as ages past
Fragmented them, that nothing in due time
Could ever have been conceived from them and brought
Into the full maturity of life.   555
For we see things can be dissolved more quickly
Than reconstructed. Therefore what past years
And bygone days of all eternity
Had broken up before now, dissolved and shattered,
In time remaining could never be made new.   560
But as it is, a certain end is given
Of breaking, since we see all things renewed,
And fixed times stand for things after their kind
In which they can attain the flower of life.

    And here's another point. Though atoms of matter   565
Are completely solid, yet we can explain
Soft things—air, water, earth, and fire—
How they are made and what force works in them,
When once we see that void is mixed with things.
But on the other hand, if atoms are soft,   570
No explanation can be given how flints
And iron, hard things, can be produced; for nature
Will utterly lack a base on which to build.
Their pure solidity gives them mighty power,
And when they form a denser combination
Things can be knit together and show great strength.   575

    Moreover, if no limit has been set
To the breaking-up of bodies, nevertheless
You must admit that after infinite time
Bodies do survive of every kind of thing,
Not yet attacked by any form of danger;   580
But since by definition they are breakable,

It is inconsistent to say they could have lasted
Through time eternal struck by endless blows.

    Again, since a limit has been set
585 For the growth of things and for their hold on life,
Each after its kind, and since it stands decreed
What each by nature can do and cannot,
And nothing changes, but all things are constant
So much that every kind of bird displays
590 Its own specific markings on its body,
They must for sure consist of changeless matter.
For if the primal atoms could suffer change,
Under some strange compulsion, then no more
Would certainty exist of what can be
And what cannot, in a word how everything
595 Has finite power and deep-set boundary stone;
Nor could so oft the race of men repeat
The nature, manners, habits of their parents.

    To proceed with the argument: in every body
600 There is a point so small that eyes cannot see it.
That point is without parts, and is the smallest
Thing that can possibly exist. It has never existed
Separately by itself, nor ever will,
But only as one part of something else;
605 Then other and other like parts in due order
In close formation fill the atom up.
Since these can have no separate existence,
They must needs clings together in one whole
From which they can in no way be detached.
Atoms therefore are solid single wholes
610 Cohered from smallest parts close packed together,
Not compounds formed by gathering of parts,
But strong in everlasting singleness.
To them nature allows no diminution
Nor severance, but keeps them as seeds for things.

615   Besides, unless there is some smallest thing,
The tiniest body will consist of infinite parts,
Since these can be halved, and their halves halved again,
Forever, with no end to the division.
So then what difference will there be between

The sum of all things and the least of things?
There will be none at all. For though the sum of things   620
Will be completely infinite, the smallest bodies
Will equally consist of infinite parts.
But since true reasoning protests against this,
And tells us that the mind cannot believe it,
You must admit defeat, and recognize
That things exist which have no parts at all,   625
Themselves being smallest. And since these exist
You must admit that the atoms they compose
Themselves are also solid and everlasting.

　　Lastly, if nature, great creatress, forced
All things to resolve into their smallest parts,
She would have no power to rebuild anything from them.   630
For partless objects must lack the properties
That generative matter needs—the various
Connections, weights, blows, concourses, and movements
By which all things are made and operate.

　　Therefore those that have thought that the substance of things   635
Is fire, and the universe consists of fire alone,
Have fallen far from valid reasoning.
Of these the champion, first to open the fray,
Is Heraclitus, famed for his dark sayings
Among the more empty-headed of the Greeks
Rather than those grave minds that seek the truth.   640
For fools admire and love those things they see
Hidden in verses turned all upside down,
And take for truth what sweetly strokes the ears
And comes with sound of phrases fine imbued.

　　For why, I ask, are things so various   645
If they are made of nothing but pure fire?
Let fire be denser or more rarefied,
So long as the parts do not differ from the whole
Nothing would be achieved.
The heat would be fiercer with the parts compressed   650
And fainter with them spread out and dispersed.
That is all. In such conditions nothing more
Could we expect, much less this world of ours,
So various, be made from fire more dense or less.

655 There is this also: if they admit that void
Is mixed with things, then it is possible
For fire to be condensed and rarefied;
But since they see so many obstacles,
They shrink from leaving pure void in things.
Fearing the heights, they lose the path of truth.

660 Nor do they see that, once void is removed,
All things must be condensed and everything
Become one single body, that cannot throw off
Anything from itself in rapid movement,
As blazing fire throws off both light and heat.
So you may see that fire does not consist
Of parts close-packed and all compressed together.

665   But if they think that in some other way
Fires can be quenched and have their substance changed,
If they insist on this, then all heat totally
Will manifestly perish into nothing,
And what is then created will come from nothing.

670 For things have limits fixed; if they by change
Transgress them, then death follows instantly.
Therefore within them something must remain
Safe and secure, or you will find all things
Return quite into nothing, and from nothing
The stock of things reborn and growing strong.

675 So therefore there are certain definite bodies
Which keep their nature unchanged, everlasting;
These by their comings and goings and changing order
Can change their nature and transform themselves.
And these atoms are, for sure, not made of fire.

680 For it would make no difference if some
Should split off and depart and others be added
Or change positions, if nevertheless
They all possessed and kept the nature of fire.
For everything they made would still be fire.
The truth I think is this: there are certain bodies

685 Which by their impacts, movements, order, position, and shapes
Produce fire, and which when their order is changed
Are changed themselves, and are not like fire,
Nor anything else that can send out particles
To our senses, and by impact touch our sense of touch.

To say moreover that all things are fire,   690
And nothing in this world is real except fire,
As this man does, seems utter lunacy.
He uses the senses to fight against the senses,
And undermines what all belief depends on,
By which he knows himself this thing that he calls fire.   695
He believes that the senses truly perceive fire,
But not the rest of things that are no less clear,
Which seems to me both futile and insane.
For what shall we appeal to? What can there be more certain
Than the senses to distinguish false from true?
And why should one remove everything else   700
And leave only fire, rather than deny
That fire exists and leave some other thing?
Both propositions seem equally insane.

Those therefore who have thought that fire   705
Is the substance of things, and that the universe
Can consist of fire, and those who have maintained
That air is the principle for the growth of things,
Or that water forms things by itself alone,
Or earth makes all things and changes into them,
These men have clearly strayed far from the truth.   710
Add those who make the elements twofold
Combining air with fire and earth with water,
And those who take the view that everything
Can grow from four—fire, water, air, and earth.   715
Foremost among these is Empedocles
Of Acragas, whom that great island bore
In its three-cornered coasts, around which flows
The Ionian deep with many a twisting firth
And splashes salt spray from its green grey waves.
Here by a narrow strait the racing sea   720
Severs its coastline from the Italian shore;
Here ruinous Charybdis seethes, and here
Etna's deep murmurs threaten once again
To muster flaming wrath, so that once more
Its violence may vomit bursting fires,
Once more dark lightning flashes to the sky.   725
But though this mighty isle seems wonderful
In many ways to nations of mankind,

Known as a land to see, rich in good things,
And guarded by a mighty force of men,
Yet nothing, as I think, more glorious
Has it possessed than this man, nor more holy,
730 More wonderful, more precious. From his heart
Divine, songs ring out clear, and tell the world
Of his illustrious discoveries,
So that he seems scarce born of human stock.

Yet he, and those of whom I spoke before,
735 So much inferior, so much less than he,
Though much they found out excellent and divine
And from their hearts' deep sanctuary gave forth
Answers more holy, on surer reason based,
Than those the Delphic prophetess pronounced
Amid the laurels of Apollo's tripod,
Yet these about the origin of things
740 Have crashed: great men, and great there was their fall.
Their first mistake is this: that they assume
Movement exists though void has been removed,
And allow things to be soft and rarefied—
Air, sun, earth, rain, and animals and crops—
745 While not admixing void within their bodies.
The second, that they acknowledge no limit at all
To the splitting of things, nor respite to their breaking,
Nor any least of things, the primal atoms;
Though we see that all things have an ultimate point
750 Which is the smallest thing our eyes can grasp,
From which you may deduce that invisible things
Have also an ultimate point which is the smallest.
Moreover, these first elements of theirs
Are soft: things that we see have birth, and bodies
755 Of wholly mortal nature; so by now
The universe must have returned to nothing,
And all things been reborn anew from nothing.
That both these views are false you know already.
Then too, these elements in many ways
Are hostile and pure poison to each other;
760 So when they meet, then either they will perish
Or fly apart, as we see lightning flashes

And thunderstorms and winds all fly apart
When they have been driven together by a storm.

    And then again, if all things were created
Out of four things, and resolved back into them,
Why should we call them elements of things   765
Rather than, thinking in reverse, maintain
That other things are elements of them?
For they are born from each other, and change colour
And their whole natures among themselves for ever.
But if you think that fire and earth and wind,   770
The breezes of the sky, the dew that lies,
Can so combine that in their combination
Their natures are not changed, then clearly nothing
Could be created from them, no animal
Nor anything inanimate, like a tree.
For in the mingling of this diverse mass   775
Each element in its own nature will display:
Air will then be seen mixed up with earth
And fire persisting side by side with moisture.
But primal atoms in begetting things
Must bring a nature secret and unseen,
That nothing may stand out to bar and thwart   780
Each thing that's made from being its proper self.

    Indeed these men trace all things back to heaven
And heaven's fires, and hold that fire first turns
Itself into breezes of the air, that rain
Is generated thence, and earth from rain
Created, then all things return again   785
From earth, reversing order, moisture first
Next air, then heat, and these things never cease
Their mutual changes, moving from the sky
To earth, from earth back to the stars of heaven.
This primal atoms never ought to do.
For something must survive unchangeable   790
Lest all things utterly return to nothing.
For all things have their boundaries fixed and sure;
Transgress them, and death follows instantly.
Therefore since those things we mentioned earlier
Undergo change, then they must needs consist   795

Of other things that cannot change at all,
Of you will find all things return to nothing.
Why not rather assume that atoms exist
Of such a nature that if they have produced fire
800 Then with a few more added or taken away
And motions and positions changed, they make air,
And in this way things change from one to another?

'But', you will say, 'the plain facts clearly show
That from the earth into the winds of air
All things grow, and from earth all take their food.
805 And unless the season with propitious hour
Makes way for rain and trees reel as storm clouds break,
And sunshine cherishes and brings them warmth,
Crops, trees, and animals can never grow.'
Yes, and unless we ourselves by solid food
And tender juices were sustained, at once
810 Our body would waste away, and all our life
From all our bones and sinews be dissolved.
For certainly we are ourselves sustained and fed
By fixed and certain things; and other things
And others again by certain other things.
No doubt the reason is that many atoms
815 Common in many ways to many things
Are mixed in many things, commingled with them,
So different things are fed from different sources.
And often it is a matter of great importance
How these same atoms combine, in what positions
They are held, what motions they give and take.
820 For these same atoms form sky, sea, land, rivers, sun,
The same compose crops, trees, and animals,
And have different motions, different combinations.
Why, in my verses everywhere you see
Are many letters common to many words,
825 But yet you must admit that words and lines
Differ in meaning and the sounds they make.
Such power have letters through mere change of order;
But atoms can bring more factors into play
To create all things in their variety.

830 Now let us examine Anaxagoras'
Homoeomeria, named so by the Greeks,

Which in our language is without a name
Because of the poverty of our native tongue.
However, it is easy to explain the thing.

First, when he talks about homoeomeria,
You must understand him to believe that bones
Are made of very small and tiny bones,   835
And flesh of small and tiny bits of flesh,
And blood created out of many drops
Of blood combined together, and that gold
Can be built up from grains of gold, and earth
Grows out of little earths, and fire from fires,   840
Water from water drops, and all the rest
He fancies are formed on the same principle.
But he does not conclude that void exists,
Nor any limit to the division of things.
Therefore on both these points he plainly errs   845
Just as those did of whom I spoke before.

Add that he makes his elements too frail,
If elements they are that are endowed
With a nature similar to the things themselves,
Suffer like them and perish, nowhere reined back
By anything from ruin and destruction.
Which of them under huge pressure will endure   850
And escape destruction right in the jaws of death?
Will fire or air or water? Which of them?
Will blood or bones? Not one, in my belief,
But everything alike will in its essence
Be as perishable as those things we clearly see   855
Visibly perishing, vanquished by some force.
I call to witness what I proved before:
That nothing ever can be reduced to nothing
Nor anything again grow out of nothing.

Again, since food builds up the body and nourishes it,
Plainly our veins and blood and bones and sinews
Must needs be made of parts unlike themselves.   860
Or if they say that all food is a mixture
Incorporating little bits of bones
And sinews, yes, and little drops of blood,
All food both solid and liquid must be held

865   To be composed of things unlike itself,
       A mixture of bones and sinews, pus and blood.
       And all those things that grow out from the earth,
       If they are in the earth, earth must consist
       Of things unlike itself that spring from it.
870   Take other cases, and the same words will apply
       If flame, smoke, ashes lurk unseen in wood
       It follows that the wood must be composed
       Of things unlike itself, that rise from it.

875   And here is left some small chance of escape
       Which Anaxagoras puts to good use.
       All things, he holds, lie hidden in all things
       Mixed up with them, but only one is seen,
       The one that has the most parts in the mixture,
       Set on the surface, readier to see.
880   But this is very far removed from truth.
       For then it would be natural that corn
       Ground by the millstone's crushing strength would show
       Some signs of blood or other substances
       Which find their nourishment within the body;
       And that, when we rub stone on stone, then blood should trickle,
885   And grass and water likewise should emit
       Drops sweet and flavoured like the milk of sheep.
       And often too when clods of earth are crumbled
       One should see various plants and corn and leaves
890   Lurking in miniature amid the soil.
       Lastly, when wood is broken one should see
       That ash and smoke and tiny flames lie hid.
       But plain facts show that none of this occurs.
       It follows therefore that one sort of thing
       Is not mixed with another in this way.
       No. But seeds common to many things
895   In many ways must needs lie hid inside them.

           'But often on great mountains', you will say,
       'It happens that the high tops of tall trees
       Are rubbed together, forced by strong south winds,
900   Until they blaze in bursting flower of flame.'
       Agreed. But fire is not implanted in the wood,
       But there are many seeds of heat which the friction

Concentrates, to make the forest fires.
If flame were hiding in forests ready-made,
Not for one moment could the fires be hid, 905
But everywhere they'ld burn the woods, turn trees to ashes.
Now do you see the point I made before,
That often it is a matter of great importance
How these same atoms combine, in what positions
They are held, what motions they give and take, 910
And that these same by quite small mutual changes
Can make both fires and firs? As the words themselves
Consist of elements a little changed
When we say fires or firs with different sounds?

And if you cannot explain the things you see 915
Without inventing tiny parts of matter
Endowed with the same nature as the whole,
This reasoning puts an end to all your atoms.
They'll simply shake their sides and rock with laughter,
And salt tears run in rivers down their cheeks. 920

Come now, and learn what follows, and listen to it
More keenly. I know how dark these matters are.
But the high hope of fame has struck my heart
Sharply with holy wand and filled my breast
With sweet love of the Muses. Thus inspired
With mind and purpose flourishing and free 925
A pathless country of the Pierides
I traverse, where no foot has ever trod.
A joy it is to come to virgin springs
And drink, a joy it is to pluck new flowers
To make a glorious garland for my head
From fields whose blooms the Muses never picked
To crown the brows of any man before. 930
First, since of matters high I make my theme,
Proceeding to set free the minds of men
Bound by the tight knots of religion.
Next, since of things so dark in verse so clear
I write, and touch all things with the Muses' charm.
In this no lack of purpose may be seen. 935
For as with children, when the doctors try
To give them loathsome wormwood, first they smear

Sweet yellow honey on the goblet's rim,
That childhood all unheeding may be deceived
At the lip's edge, and so drink up the juice
940 Of bitter medicine, tricked but not betrayed,
And by such means gain health and strength again,
So now do I: for oft my doctrine seems
Distasteful to those that have not sampled it
And most shrink back from it. My purpose is
945 With the sweet voices of Pierian song
To expound my doctrine, and as it were to touch it
With the delicious honey of the Muses;
So in this way perchance my poetry
Can hold your mind, while you attempt to grasp
The nature of the world, and understand
950 The great design and pattern of its making.

And now, since I have shown that primal atoms
Completely solid unimpaired for ever
Fly everywhere around, let us unfold
Whether or not there is a limit to their number.
Likewise the void which we have found to exist,
955 Or place or space, in which all things occur,
Let us see whether its extent is limited
Or stretches wide immeasurable and profound.

We find then that the universe is not bounded
In any direction. If it were, it would need to have
An extremity. But nothing can have an extremity
960 Unless there is something outside to limit it,
Something beyond to bound it, some clear point
Further than which our senses cannot reach.
Now since we must admit that there is nothing
Beyond the sum of things, it has no extremity.
Therefore it has no end, nor any limit.
965 Nor does it matter in what part of it
You stand: wherever a man takes his place
It stretches always boundless, infinite.
Suppose moreover that the whole of space
Were finite, if one ran right to the edge,
970 Its farthest shore, and threw a flying lance,
Which would you rather say, that hurled amain

It flies straight on, as aimed, far far away,
Or that something can check it and block its path?
One or the other you are bound to choose.
But each cuts off your escape route, and compels you
To concede that the universe continues without end.
For whether there is some object that can thwart
Its flight, so that it cannot reach the boundary,
Or whether it passes straight on unimpeded,
Its starting point is not the boundary.
And I'll pursue you further, and I'll ask,
Wherever you may place the furthest shore,
What happens to the lance? The upshot is
That nowhere in the universe can be
A final edge, and no escape be found
From the endless possibility of flight.

    And here's another thing. If all the space
In the universe stood shut in on all sides
By fixed and certain boundaries limited,
The store of matter everywhere by now
By its own solid weight borne down, compressed,
Would all have flowed together to the bottom,
And nothing could happen under the vault of heaven,
No sky at all could be, not light of sun,
Since all the sum of matter in a heap
Would lie, through ages infinite sunk down.
But as it is, no rest for sure is given
To primal atoms, since there is no bottom
No base at all, on which they can as it were
Accumulate and set up their abode.
Always in everlasting motion all things move
In every part, and from below supplies come in
Of matter, summoned from the infinite.

    Our eyes tell us that one thing bounds another.
Air fences in the hills, the mountains air,
And land sets bounds to sea, and sea to lands,
But nothing outside it bounds the universe.

    Therefore there is a vast abyss of space
So wide and deep that flashing thunderbolts
Can neither in their courses traverse it

975
980
985
990
995
1000

Though they may fall through endless tracts of time,
Nor by their travel make one whit the less

1005   The distance still to go. So huge extends
Capacity of space on either side,
No bounds at all, no limit anywhere.

Further, nature prevents the universe
From setting any limit to itself.

1010   Body is bounded by void and void by body,
Thus in their interchange the universe
Is infinite, or else one of the two,
If the other does not bound it, by itself
Must stretch away alone illimitable.
Since space is infinite, so must matter be.
Else neither sea nor land nor the bright realms of heaven

1015   Nor race of men nor holy forms of gods
Could stand for one brief fraction of an hour,
For matter, its close union all shattered,
Would rush dissolving through the mighty void
Or rather it could never have grown together
So as to form anything, since thus dispersed

1020   It could never have been brought to form a union.

For certainly not by design or mind's keen grasp
Did primal atoms place themselves in order,
Nor did they make contracts, you may be sure,
As to what movements each of them should make.
But many primal atoms in many ways
Throughout the universe from infinity

1025   Have changed positions, clashing among themselves,
Tried every motion, every combination,
And so at length they fall into that pattern
On which this world of ours has been created.
And this preserved through cycles of the years

1030   When once set going in appropriate movements
Causes the rivers to refill the sea,
The greedy sea, with lavish waters, and earth
Warmed by the sun's caress renews its fruits.
And all the race of animals springs up
And grows; the gliding fires of ether live.

1035   And this they could by no means do, unless

A store of matter from the infinite
Could spring, from which in turn in season due
All that is lost could be made good again.
For just as living creatures lacking food
Lose flesh and waste away, so must all things
Decay, as soon as matter, for some reason
Turned from its course, has ceased to be supplied.   1040

Whatever world atoms have combined to form
Blows from outside cannot preserve entire.
They can strike it frequently and hold back a part
Till others come and keep the whole filled up;   1045
Yet sometimes they must needs rebound, and give
The primal atoms space and time for flight
To freedom from the union they have created.
Wherefore again and yet again I say
That atoms in great numbers must come up;
Indeed the blows themselves must fall away   1050
Unless the supply of matter is infinite.

One thing you must reject from all belief,
Good Memmius, is the theory which some hold,
That all things press towards the centre of the universe,
And that for this reason the world stands fast
Without impacts from outside, and that the top   1055
And bottom are not free to move in any direction,
Since everything is pressing towards the centre—
If you can believe that anything rests upon itself—
That all the heavy things below the earth
Press upwards and rest upside down upon it,
Like images of things reflected in water.   1060
And likewise they contend that animals
Wander about head downwards and cannot fall
Off from the earth into the sky below
Any more than our bodies of themselves can fly
Upwards into the regions of the sky;
That when they see the sun, the stars of night   1065
Are what we see, and that they share the hours
Of the wide heavens alternately with us,
And pass nights corresponding to our days.
But error has given these false ideas to fools,

Embraced by them with reasoning askew.
1070　For since the universe is infinite,
There can be no middle. And even if there were,
Nothing could stand there, because it is the middle,
Rather than fly apart for some different reason.
For all the place and space which we call void
1075　Through middle, through non-middle, must give way
To things, wherever their movements take them.
Nor is there any place where bodies can go
And lose their weights, and stand still in the void;
Nor can void make resistance to anything
1080　But as its nature demands it must give way.
Therefore things cannot by this means be held
In combination, mastered by their longing for the middle.

　　Besides, they do not claim that all bodies press
Towards the middle, but only those of earth and water,
1085　The liquid of the sea and the great waves
That pour down from the mountains, and those things
That as it were an earthly frame contains.
They tell us by contrast that air's thin breaths
And hot fires are all borne away from the middle;
That all the ether twinkles with the stars
1090　And the sun's flame feeds on the sky's blue pastures
Because fire flying upwards from the middle
Gathers together there; and tall trees, they say,
Could never bring high branches into leaf
If food did not rise upward from the earth.

[8 lines missing]

But if it were the nature of air and fire
To move always upwards, then there is a risk
That suddenly the ramparts of the world
Would burst asunder and like flying flames
Rush headlong scattered through the empty void,
And in like manner all the rest would follow,
1105　The thundering realms of sky rush down from above,
Earth suddenly withdraw beneath our feet,
And the whole world, its atoms all dissolved,
Amid the confused ruin of heaven and earth
Would vanish through the void of the abyss,

And in a moment not one scrap be left
But desert space and atoms invisible, 1110
For at whatever point you first allow
Matter to fail, there stands the gate of death.
And through it all the crowding throng of matter
Will make its exit and pass all away.

And so, led firmly on, without great toil
You will understand these matters well and truly.
For one thing makes another clear; and night 1115
Won't snatch the path from you until you have seen
Right to the heart of nature's mysteries,
So surely things will kindle light for things.

BOOK TWO

A joy it is, when the strong winds of storm
Stir up the waters of a mighty sea,
To watch from shore the troubles of another.
No pleasure this in any man's distress,
But joy to see the ills from which you are spared,
And joy to see great armies locked in conflict
Across the plains, yourself free from the danger.
But nothing sweeter is than this: to dwell
In quiet halls and lofty sanctuaries
Well fortified by doctrines of the wise,
And look thence down on others wandering
And seeking all astray the path of life—
The clash of intellects, the fight for honours,
The lust for wealth, the efforts night and day
With toil and sweat to scale the heights of power.
O wretched minds of men! O hearts so blind!
How dark the life, how great the perils are
In which whatever time is given is passed!
Do you not see that Nature cries for this,
And only this, that pain from out the body
Shall be removed away, and mind enjoy
Sweet sense of pleasure, freed from care and fear?

Therefore we see that human nature's needs
Are small indeed: things that take pain away,
And such as simple pleasures can supply.
Nature herself demands nothing more sweet,
If golden statues of young men be lacking
Whose hands hold flaming torches through the house
Providing light for nightly revellings,
If with no gleam of gold or flash of silver
The hall shines bright, if no lyre echoes round

High gilded ceilings and fine panelled walls,
So long as men, lying in company together
On the soft grass beside a flowing stream
Beneath a tall tree's shade, at little cost   30
Find pleasure for their bodies; most of all
When weather smiles and the season of the year
Scatters the meadows and green lanes with flowers.
And fevers leave the body no more swiftly,
If figured tapestries and purple sheets   35
Are what you toss on, than if you have to lie
With plain plebeian blanket on your bed.

    Wherefore, since our bodies profit nothing
From riches or noble birth or glory of kingdom,
We must believe our minds also gain nothing.
Unless perchance the sight of mimic war
When your fine legions throng the great Parade   40
Strong in auxiliaries and cavalry,
Alike in arms, alike with ardour fired,
Or when you see the fleet come surging out
And spreading far and wide across the sea,
These things excite and thrill your mind, and drive
Religion's dread away, and fears of death   45
Leave your heart empty then, from care set free.
But if we see that all this is ludicrous,
And that in truth men's cares and haunting fears
Reck nothing of clash of arms or brutal missiles
And boldly walk with kings and potentates,   50
Nor stand in awe of the bright sheen of gold
Or brilliant splendour of a purple robe,
How can you doubt that reason has this power,
Reason alone? Our lives in very truth
Are but an endless labour in the dark.
For we, like children frightened of the dark,
Are sometimes frightened in the light—of things   55
No more to be feared than fears that in the dark
Distress a child, thinking they may come true.
Therefore this terror and darkness of the mind
Not by the sun's rays, nor the bright shafts of day,
Must be dispersed, as is most necessary,   60
But by the face of nature and her laws.

Come, listen now, and I'll explain the motions
By which the generative bodies of matter
Beget the various things and, once begotten,
Dissolve them, and by what force they are driven to do this,
65 And what power of movement through the mighty void
Is given them. Do you now mark my words.

Matter, for sure, is not one solid mass
Close packed together. We see that everything
Diminishes, and through the long lapse of time
We note that all things seem to melt away
70 As years and age withdraw them from our sight.
And yet the sum of things stays unimpaired.
This is because when particles are shed
From a thing they diminish it as they leave it,
And then increase the object that they come to.
75 They make the one grow old, the other flourish,
But do not linger there. The sum of things
Is thus forever renewed, and mortals live
By mutual interchange one from another.
Some races increase, others fade away,
And in short space the breeds of living creatures
Change, and like runners pass on the torch of life.

80 Now if you think that atoms can be at rest
And can by resting beget new movements in things,
You are lost, and wander very far from truth.
For since the atoms wander through the void,
All must be driven either by their own weight
85 Or by some chance blow from another atom.
For often when, as they move, they meet and clash,
They leap apart at once in different directions.
No wonder, since they are extremely hard
And solid, and there is nothing behind to stop them.
To see more clearly that all particles of matter
Are constantly being tossed about, remember
90 That there is no bottom to the universe,
That primal atoms have nowhere to rest,
Since space is without end or any limit.
And I have shown by many words, and proved
By surest reasoning that it extends

Boundless in all directions everywhere.
Since that stands true, no rest, we may be sure,   95
Is given to atoms in the void abyss
But rather, as unceasing different
Movements impel them, some, colliding, leap
Great intervals apart, while others recoil
Only a short distance from the impact.
And those whose union being more closely packed   100
Leap back short distances after a collision,
Being fast entangled by their own complex shapes,
These constitute strong roots of stone and the brute bulk
Of iron, and other objects of that kind.
Of the rest, which wander further through the void,   105
A few leap far apart, and far recoil
Over great intervals; these make for us
Thin air, and make the shining light of sun.
And many wander through the mighty void
Rejected from all union with others,
Unable anywhere to gain admittance   110
And bring their movements into harmony.

    An image and similitude of this
Is always moving present to our eyes.
Consider sunbeams. When the sun's rays let in
Pass through the darkness of a shuttered room,
You will see a multitude of tiny bodies   115
All mingling in a multitude of ways
Inside the sunbeam, moving in the void,
Seeming to be engaged in endless strife,
Battle, and warfare, troop attacking troop,
And never a respite, harried constantly,
With meetings and with partings everywhere.   120
From this you can imagine what it is
For atoms to be tossed perpetually
In endless motion through the mighty void.
To some extent a small thing may afford
An image of great things, a footprint of a concept.

    A further reason why you should give your mind   125
To bodies you see dancing in a sunbeam
Is that their dancing shows that within matter

Secret and hidden motions also lie.
For many you will see are struck by blows
130   Unseen, and changing course are driven back
Reversed on all sides, here, there, everywhere.
These wandering movements, you may be sure, are caused
In every case by atoms. Atoms first
Move of themselves, next bodies that are formed
135   In a small group and nearest to the force
Of the primal atoms are set moving by them,
Driven by unseen blows from them; and they
Attack in turn bodies a little larger.
The movement thus ascends from primal atoms
And comes out gradually up to our senses,
And thus it is that those bodies also move
140   That we can see in sunbeams, though the blows
That make them do it are invisible.

Now, as to the speed with which the atoms move.
This in a few words you may understand,
Good Memmius, from what I now shall tell you.
First, when dawn strews new light across the earth,
145   And the birds flying through the pathless woods
In the soft air fill with their liquid notes,
So varied and so sweet, the place below,
We see then plain and manifest to all
How suddenly the rising sun is wont
To clothe the world and flood it with his light.
150   But that heat and light serene the sun sends forth
Do not pass through empty void; and for this reason
They are compelled to go more slowly, and
To cleave their way as it were through waves of air.
Nor do the particles of heat move separately,
But in a mass all linked and massed together,
155   So that at the same time they drag each other back
And meet external obstacles, and so move more slowly.
But atoms, which are completely solid and single,
When they pass through the empty void, and nothing
Outside of them delays them, then they move
160   As single units on the course on which they started.
Therefore they must be of surpassing speed
And move much faster than the light of the sun,

And cover a distance many times as great
In the time the sun's flash takes to cross the sky.

[*Text missing*]

And not to follow every single atom   165
To see in what way everything is done.

    Some people oppose this, being ignorant of matter,
Believing that without the power of gods
Nature could never match the needs of men
So fitly as she does, so very closely,
Changing the seasons and producing crops,   170
And all those other things which pleasure divine,
The guide of life, leads mortals to enjoy,
And through the arts of Venus coaxes them
To breed, and propagate the generations,
Lest the human race should perish. But when they imagine
That gods have ordered all things for men's sake,   175
In every way they have fallen far from truth.
For even if I had no knowledge of atoms,
This from the order of the heavens itself
And many other facts I would dare assert—
That in no way for us the power of gods   180
Fashioned the world and brought it into being.
So great the faults of which it stands possessed.
This, Memmius, I will make clear to you later.
Now I'll complete my account of the motion of atoms.

    This is the place, I think, to make the point
That no material thing can by its own power   185
Ever be lifted up, or travel upwards.
Do not let the atoms that make flame deceive you.
For trees and shining crops spring into birth
Upwards and grow and make their increase upwards,
Though all weights by themselves tend downwards.   190
And when fires leap up to the roofs of houses
And with swift flame devour beams and timbers,
We must not think that of their own accord
They do this, without some force below to drive them.
Blood in the same way, let out from our bodies,
Spurts in a jet aloft and splashes gore.   195
Do you not see also the power with which water

Spits out beams and timbers? We press them down,
Deep down, many of us pushing all together
With might and main, and the harder we push them down
The more the water wants to spew them up,
And throw them back again, so that more than half
200 Emerges and shoots up above the surface.
And yet I think we have no doubt that all of them
Left to themselves would move downwards through the void.
The same thing must happen with flames. These under pressure
Can shoot up into the air, although their weights,
205 Left to themselves, must fight to drag them down.
And the nocturnal torches of the sky
Flying aloft, you see how in their wake
Long trails of flame they draw, wherever nature
Has set them on their course across the heavens.
And see how stars and meteors fall to earth.
210 And the sun also from the height of heaven
Throws its heat out and sows the fields with light.
So the sun's heat also inclines towards the earth.
Lightning you see through rainstorms flies aslant;
Now here, now there, the fires burst through the clouds
215 Headlong together; the flaming bolt falls to the earth.

   Now here is another thing I want you to understand.
While atoms move by their own weight straight down
Through the empty void, at quite uncertain times
And uncertain places they swerve slightly from their course.
220 You might call it no more than a mere change of motion.
If this did not occur, then all of them
Would fall like drops of rain down through the void.
There would be no collisions, no impacts
Of atoms upon atom, so that nature
Would never have created anything.

   If anyone believes that heavier atoms
225 Moving straight down more quickly through the void
Can fall on lighter atoms from above
And by this means produce the varied impacts
That can give rise to generative motions,
He is lost, and strays far from the path of truth.
For when things fall through water or thin air,

They must gain speed according to their weights;   230
For water's mass and air's thin nature cannot
Slow down the pace of all things equally
But must give way more quickly to the heavier.
But, by contrast, nowhere at any time   235
Can empty void make resistance to anything,
But as its nature demands it must give way.
Therefore through the calm and quiet void
All things must travel at an equal speed
Though with unequal weight. The heavier   240
Will never have the power to fall upon
The lighter from above, nor by themselves
Beget impacts that make the varied mix
Of movements by which nature fashions things.
Therefore again and again I say that atoms must
Swerve slightly, just the very least—no more—
Or we shall find ourselves imagining
A sideways movement, which the facts refute.   245
For it is plain and manifest that weights
When falling from above, left to themselves,
So far as meets the eye cannot move sideways.
But whose eye can perceive that nothing swerves
Ever so slightly from its straight course down?   250

 Again, if movement always is connected,
New motions coming from old in order fixed,
If atoms never swerve and make beginning
Of motions that can break the bonds of fate,
And foil the infinite chain of cause and effect,   255
What is the origin of this free will
Possessed by living creatures throughout the earth?
Whence comes, I say, this will-power wrested from the fates
Whereby we each proceed where pleasure leads,
Swerving our course at no fixed time or place
But where the bidding of our hearts directs?   260
For beyond doubt the power of the will
Originates these things and gives them birth
And from the will movements flow through the limbs.

 Consider racehorses. The starting gates
Fly open, the horses are strong and keen to go,

265 But can't break out as fast as their minds would wish.
For all the mass of matter must be stirred
Through the whole body, roused through every limb,
Before it can follow the prompting of the mind.
So you may see that heart begins the motion
Then mind and will join in and drive it on
270 Until it reaches all the body and limbs.

But let's suppose another man has struck us
A violent blow—he's hit us really hard—
And we move forward. That's quite different.
For all the matter then of all the body
275 Clearly against our will is forced to move,
Until the will has reined limbs back again.
Do you see the point? Though many men are driven
By an external force, compelled to move
Often in headlong rush against their will,
Yet in our breasts there's something that has the power
280 To fight against this force and to resist it.
At its command at times the mass of matter
Is forced to change direction in our limbs,
Or, reined back on its way, it comes to rest.

The same thing therefore we must admit in atoms:
285 That in addition to their weights and impacts
There is another separate cause of motion,
From which we get this innate power of ours,
Since nothing ever can be produced from nothing.
For it is weight that prevents all things being caused
Simply by external impacts of other atoms.
290 But that within the mind there's no necessity
Controlling all its actions, all its movements,
Enslaving it and forcing it to suffer—
That the minute swerving of atoms causes
In neither place nor time determinate.

The mass of matter in the universe
Was never more tightly packed than it is now,
295 Nor ever set at wider intervals.
Nothing increases it or is taken away from it.
Therefore the motions in which the primal atoms
Are now have been the same for ages past,

And in like manner they will move hereafter.
And things which the ancient custom of the world
Has brought to birth will always in like manner   300
Be brought to birth, and be and grow and flourish,
So far as to each is given by Nature's laws.
No power can ever change the sum of things.
No place exists to which any kind of matter
Could escape from the universe, nor any place   305
From out of which some new force building up
Could break into the universe, and change
The nature of all things, and reverse their movements.

   And here's a thing that need cause no surprise:
That though all atoms are in ceaseless motion
Their total seems to stand in total rest,   310
Except so far as individual objects
Make movements by the movements of their bodies.
For all the nature of the primal atoms
Lies hidden far beneath our senses; therefore since
You cannot see them, you cannot see their movements.
Indeed things we can see, if some great distance   315
Divides them from us, oft conceal their movements.
You see sheep on a hillside creeping forward
Cropping the fresh green grass new-pearled with dew
Where pastures new invite and tempt them on,
And fat lambs play and butt and frisk around.   320
We see all this confused and blurred by distance,
A white patch standing still amid the green.
And when in mimic war the mighty legions
Fill all the plain with movements far and wide,
And sheen of armour rises to the sky;   325
Earth flashes with bronze; the tramp of marching feet
Resounds on high; the hills struck by the noise
Throw back the echoes to the stars of heaven;
And wheeling horsemen gallop, and suddenly
Charge, and shake all the plain with their attack—   330
And yet among high mountains there's a place
From which they seem to stand still, motionless,
A flash of brightness on the plain below.

   Now let us consider the qualities of atoms,
The extent to which they differ in their shapes

335 And all the rich variety of their figures.
    Not that there are not many of the same shape,
    But all by no means are identical.
    Nor is this strange. For since their multitude
    As I have shown has neither sum nor end,
340 Not all, for sure, must be the same in build
    As all the rest, nor marked by the same shape.

    Consider the race of men, and silent shoals
    Of scaly fish, fat cattle, and wild beasts,
    And all the varied birds that throng the waters
345 By joyful lakes and streams and river banks,
    And flock and fly among the pathless woods.
    Take any one you will among its kind,
    And you will find they all have different shapes.
    This is the only way the young can know
350 Their mothers, and the mothers know their young.
    And this we see they do; no less than men
    They recognize each other readily.
    For oft in front of noble shrines of gods
    A calf falls slain beside the incensed altars,
    A stream of hot blood gushing from its breast.
355 The mother wandering through the leafy glens
    Bereaved seeks on the ground the cloven footprints.
    With questing eyes she seeks if anywhere
    Her lost child may be seen; she stands, and fills with moaning
    The woodland glades; she comes back to the byre
360 Time and again in yearning for her calf.
    Nor tender willows nor meadows lush with dew
    Nor those sweet rivers brimming to their banks
    Can charm her mind or ease the sudden care,
    Nor sight of other calves in happy pastures
    Divert her mind and lift the care away,
365 So does she seek what was her own, her darling,
    So steadfastly the child she knows so well.
    And tender kids with trembling voices know
    Their horned mothers well, and playful lambs
    The bleating ewes. So each as Nature bids
    To its own udder scampers back for milk.
370 Lastly, consider corn of any kind.
    Not every grain you'll find is quite the same,

But through their shapes there runs some difference.
So likewise all the various shells we see
Painting the lap of earth, the curving shore
Where waves beat softly on the thirsty sands.   375
Therefore again and yet again I say
That in the same way it must be that atoms,
Since they exist by nature and are not made by hand
To the fixed pattern of a single atom,
Must, some of them, be different in their shapes.   380

    With this in mind it is easy to explain
Why the fire of lightning penetrates much further
Than our fire does which springs from earthly torches.
For you could say that the heavenly fire of lightning
Is finer, being composed of smaller shapes
And therefore passes through apertures impassable   385
By our fire sprung from wood and lit by torch.
Besides, light passes through a pane of horn, but rain
Is thrown off. Why? Because the atoms of light
Are smaller than those that make life-giving water.   390
And though we see wine pass quickly through a strainer,
Yet olive oil by contrast lags and lingers;
No doubt, either because its atoms are larger
Or they are more hooked and more closely interwoven,
And therefore cannot separate so quickly   395
And trickle through the holes each one by one.

    And here's another thing. Honey and milk
Rolled in the mouth have a delightful taste;
But bitter wormwood and harsh centaury
Quite screw the face up with their loathsome flavour.   400
So you can easily see that smooth round atoms
Make up things which give pleasure to our senses,
But, by contrast, things that seem harsh and bitter
Are more composed of atoms that are hooked,
Which therefore tear their way into our senses,   405
And entering break the surface of our bodies.

    There is conflict between those things that strike the senses
As good or bad, because their shapes are different.
The strident rasping of a screeching saw
You must not think consists of elements

As smooth as melodies musicians shape
Waking the tuneful lyre with nimble fingers.
Nor must you think that atoms of the same shape
Enter men's nostrils when foul corpses burn
As when Cilician saffron o'er the stage
Is freshly cast, or when a near-by altar
Exhales the perfumes of Arabia.
And colours too, whose beauty feeds the eye,
Cannot be composed of atoms similar
To those that prick the pupil and force tears,
Or bring through ugliness disgust and loathing.
For everything that charms the senses must
Contain some smoothness in its primal atoms.
But by contrast things that are harsh and painful
Are found to have some roughness in their matter.
Some atoms are rightly thought to be neither smooth
Nor altogether hooked, with curving points,
But rather to have angles projecting slightly;
These tickle our senses without harming them.
Of such kind are wine-lees and piquant endive.
And fire with heat and frost with cold have teeth
That bite our senses in quite different ways,
As touch in each case indicates to us.
For touch (by all the holy powers of heaven!),
Touch is the body's sense, whether from outside
A thing slips in, or something inside hurts us,
Or pleasure comes when something issues forth
In procreative acts of Venus, or when some blow
Upsets the body's atoms and we feel
Disordered by their ferment—and for proof
Hit yourself anywhere with your own hand!
So atoms must have widely different shapes
Since they can cause such varying sensations.

Again, things that seem hard and dense must be
Composed much more of atoms hooked together
Held tight deep down by branch-like particles.
First in this class and in the leading rank
Stand diamonds, well used to scorn all blows.
Next come stout flints and the hard strength of iron
And bronze that fights and shrieks when bolts are shot.

415
420
425
430
435
440
445
450

But liquids in their fluid composition
Must consist more of atoms smooth and round.
You can pour poppy seeds as easily as water,
The tiny spheres do not hold each other back,
And if you knock a heap of them they run
Downhill in the same way as water does.
And all those things you see that in an instant   455
Disperse, like smoke or clouds or flames, must be,
If not composed entirely of smooth round atoms,
At least not hampered by a close-knit texture,
So they can sting the body and pass through stones   460
Without adhering together. So you can see
That all things of this kind that prick the senses
Are made of atoms sharp but not enmeshed.
And some things too can be both fluid and bitter,
Like the salt sea. This should cause no surprise.   465
For, being fluid, it consists of smooth round atoms,
And rough ones are mixed with them, thus causing pain.
There is no need for them to be hooked together.
You must know that they are round as well as rough
And so can roll and also hurt the senses.   470
It can be shown that Neptune's bitter brine
Comes from a mixture of atoms, rough with smooth.
There is a way to separate them. You can see
How the sweet water, when the same is filtered
Through many layers of earth, runs separately
Into a pit and loses all its saltness.
The atoms of nauseous salt are left on top.   475
Since being rough they adhere more to the earth.

   Now I have explained this I will link a fact
Associated with it and gaining credence from it:
That atoms have a finite number of shapes.
If this were not so, then inevitably   480
Some atoms will have to be of infinite size.
Within the small space of a single atom
There can be no large variety of shapes.
Suppose that atoms consist of three minimal parts,   485
Or make them larger by adding a few more,
When you have taken those parts of a single body
And turned them top to bottom, changed them right and left,

And have worked out in every possible way
What shape each order gives to the whole body,
Then, if you wish perhaps to vary the shapes,
You must add other parts; thence it will follow
That if you wish to change the shapes still further
The arrangement in like manner will need others.
Therefore novelty of shape involves
Increase in size. And so you cannot believe
That atoms differ infinitely in shape
Or you will make some have enormous magnitude,
Which I have proved above to be impossible.

Were it not so, the Orient's richest robes
And gleaming silks of Meliboean purple
Dyed with the hues of shells of Thessaly,
And peacocks' golden breed of laughing beauty,
All, put to shame, would pale before new colours.
Myrrh's scent and honey's taste would be despised,
The swan's sweet song, the high-wrought melodies
Of Phoebus' lyre would vanish, crushed and silent.
Always there would be something more excellent.
And as we see good things would yield to better,
So turning back, they might give way to worse.
Things might well come successively more filthy
And foul to eyes and ears and mouth and nostrils.
Since this does not occur, but things are bound
By limits at each extreme, you must admit
A limit too for matter's different forms.

The path that leads from fires to icy frosts
Also is finite, and the way back is finite.
There are heat and cold and middle temperatures
Between the two which make the range complete.
A finite distance governs their creation,
And two points mark the extremes at either end,
Where flame scorches the one and frost the other.

Now I have explained this I will link a fact
Associated with it, and gaining credence from it:
That atoms which are made of similar shapes
Are infinite in number. Since the variety
Of shapes is finite, then of necessity

The number of similar shapes must be infinite,
Or else the sum of matter would be finite,
Which I have proved it not to be, and in my verses
Have shown that the universe is held together
From infinity by particles of matter
In endless chain of impacts everywhere.   530

You can see that certain animals are rarer,
And nature grants them less fertility;
Yet other climes and places, distant lands,
Breed many of that kind, to swell the total.
Of quadrupeds among the first we see   535
Snake-handed elephants, where India
Lies safe behind a wall of countless thousands,
Of ivory, a rampart none can pass.
So huge the number is of those great beasts,
Of which we see but very few examples.   540

Let me concede this too: let us suppose
One thing exists alone, unique from birth,
That has no likeness in the whole wide world.
Unless there is an infinite supply
Of matter to conceive it, give it birth,   545
It would have no chance of ever being created,
Still less of growth and further nourishment.
Let us assume also that a finite number
Of atoms generative of one single thing
Exists, dispersed at large through the universe,
Then whence, then where, by what force, in what way
Shall they combine and meet in that vast sea,
That alien turmoil of endless matter?
They have no means, I think, of union ever.   550
Observe, when some great flotilla has been wrecked
How the sea throws up pieces everywhere,
And scatters thwarts, ribs, masts, yards, oars adrift,
And every shore along the coast can see   555
Stern-posts a-floating, warning mortal men
To shun the snares and violence and guile
Of the false faithless sea, and never trust
A calm sea's smiling treacherous blandishments.
So, if you once decide that certain atoms   560

Are in number finite, through all time they must be tossed
And scattered on conflicting tides of matter,
Unable ever to join and form connections
Or stay connected or to grow by increase.
565 But plain fact shows that both these things do happen:
Things can be born, and being born can grow.
Therefore it is obvious that an infinite number
Of primal atoms exists of every kind
So as to maintain the supply of everything.

Thus never can the motions of destruction
570 Prevail for ever, entombing life for ever,
Nor can the motions of creation and growth
Forever keep intact what they have fashioned.
Thus the war waged between the primal atoms
Is fought from infinity on equal terms.
575 Now here, now there, the vital powers in things
Vanquish and in turn are vanquished. The funeral dirge
Blends with the wailing of the infant child
When first newborn it sees the shores of light.
No night has followed day, no dawn a night,
That has not heard, mixed with those fretful cries,
580 Laments that march with death and death's dark obsequies.

Now here's another thing you should keep signed and sealed
And locked and treasured in your memory:
That there is nothing, among all things visible,
That consists of one kind of atom only;
585 Nothing that is not a mixture of elements.
The more qualities and powers a thing possesses,
The more it tells that it has great quantity
Of different atoms and of varied shapes.

Firstly, the earth holds atoms in itself
590 From which the springs, their coolness welling forth,
Continually renew the boundless sea.
It holds those atoms too whence fires are born.
The surface of the earth in many a place
Is set alight and burns, while from deep down
The fires arise that kindle Etna's fury.
Further, it holds the means to raise bright crops
595 And joyful orchards for the race of men,

And rivers too and leaves and joyful pastures
For creatures of the wild that range the hills.
Therefore the earth and earth alone is named
Great Mother of the Gods, Mother of beasts,
And procreatress of our human frame.

   Of her of old the Grecian poets sang   600
Learned in ancient lore; a goddess she
In chariot seated by two lions drawn;
Teaching thereby that the world's mighty mass
Hangs fast in space, and earth cannot rest on earth.
They yoked wild beasts to show that stubborn children
Must be subdued by parents' loving care.   605
Upon her head they set a mural crown
Because established safe on chosen heights
Well fortified she bears the weight of cities.
In solemn state the image thus adorned
Of the holy Mother is borne now through the world.
And different peoples in their ancient rites   610
Name her Idaean Mother; and Phrygians
They appoint escort since from there, they say,
First came the corn that spreads now through the world.
Eunuchs they give her, wishing thus to show
That those who violate the Mother's godhead   615
And have been found ungrateful to their parents
Must be accounted shameful and unworthy
To bring live offspring into the shores of light.
On tight-drawn drums palms thunder, cymbals clash,
Horns blare their hoarse threats out, the hollow pipe
Thrills every heart with Phrygian melodies.   620
Next spears are borne before her, savage signs
Of force, to terrify the crowd's ungrateful minds
And impious hearts with fear of power divine.
Therefore when first she rides through some great city,
And silent, with unspoken benediction   625
Blesses mankind, much copper then and silver
They strew along her way in rich largesse,
And with a snow of roses falling, falling
Shadow the Mother and her retinue.
Next comes an armed band dancing, fired with blood,
Leaping in rhythm midst the Phrygian throng,   630

Shaking their awful crests with nodding heads.
These the Greeks name Curetes. They recall
Dicte's Curetes who, the story tells,
In Crete once drowned the infant cries of Jove.
635   A band of boys around the baby boy
All armed and nimbly dancing, keeping time,
Clashed bronze on bronze, lest Saturn find the child
And seize and crush him in his jaws, and deal
The Mother's heart an everlasting wound.
640   Therefore in arms the Great Mother they escort,
Or else to show the goddess' high command
That they in arms and valour strong be ready
To defend their native land, and to their parents
Protection give and pride for all to see.

     All this is well and admirably told.
645   It is, however, far removed from truth.
For perfect peace gods by their very nature
Must of necessity enjoy, and immortal life,
Far separate, far removed from our affairs.
For free from every sorrow, every danger,
650   Strong in their own powers, needing naught from us,
They are not won by gifts nor touched by anger.
Indeed the earth is now and has been always
Devoid entirely of any kind of feeling.
The reason why it brings forth many things
In many ways into the light of sun
Is that it holds a multitude of atoms.
655   If anyone decides to call the sea Neptune,
And corn Ceres, and misuse the name of Bacchus
Rather than give grape juice its proper title,
Let us agree that he can call the earth
Mother of the Gods, on this condition—
That he refuses to pollute his mind
660   With the foul poison of religion.

     We often see grazing the fields together
Under the same wide canopy of heaven
Sheep in their woolly flocks, the martial breed
Of horses, and the horned herds of cattle,
Quenching their thirst all from a single stream,

And yet to each life gives a different shape, 665
And each retains the nature of its parents,
Each after its kind copies their behaviour.
So great is the variety of matter
In every kind of herbage, every river.
Moreover every animal of every kind
Is made of bones, blood, veins, heat, moisture, flesh, and sinews, 670
And all of these are widely different,
Being formed of atoms differently shaped.
Again, whatever can be set on fire
And burnt, for sure must hide within its body,
If nothing else, at least the matter needed
To generate flame and fire and send out light, 675
And make sparks fly and scatter glowing embers.
And all the rest, if with like reasoning
You run through them in your mind, you'll find they have
The seeds of many things hidden inside them
And make combinations of atoms of various shapes.

Again, you see many things have colour and taste 680
Together with smell. Chief among these might be
Burnt offerings smoking on some holy altar.
These therefore must be made of various shapes.
For scent can permeate the human frame
Where colour cannot go; and colour glides
Into the senses separately from taste.
Thus you'll recognize that their atoms have different shapes. 685
Different shapes therefore combine in a single mass
And all things are composed of a mixture of seeds.

Everywhere in my verses you can see
Many letters common to many words,
Although it is obvious that both words and verses 690
Are different and composed of different letters.
Not that there are not many letters common
To separate words, or that no two words consist
Of the same letters, but as a general rule
Words are not made up of the same letters.
Likewise in other things, though many atoms 695
Are common to many things, yet combined together
They can make a whole quite different in substance.

So that the human race and crops and fruitful trees
We may rightly think are made from different elements.

700   Do not imagine that atoms of every kind
Can be linked in every sort of combination.
If that were so, then monsters everywhere
You'ld see, things springing up half-man, half-beast,
Tall branches sprouting from a living body,
Limbs of land animals joined with those of sea.
705   Chimaeras breathing flame from hideous mouths
Nature would feed throughout the fertile earth,
Too fertile, generating everything.
That these things do not happen is manifest.
We see all things created from fixed seeds
By a fixed parent and able as they grow
To keep true to the stock from which they sprang.
710   All this, for sure, fixed laws of nature govern.
Each thing contains its own specific atoms
Which, fed by all its food, spread through the body
Into the limbs and there, combined together,
Produce appropriate movements. By contrast
Alien elements are thrown back by nature
Into the earth; and under the impact of blows
715   Invisible particles fly off from the body
In quantity, unable anywhere
To combine with it, or feel the vital motions
That are in the body so as to copy them.

However, you must not think these laws apply
Only to animals. The same principle
Determines everything that is in the world.
720   All things created differ from each other
By their whole natures; each one therefore must
Consist of atoms differently shaped.
Not that there are not many atoms endowed
With the same shape, but as a general rule
Things do not consist wholly of the same atoms.
725   Further, since the seeds are different, different also
Must be their intervals, paths, weights, and impacts,
Connections, meetings, motions. These separate
Not only animals, but land from sea,
And hold the expanse of heaven apart from earth.

Now here's a matter which with labour sweet
I have researched. When you see before your eyes
A white thing shining bright, do not suppose
That it is made of white atoms; nor when you see something black
That it is made of black atoms; or that anything
Imbued with colour has it for the reason
That its atoms are dyed with corresponding colour.
The atoms of matter are wholly without colour,
Not of the same colour as things, nor of different colour.
And if you think the mind cannot comprehend
Bodies of this kind, you wander far astray.
Men blind from birth, who have never seen the light of sun,
Nevertheless can recognize by touch
Things that from birth they have not linked with colour.
In the same way bodies not marked by any hue
Are able to form a concept in the mind.
We ourselves, when we touch a thing in the dark,
Do not feel that it possesses any colour.

    Since I have proved this, now I will show there are

        [One or more missing lines]

Any colour can change completely into another,
Which primal atoms never ought to do.
For something must survive unchangeable
Lest all things utterly return to nothing.
For all things have their own fixed boundaries;
Transgress them, and death follows instantly.
Therefore beware of staining atoms with colour
Lest you find all things utterly return to nothing.

    If atoms are by nature colourless
But possess different shapes from which they make
Colours of every kind in varied hues—
A process in which it is of great importance
How they combine, what positions they take up,
What motions mutually they give and take—
That gives you at once a simple explanation
Why things that were black a little while before
Can suddenly become as white as marble,
As the sea when strong winds beat upon its surface
Turns into white wave-crests of marble lustre.

730

735

740

745

750

755

760

765

You could say that often what we see as black,
When its matter has been mixed and the arrangement
770   Of atoms changed, some added, some taken away,
Immediately is seen as white and shining.
But if the atoms of the sea's wide levels
Were blue, they could not possibly be whitened.
Stir up blue matter anyway you will,
775   It can never change its colour into marble.
Or if the different atoms that compose
The single unmixed brightness of the sea
Are dyed with different colours, as a square,
A single shape, may be made up of parts
Of different shape and form, it would be right
780   That, as in the square we see the different shapes,
So on the surface of the sea, or in
The unmixed brightness of some other object,
We should see various colours, widely different.
Besides, the different shapes of various parts
785   Do not prevent the whole from being a square;
But different colours make it impossible
For a thing to possess one single brightness.

The argument that sometimes entices us
To attribute colours to atoms, falls apart;
790   For white things are not made from white, nor black
From black, but both from different colours.
White obviously comes much more easily
From no colour than from black, or any other
Colour that interferes with it and thwarts it.

795   And since there can be no colour without light
And atoms do not emerge into the light,
You can be certain that no colour clothes them.
What colour can there be in total darkness?
It is light itself that produces change of colour
As things are lit by rays direct or slanting.
800   The feathers of a pigeon in the sunshine
Around its neck, crowning its lovely head,
Sometimes you see them gleaming bronze and ruby,
At other times, viewed from a certain angle,
805   They mix sky blue with green of emeralds.

A peacock's tail, when filled with bounteous light,
In the same way changes colour as it turns.
These colours are made by incidence of light;
Without it certainly no colour could exist.

When the eye is said to see the colour white,   810
The pupil receives a certain kind of impact,
And another when it sees black and all the rest;
But when you touch things, it matters not at all
What colour they have but only what the shape is.
For sure then, atoms have no need of colour,   815
But their different shapes and forms produce
Various sensations of touch and different feelings.

There is no direct connection between colour and shape,
And all formations of atoms can exist in every hue;
Why therefore are things composed of them,   820
Not tinted all with every kind of colour?
You would see ravens flying through the air
Emit a snowy sheen from snowy wings,
And swans turn black, their atoms being black,
Or any colour uniform or mixed.

Again, the more a thing is divided up   825
Into minute parts, the more you see the colour
Fades gradually away and is extinguished.
When purple cloth for instance is pulled to pieces
Thread by thread, the purple and the scarlet,
Brightest of colours, are totally destroyed.   830
So that you may see that, before its particles
Are reduced to atoms, they breathe out all their colour.

Finally, since you accept that certain things
Emit neither noise nor smell, for this reason   835
You do not attribute sound or scent to everything.
So, since our eyes cannot see everything,
You may be sure that certain things exist
Which have no colour, any more than scent or sound.
And these the intelligent mind can comprehend   840
No less than things that lack some other quality.

Do not suppose that atoms are bereft
Only of colour. They are quite devoid
Also of warmth and cold and fiery heat.

Barren of sound and starved of taste they move.
845 Their bodies emit no odour of their own.
When you set out to make a pleasing scent
From marjoram or myrrh or the sweet flower
Of spikenard breathing nectar to our nostrils
Among the first things that you need to seek
850 Is an oil that is, so far as you may find one,
Odourless and emits no breath of anything.
For this will least with harsh taint of its own
Corrupt the scents concocted with its substance.
For the same reason atoms must not bring
855 An odour of their own in making things,
Nor sound, since they can emit nothing from themselves,
Nor similarly taste of any kind,
Nor cold likewise nor heat nor gentle warmth
And all the rest. All these are perishable—
The softness of their substance makes them pliant,
860 Its hollowness porous, its brittleness makes them crumble—
All must be kept well separate from atoms,
If we wish to lay a strong and sure foundation,
Immortal, on which the sum of life may rest;
Lest you find all things utterly returned to nothing.

865   Now here is another point. Things that we see have feeling
Consist of atoms that are devoid of feeling.
Nor do things plainly known to us
And manifest refute this or fight against it.
Rather they take us by the hand and make us believe
870 That living things, as I say, are born from insentient atoms.
Why, you can see that living worms emerge
From filthy dung when the wet earth is soaked
And rotted by unseasonable rains.
All other things are seen likewise to change.
875 Rivers and leaves and joyful pastures change
Into cattle, and cattle change into our bodies,
And often too our bodies build the strength
Of wild beasts and winged masters of the air.
So nature turns all foods to living bodies
880 And from them makes all the senses of animals
In much the same way as she makes dry logs
Unfold in flames and turns them into fire.

Now do you see how very important is
The order in which all the atoms are placed,
How they combine, what motions they give and take? 885

What is it then that strikes the mind itself
And moves it, and compels it to express
Ideas which forbid you to believe
That the sentient comes from the insentient?
Doubtless it is that a mixture of water and logs
And earth cannot produce a vital sense. 890
And here you will please bear this in mind:
I do not say that all the substances
Which produce sentient bodies always do so.
It all depends how small the atoms are
That make a sentient thing, what shapes they have, 895
What motions and arrangements and positions.
None of these things is found in wood or clods,
Yet these, when rotted as it were by rain,
Produce small worms, because the bodies of matter,
Moved by a new thing from their ancient order, 900
Combine in a way that must make living creatures.

Further, those who maintain that sentient things
Can be created from things sentient,
Themselves from other sentient things created,
Make the foundations of our senses perishable,
Because they make them soft; for all sensation
Is linked with flesh, veins, sinews, all of which 905
Being soft consist of substance which is mortal.

However, let us assume, for the sake of argument,
That these things last for ever. Then they must
Either have the sensation of a part
Or else instead be like whole animals.
But parts can have no feeling by themselves: 910
Sensation in our limbs involves the whole body.
A hand or any part severed from the body
Cannot retain sensation on its own.
It follows that they are like whole animals.
So they must have the same feelings as ourselves 915
So as to share in all our vital senses.
How then can they be called first elements

And escape the paths of death? They are animate,
And animate and mortal are the same.

920 Even if they could, their unions and combinations
Would make nothing more than a crowd of living things,
Any more than men and cattle and wild beasts
By combination could make anything.
But if they were to give up from their bodies
Their own power of feeling, and acquire another one,

925 What was the point of giving them in the first place
What is taken away? Besides, as we saw before,
Since we see eggs of birds produce live chicks
And worms swarm out when by untimely rains
Earth has been rotted, then we may be sure

930 That sense can be produced from the insentient.

Suppose, however, someone should maintain
That sense can indeed arise from the insentient,
But is produced by some process of change
Or by some kind of birth that gives it being,
It will suffice to prove quite clearly to him

935 That birth does not occur without previous union,
And nothing changes except by combination.
There can be no sensation in any body
Until the living thing itself is born;
Because of course its matter is held dispersed

940 In air and rivers and earth and earth-born things,
And has not yet assembled, nor combined
Within itself the vitalizing motions
By which the all-perceiving senses kindled
See to the safety of all living things.

Consider this also: some living creature
Is suddenly prostrated by a blow

945 More powerful than its nature can withstand,
And all the senses then of mind and body
Are stunned, and thrown at once into confusion.
For all the arrangements of the primal atoms
Are broken up, the vital motions checked
Deep down inside, until the substance fails,
Battered through every limb, and loosens all

950 The vital knots that bind the soul to body

And scatters it, forced out through every pore.
What else are we to think a blow can do
Than shatter what it strikes and break it up?
And often, when a blow strikes with less force,
The vital motions that remain will win,   955
Yes, win, and calm its vast disturbances,
Recalling every part to its own course
And shattering the impetus of death
Now all but lord and master of the body,
Kindling once more sensations almost lost.
How else could creatures at the door of death   960
Return to life, their minds restored again,
Rather than make their exit by a route
They have travelled almost to the end, and pass away?

   Pain occurs when particles of matter
Attacked by some force in the limbs and flesh
Quiver and tremble in their deep abodes;   965
And when they settle back into their places
That is a soothing joy. So you may know
That atoms cannot suffer any pain
Nor in themselves experience any pleasure,
Since they possess no primal particles
From whose new movements they might feel distress   970
Or reap some fruit of life-giving delight.
Therefore they cannot be endowed with senses.

   And if, to enable animals to feel,
We must attribute senses to their atoms,
What are we then to say about those atoms
Which give the human race its character?   975
Doubtless they shake their sides and rock with laughter
And weeping oft bedew their cheeks with tears,
Engage in long and brilliant disputation
About the mix of things that makes the world,
And then proceed to enquire about themselves
To find what atoms they themselves are made of.
For if they resemble complete mortal men,   980
They must also consist of other particles
And those in turn of others, and then others;
There's nowhere you could dare to call a halt.

Indeed, I will follow you in your argument
And say that whatever speaks and laughs and thinks
Must be composed of parts that do the same.
985   But if we see that this is raving madness,
That a man can laugh who has no laughing atoms,
And think and proffer learned arguments
Though sprung from seeds not wise or eloquent,
Why should not things we see possessing feeling
990   Be made of seeds entirely without senses?

Lastly, we are all sprung from heavenly seed,
All from the same one father, him from whom
Life-giving mother, kindly earth, receives
Sweet showers of moisture, by which fertilized
She brings forth shining crops and joyful trees,
995   Brings forth mankind and all the breed of beasts,
And yields the food on which all feed their bodies,
To lead sweet lives and propagate their kind.
Wherefore she rightly has earned the name of mother.
And what before was made from earth returns
1000   To earth, and what came down from ether's shores
Borne back again the halls of heaven receive.
And death does not destroy things when they die
So as to bring destruction to their atoms,
But breaks their combination everywhere,
And then makes new conjunctions, making all things
1005   To change their shapes and colours and receive feeling,
And in an instant yield it up again.
So you may recognize how much it matters
How these same atoms combine, in what positions,
What motions mutually they give and take.
1010   Then you will not suppose that what we see
Floating upon the surface of things, sometimes
Being brought to life, then dying suddenly,
Are qualities of everlasting atoms.
Moreover in my verse it matters much
How letters are arranged and linked with others.
1015   The same denote sky, sea, land, rivers, sun,
The same denote crops, trees, and animals,
And, if not all, by far the greater part
Are alike; but the position decides the meaning.

So with real things, when the combination of their atoms,
Their motions, order, forms, shapes, and positions   1020
Are changed, the thing itself must change.

    Now give your mind, please, to true reasoning.
A new thing now is struggling urgently
To reach your ears, a new aspect of creation
Is striving to reveal itself.   1025
But nothing is so simple that at first
It is not more difficult to believe it than to doubt it,
And nothing so mighty and so marvellous
That men do not in time abate their wonder.
Take first the bright pure azure of the sky   1030
And all the sky contains—the wandering stars,
The moon, and glorious radiance of the sun—
If all these suddenly, unexpectedly,
For the first time appeared to mortal men,
What would they name more wonderful, what less likely   1035
That men before they saw it should believe it?
Nothing, I think—so marvellous the sight.
But now, long sated with this glorious vision,
Men do not care, and no one lifts his head
To look up to the shining realms of heaven.
Therefore forbear, dismayed by novelty,   1040
To thrust out reason from your mind. No. Weigh it
With judgement keen, and then if it seems true
Give in, or if false, gird yourself to fight.
For since the sum of space is infinite
Spreading beyond the ramparts of the world,   1045
The mind desires by reasoning to find
What may exist there far away, the bourne
To which the exploring intellect aspires,
To which the mind's thrust flies forever free.

    This is my first point. Everywhere around us
On either side, above, below, throughout the universe,
There is no end. I have proved this, and the facts themselves 1050
Shout it aloud. Deep space shines clear to see.
Now since space lies in all directions infinite
And seeds in number numberless for ever
Fly all around in countless different ways

Through an unfathomable universe
1055 Perpetually driven by everlasting motion,
It must be deemed in high degree unlikely
That this earth, this sky, alone have been created,
And all those bodies of matter outside do nothing.
And added proof of this lies in the fact
That nature made this world. The seeds of things
In random and spontaneous collision
1060 In countless ways clashed, heedless, purposeless, in vain
Until at last such particles combined
As suddenly united could become
The origins always of mighty things,
Of earth, sky, sea, and breeds of living creatures.
Wherefore again and again I say you must admit
That in other places other combinations
1065 Of matter exist such as this world of ours
Which ether holds in ardent fond embrace.

And note this too—when matter is abundant
And space is there, and nothing checks and hinders,
Then action and creation must take place.
1070 And if there exists so great a store of atoms
As all the years of life on earth could never number,
And if the same great force of nature stands
Ready to throw the seeds of things together
In the same way as they have here combined,
Then of necessity you must accept
1075 That other earths exist, in other places,
With varied tribes of men and breeds of beasts.

Add to this that nothing in the universe
Is born unique and grows unique, alone,
But all belong to a species, very many
1080 Of the same kind. Consider animals:
You'll find this rule applies to the wild beasts
That roam the mountains, to the human race,
To the dumb shoals of fish, to all things that fly.
Therefore likewise one must accept that sky
1085 And earth and sun, moon, sea, and all else that exists
Are not unique, but in number numberless.
No less a deep-set boundary stone of life

Awaits them, no less from a birth their bodies sprang,
Than those that here on earth of every kind
Abound, and multiply their generations.

    If you know these things well, you'll see at once   1090
That nature is free, no slave to masters proud;
That nature by herself all things performs
By her own will without the aid of gods.
For—by the gods who in their tranquil peace
Live ever quiet in a life serene—
Who has the strength to rule the sum of things
Immeasurable, to hold beneath his hands   1095
Bridled and reined the unfathomable deep,
To turn the firmaments of all the heavens,
Warm all the fertile worlds with heavenly fires,
At all times present and in every place,
That can make darkness with his clouds, and shake
The sky serene with thunder, and with lightning   1100
Oft shatter his own temples and then departing
Let fly at deserts, raging with that bolt
That often spares the guilty, but brings death
To men whose lives are innocent and blameless?

    Since the first natal hour of the world,   1105
The day when earth and sea were born, and sun
Had first its rising, atoms have been added
In multitudes from outside, many seeds
Added from out the mighty universe,
Thrown all together by its ceaseless motion;
That increase might be given to land and sea,
The realms of sky extend their bounds, and lift   1110
Their lofty buildings far above the earth;
That air might rise. For blows from every side
Supply to each thing its own special atoms.
All join their own kind; water goes to water,
Earth is increased by elements of earth,
And fires are forged by fire, and ether by ether,   1115
Until to the utmost limit of their growth
Nature at last has brought them, great perfectress,
Great mother and creatress of the world.
And this is reached when into the veins of life

No more is given than passes out away.
1120 Here for all things the advance of life must halt,
Here nature checks the increase of her powers.
For all things that you see in cheerful growth
Scale step by step the ladder of ripe years,
Take into themselves more things than they discharge,
1125 While food flows smoothly into all the veins
And they themselves are not so loosely knit
As to shed matter freely and to squander
More than their life absorbs in nourishment.
For though we must accept that many bodies
Flow off from things and pass away, more must be added,
1130 Until they have touched the topmost peak of growth.
Then the strong vigour of maturity
Age slowly breaks and melts into decay.
And when growth stops, the larger a thing is
And wider, the more particles it throws off
1135 And scatters them on all sides everywhere.
Food does not easily penetrate the veins,
Nor in proportion to the flow outpoured
Is there enough to bring to birth again
All that is needed, and make good the loss.

So death comes rightly, when by constant flow
1140 All things are thinned, and all things, struck from without
By an increasing hail of blows, succumb;
Since at the end great age finds food to fail,
And without ceasing bodies from outside
Beating on things subdue them and destroy them.

1145 So shall the ramparts of the mighty world
Themselves be stormed and into crumbling ruin
1150 Collapse. Even now the world's great age is broken
And earth worn out scarce bears small animals,
She who created all the generations
And brought to birth huge bodies of wild beasts.
No golden chain, I think, from heaven on high
Let down the breeds of mortals to the fields;
1155 Nor sea nor waves that break upon the rocks
Created them. From the same earth they sprang
That now supplies their nurture from her body.

Herself the shining crops and joyful vineyards
By her own will first made for mortal men;
Herself gave forth sweet fruits and joyful pastures,
Which now our toil scarce brings to growth and increase.   1160
We wear out oxen, wear out the strength of farmers,
Wear down the ploughshare in fields that scarce can feed us,
So do they grudge their fruits and multiply our toil.
And now the aged ploughman shakes his head
With many a sigh that all the weary labour
Of his strong arms has fallen away in vain,   1165
And when he compares times present with times past
Oft praises then the fortunes of his father.
And looking on his old and worn-out vines,
The husbandman bewails the march of time
And rails at heaven, and grieves that men of yore
In old god-fearing days could easily   1170
Within the confines of a narrow plot,
Far smaller then than now, support their lives.
He does not know that all things in decay
By slow degrees are moving towards their end
Worn by the age-old passage of the years.

BOOK THREE

You, who from so great darkness could uplift
So clear a light, lighting the joys of life,
You, glory of the Greeks, I follow you
And in your footprints plant my footsteps firm,
Not in desire of rivalry, but love
Drives me to yearn to copy you. The swallow
Can't vie with swans. What would a trembling kid
Do in contest with a strong swift horse?
You, father, have revealed the truth, and you
A father's precepts gave us in your pages.
As bees in flowery glades sip every bloom,
So we, like them, feed on your golden words,
Golden, most worthy of eternal life.
For once your reason, born of mind divine,
Starts to proclaim the nature of the world
The terrors of the mind flee all away,
The walls of heaven open, and through the void
Immeasurable, the truth of things I see.
The gods appear now and their quiet abodes
Which no winds ever shake, nor any rain
Falls on them from dark clouds, nor ever snow
Congealed with bitter frost with its white fall
Mars them; but always ever-cloudless air
Enfolds and smiles on them with bounteous light.
There nature everything supplies, and there
Through all the length of ages nothing comes
To vex the tranquil tenor of their minds.
But in contrast nowhere at all appear
The halls of Acheron, though earth no bar
Opposes, but lets all be clearly seen
That moves beneath our feet throughout the void.
And now from all these things delight and joy,

As it were divine, takes hold of me, and awe
That by your power nature so manifest
Lies open and in every part displayed.

                                                                    30

   And since I have taught the beginnings of all things,
What kind they are, and how in varying forms
Of their own accord, driven by everlasting
Motion, they fly, and how all things from them
Can be created, next and following this
The nature of mind and spirit by my verses   35
Must be made clear, and headlong out of doors
That fear of Hell be thrown, which from its depths
Disquiets the life of man, suffusing all
With the blackness of death, and leaving no delights
Pure and unsullied. This man it persuades
To break the bonds of friendship and another   40
To violate honour, and in a word   83
To turn all morals upside down. Traitors
To country and to parents men have been
For fear, the appalling fear, of Acheron.
                                                                    86
For when men say a life of infamy
And foul diseases is more terrible
Than death's deep pit, and that they know that blood
Is what the spirit is made of, or even wind,
(If so the fancy takes them) and that they have
No need of what my reasoning tells them, then
I'll show you that they speak thus seeking praise,   45
Boasting, and not because the matter's proved.
These men in exile, banished from their homes,
Far from the sight of men, stained by foul charges,
Cursed, in a word, by every misery,
Yet live; and despite their words they sacrifice
To their ancestral gods, they slay black cattle,   50
They send oblations to the ghosts below,
And in their bitter straits they turn their minds
More keenly now than ever to religion.
Thus, when in perils and adversity
A man has fallen, it's more useful then   55
To look at him and easier to know him.
For only then from out the heart's deep core
True voices rise, the mask's stripped off, the man

Remains. Greed and blind lust for fame
Moreover, which compel men to transgress
60   The bounds of law, and often times make them,
Allies and ministers of crime, strive night and day
With toil and sweat to gain the heights of power,
These wounds of life in no small part are fed
By fear of death. For 'tis the common view
That shameful scorn and bitter poverty
65   Are far removed from a sweet and stable life,
And, as it were, are simply lingering
Before the gates of death. From which, when men
Driven by groundless fear desire to flee
And to remove themselves far, far away,
70   By civil strife they make wealth for themselves
And heap up riches, murder upon murder
Piling in greed. A brother's death gives joy.
A kinsman's board supplies both hate and fear.
By similar reasoning, born of the same fear,
75   Envy consumes them; that he before their eyes
Gets power, is known, parades in pomp and show,
While they the while in darkness and in filth
Lie wallowing—that's their complaint, you see!
Some die to get a statue and a name.
And often too, crazed by the fear of death,
80   Such hate of life and light possesses them
That their own deaths they plan, with sorrowing heart,
82   Forgetting that this fear begets their woes.
87   For we, like children frightened of the dark,
Are sometimes frightened in the light—of things
No more to be feared than fears that in the dark
90   Distress a child, thinking they may come true.
Therefore this terror and darkness of the mind
Not by the sun's rays, nor the bright shafts of day,
Must be dispersed, as is most necessary,
But by the face of nature and her laws.

First I say that the mind, which we often call
The intelligence, in which is situated
95   The understanding and the government
Of life, is a part of man, no less than hands
And feet and eyes are part of the living being,

Though many wise philosophers have thought
That it is not placed in a definite part, but is
A sort of vital essence of the body,
Called harmony by the Greeks, which makes us live   100
Endowed with feeling, though the intelligence
Is not in any part; as when the body
Is said to be in good health, but health is not
A part of it, so in no definite place
They place the mind—and here they plainly err
Exceedingly, in many different ways.   105
For often the body, which we see, is sick
And yet in another part, which we cannot see,
We're happy. And conversely, in its turn,
The opposite applies, as when a man
Though sick in mind in body flourishes.
Let's take another case—a man hurts his foot,   110
It doesn't mean he gets a headache too!
Again, when limbs are given to gentle sleep
And body without senses lies outstretched,
There's something in us all the time that feels
In many ways, and takes into itself
Movements of pleasure and the heart's vain cares.   115

Next, that the spirit also you may know
Lies in our limbs, and that it is not harmony
That makes the body feel, firstly it happens
That if a great part of the body be taken away
Yet oft within our limbs life still remains.   120
Again, when a few particles of heat
Have fled abroad, and outwards through the mouth
Air is expelled, at once this same spirit
Deserts the veins and leaves the bones. From this
You will recognize that not all particles
Work the same way or support life equally.   125
But those that are seeds of wind and warming heat
Secure that life still lingers in our limbs.
Therefore there is within the body heat
And vital wind which at the point of death
Deserts our frame and causes us to die.

Well then, since we have recognized that mind   130
And spirit are in some way a part of man,

Give back the name of harmony, brought down
To those musicians from high Helicon;
Maybe they found it somewhere else, and gave
The name to something till then nameless. Anyway
Whatever it is, let them keep it. And you
135   Please listen to the rest of what I say.

I tell you now that mind and spirit are
Conjoined and in one single nature fixed,
But head and master as it were of all
The body, is the understanding, which we call
Mind and intelligence. It has its seat
140   Placed in the middle region of the breast.
For here throb fear and terror, here abides
Sweet melting joy, and therefore intelligence
And mind are. And the rest of the spirit,
Through the whole body diffused, obeys the will
Of mind and working of intelligence.
Mind by itself alone has sense, alone
145   Rejoices for itself, when nothing moves
Spirit or body. And just as when our head
Or eye is hurt by an attack of pain,
The whole body is not tormented, so
The mind sometimes itself alone is hurt
150   Or thrills with joy, while the spirit's other part
Throughout our limbs and frame remains unmoved.
But when the mind is strongly gripped by fear
We see the whole spirit throughout the frame
Share the same feeling; we sweat, grow pale,
155   Our speech is broken, the voice dies away,
Our eyes grow dark, our ears are filled with noise,
Our limbs give way; in short, through mental terror
We see men fall to the ground. From this we know
That spirit is linked with mind; when struck by mind
160   The spirit drives the body and compels it.
This reasoning likewise shows that mind and spirit
Are bodily, for when we see that limbs are moved,
The body snatched from sleep, the countenance
Changed, the whole man ruled and steered, a thing
165   Impossible without touch, and touch in turn
Impossible without body, must we not

Admit that mind and spirit are bodily?
Moreover you can see the mind to suffer
Along with the body, and to share its feeling.
If the grim power of a javelin,
Driven deep into the bones and sinews, fails   170
To take the life, yet weakness follows, then
A fall to the ground, and on the ground a storm
In the mind, and sometimes as it were
A faint desire to rise. The nature of mind
Must therefore in itself be bodily,
Since blows upon the body make it suffer.   175

This mind, I now propose to explain to you,
What kind of thing it is, and whence derived.
Most delicate it is I say and formed
Of atoms most minute. That this is so
The following example may convince you.   180
Nothing is done so swiftly as the mind
Determines it to be done, and acts itself;
More quickly then the mind bestirs itself
Than anything else that comes before our eyes;
But what is so readily moved must needs consist   185
Of seeds extremely round and most minute
So that a force though very small can move them.
Water moves easily and flows with little force
Because it is formed of smooth and rolling shapes.
Honey conversely has more stability,   190
Its fluid is more sluggish and its movement
Slow, because the whole mass of its matter
Coheres more slowly, since it is not made
Of atoms so smooth and delicate and round.
Take poppy seeds, a big high heap of them,   195
A breath of wind can make the top slide down,
But take a heap of stones or ears of wheat,
It cannot move them. So, you see, so far
As atoms are extremely small and smooth,
They have the power of motion; but heavy things   200
And things that are rough have more stability.

Now therefore, since we have found the mind to be
Extremely mobile, of necessity

It must consist of atoms extremely small
And smooth and round. If this be known to you
My friend, you'll find it helps in many ways,
And you will call it valuable and useful.
This also shows its nature and how fine
Its texture is, and how minute a space
It would occupy if it could be massed together—
As soon as death's calm quiet takes a man
And mind and spirit have departed, then
Nothing from all the body can you see
Diminished, not in look nor weight, but death
Presents it all, less only sense and warmth.
Therefore the entire spirit must consist
Of seeds extremely small, through veins, flesh, sinews,
Woven; wherefore, when all of it has left
The body, none the less the shape of limbs
Remains intact; no whit of weight is lost.
The bouquet of wine is an example, or
The scent of ointment, or the flavour of something;
They disappear, but all the same no whit
Smaller the thing seems to our eyes, nor less
Is it in weight; no wonder, since minute
Seeds are what make the flavour and the scent.
Wherefore again and yet again I say
The nature of the mind and spirit must
Of seeds extremely small be constituted,
Since when it flees it takes no weight away.

But do not suppose that this nature is single.
When a man dies, a kind of thin breath, mixed
With heat, deserts him, and the heat draws air
Along with it. Nor is there any heat
That is not mixed with air, for since its nature
Is rarefied, then of necessity
First elements of air must needs move through it.
Already therefore we have found that mind
Is threefold; but these three are not enough
To engender feeling, since no one of them
Is able to make the motions that bring sense,
Still less the thoughts that come into our minds.
Therefore a fourth thing of some kind must be

Added, and this is wholly without name.
Nothing exists more easily moved than this,
Nor thinner nor made of elements more small
And smooth, and this first transmits through our limbs   245
Sense-giving motions. For this first is moved
Being smallest, next heat and the blind power of wind
Take on the movement, then the air, then everything
Is moved, the blood is stirred, the flesh is thrilled
All through with feeling, bones and marrow feel   250
Pleasure perhaps, or pleasure's opposite.
Nor can pain penetrate thus far, or violent ill,
But that they cause so much disquiet that
No place is left for life, the spirit flees
Dispersed through all the channels of the body.   255
But usually, as it were at the body's surface
These movements end; so we keep hold on life.

    Now when I long to explain how these things are
Mingled among themselves, and in what ways
Arranged they are active, then against my will
The poverty of our language holds me back.   260
But the chief points I'll touch on, as best I can.
The first beginnings move among themselves
So closely that no single one of them
Is separate or has power to act alone
Divided from the rest, but many of them
Compose together a kind of single body.   265
As in the flesh of any animal
There is a certain scent and heat and flavour
Yet from all these one body is made complete,
So heat and air and the blind power of wind
Mixed form one nature, with that moving force   270
Which from itself dispenses the beginning of motion,
The sense-bringer, from which through all the body
Movement first begins. For deep deep down
This nature hidden lies, and far beneath;
Nothing so deep in all our body lies,
The spirit of the very spirit itself.   275
Just as, mixed in our limbs and all our body,
The force of mind and power of spirit lies hid,
Made as it is of few small elements,

280   So does this nameless force made of minute
      Atoms lie hid, spirit of spirit, and lord
      Of all the body. So likewise must wind
      And air and heat all mingled interact
      Throughout our limbs, one yielding place to another
      Or rising in such a way that a unity
285   Is made of all; for else must heat and wind
      Apart, and the power of air apart, destroy
      The senses and apart dissolve them.
      That heat is also in the mind when anger
      Boils, and fire flashes fiercely from the eyes;
290   And cold is too, fear's chill companion, when
      It makes the flesh to creep and shakes the limbs.
      And then there is that calm and peaceful air
      Which comes from tranquil heart and face serene.
      But more of heat there is in those whose hearts
295   And bitter minds flash easily into wrath.
      Lions are most like this, that growl and roar
      And cannot contain the fury in their breasts.
      But the cold mind of the stag has more of wind
300   That sends cold airs more quickly through his flesh
      Which cause a quivering movement in the limbs.
      But the cow lives more by peaceful air. She's not
      Too much excited by the smokey torch
      Of anger spreading darkness all around,
305   Nor pierced and frozen with cold shafts of fear.
      She stands between the two—stags and fierce lions.
      So also is it with the race of men.
      By schooling many achieve an equal gloss,
      But the character they're born with still remains.
310   And faults you cannot tear up by the roots,
      So that one man can hold his temper better,
      Another be less of a coward or a third
      Accept insults too readily. For men
      In many other ways must differ, and
315   Their habits follow from their different natures.
      I cannot now explain the causes of these
      Or list the names of all those primal things
      Which give to nature such variety.
      One thing for sure I can affirm is this:

The traces of these things which stay in us
Beyond the power of reason to expel 320
Are so minute that nothing can prevent
Our living lives on earth like those of gods.

   This spirit then is contained in every body,
Itself the body's guardian, and source
Of its existence; for with common roots
They cling together, and without destruction 325
Cannot be torn apart, like frankincense,
You can't tear out the scent from lumps of it
Without its very nature being destroyed.
So from the body if mind and spirit be
Withdrawn, total collapse of all must follow, 330
So interwoven are the elements
From their first origin, which constitute
Their common life; and neither body nor mind
Has power of feeling, one without the other,
But by the joint movements of both united
Sensation is kindled for us in the flesh. 335
Besides, a body is never born by itself
Nor grows, nor ever lasts long after death.
For not as water when it gives off heat
Does not disintegrate, but remains entire,
Not thus I say can the body endure division 340
From the spirit which has left it. But utterly
It perishes convulsed and rots away.
Likewise, when life begins, in a mother's limbs
And womb, body and spirit learn so well
The ways of life, that if they are separated 345
Damage and ruin follow instantly.
So since their life depends upon this unity
Their nature also must be unified.
Also, if anyone denies that body can feel
And believes that spirit, mixed through the whole body, 350
Creates this motion which we name feeling,
He fights against things manifest and true.
For who can ever make clear what it is
For the body to feel, if not the obvious
Experience which the body has given us?
But once the spirit has left it, then the body 355

Lacks feeling in every part, because it loses
That which in life was not its property;
And many other things it loses too.

    Moreover to say that eyes can see nothing
360 But through them mind looks out, as through a door,
Is difficult, when sense clearly rejects it.
For sense propels us to the object seen;
Especially since we often cannot see
Bright things because of glaring brightness, a thing
Which never happens with doors. For an open door
365 Through which we look presents no difficulty.
Moreover, if our eyes act as a door
Well, take the eyes away, doorposts and all,
And then you'll find the mind should see more clearly.

370   Now here's a thing you never could accept,
A view held by the great Democritus,
That primal atoms of body and mind are placed
One beside one alternately in pairs
And in this manner bind the frame together.
375 For, while the seeds of spirit are much smaller
Than those which make our body and our flesh,
Also they are fewer in number and are placed
Only at wide intervals through the frame.
The intervals at which these atoms lie
Equal in size the size of the smallest thing
380 That can produce sensation in our bodies.
Sometimes we do not feel a speck of dust
Clinging to the body, or chalk-powder whitening
Our limbs, nor mist at night; nor spider's webs
When we move into them, or the web's fine threads
385 Falling upon our heads, nor feathers of birds
Or flying thistledown, which are so light
They scarce can fall to the ground. A caterpillar
Or other creeping thing, we can't feel it walking;
390 Nor the separate footsteps of a gnat or fly.
So fine it is that many particles
Must be moved in us before, spread through our limbs,
The first beginnings of spirit can be touched
And feel, and bouncing across those intervals
395 Combine and couple and spring apart in turn.

The mind more strongly holds the barriers
Of life, than does the spirit, and is lord
Of life more than the spirit is. For without
Mind and intelligence no particle
Of spirit for the smallest length of time
Can stay in our limbs, but all too easily
Follows its companions into the air away
And leaves the limbs cold in the chill of death.   400
But he remains in life to whom the mind
And intelligence remain. Though he may be
A mutilated trunk dismembered, and
The spirit fled and banished from the limbs,
Yet he lives, and breathes the air of life. Cut off   405
If not from all yet from the greater part
Of the spirit, yet he lingers, and clings to life.
Consider the eye, if it is cut all round,
Provided that the pupil stays unhurt
The lively power of seeing abides intact;
Unless, that is, you damage the whole eyeball   410
And slicing round it leave it quite cut out,
For that results in ruin to them both.
But if that tiny spot in the middle of the eye
Is eaten through, at once the light is out
And darkness follows, however bright it be
With eyeball safe. Such is the bond by which   415
The mind and spirit are forever bound.

Well now, that you may know that mind and spirit
Are born in living creatures and are mortal,
Verses which I with labour sweet and long
Have wrought, I'll give you, worthy of your name.   420
Please now apply both these names to one thing;
When for example I speak of spirit and show
That it is mortal, understand me also
To speak of mind since it is one with the other
And the whole is combined. First, as I have shown
That it is thin, composed of tiny atoms,
And of much smaller elements consists   425
Than the liquid of water, or cloud or smoke,
For it moves far more quickly and behaves
As if struck by some more delicate force, for dreams

430 Of smoke and mist can move it, imaginations
     We have in sleep of altars burning and smoke
     Coming from them (since beyond doubt these are
     Images borne to us that we see in sleep)—
     Now therefore, when you see from a broken pot
435 Water or liquid spread out all around
     And see how cloud and smoke dissolve into air,
     Believe that the spirit also is diffused
     And much more quickly dies and is dissolved
     Into its primal atoms once it has left
440 The limbs. And if the body which is its vessel,
     As it were, cannot hold it when broken up
     By anything, or rarefied when blood
     Flows out from the veins, how then do you suppose
     That any air could hold it? How could a thing
     More rarefied than our body ever hold it?

445   We feel moreover that the mind is born
     Together with the body and grows up with it,
     And ages with it. Children run about
     With weak and tender bodies, and their minds
     Are tender too. Next, when maturing years
     Have given them strength, the wisdom and the power
     Of mind grows stronger also. Last, when time
450 With its strong hours has marred them, and the limbs
     Have fallen beneath its blows, the intelligence
     Limps, the tongue rambles, the mind gives way,
     All fails and in one single moment dies.
455 Therefore it follows that like smoke the spirit
     Is melted into air, into thin air,
     Since with the body equally it is born
     And grows, and dies when old age wearies it.

         Another point: just as the body itself
460 Is prone to foul diseases and harsh pain,
     So we can see the mind to suffer also
     Anxiety and grief and fear; it follows
     That the mind equally partakes of death.
     Moreover, even in bodily diseases,
     Often the mind wanders astray, demented,
     Delirious; sometimes the heavy weight

Of lethargy brings everlasting sleep, 465
Closed eyes and drooping head; no voices now
He hears, nor looks can recognize, of friends
Standing beside the bed, calling him back
To light and life, their cheeks bedewed with tears.
Wherefore you must confess that the mind also 470
Is dissolved, since the contagion of disease
Penetrates into it, and disease and pain
Make death, as well we have been taught ere now.
Now let's consider wine. When its strong power 475
Has entered into a man and through the veins
Its fire has spread, then what a weight is there
In all his limbs! His legs give way, he staggers,
His speech is slow, his mind is sodden, his eyes
Swim, and he shouts and belches and fights. He's drunk. 480
Why does this happen, why, I say, unless
Because the spirit, whole still in the body,
Is shaken by the violence of wine?
But this confusion and impediment
Shows that if something slightly stronger should 485
Find its way in, then robbed of his future life
The man must die. Now, take another case—
A man's struck suddenly before our eyes
As if by lightning, falls to the ground and foams
At the mouth, shudders and groans and raves, grows rigid,
Twists, pants, convulsions rack him. Why? for sure 490
Because the force of the disease spread through the limbs
Tears him and spews the spirit out in foam,
As when the sea is lashed by violent waves.
Groans are forced out since limbs are racked with pain, 495
And gathering in the mouth the seeds of voice
Rush out, as it were along the road they know.
Raving occurs because the mind and spirit
Are racked and torn and, as I have shown, divided 500
By that same poison, drawn apart, split up.
Then when at last the disease is spent, and back
To its secret haunts the bitter humour goes
Of the corrupted being, swaying then
A man begins to rise, and by degrees
Returns to his full senses and receives

505 His spirit back. Now therefore, since the spirit
Within the body itself by such diseases
Is tossed about and worn and torn apart,
Why do you think that without a body the same
In the open air, blown by strong winds, can live?
510 And when we see that the mind like a sick body
Can be restored to health by medicine,
This also shows that the living mind is mortal.
For if a man sets out to change the mind
515 Or anything in nature, then he must
Remove a part, however small, or add one,
Or change its position. But what is immortal
Suffers no change of its parts, nor anything added
Or taken away. Its boundaries are fixed;
520 Transgress them, and death follows instantly.
Therefore, as I have taught, a sick mind shows
Signs of mortality and equally
A mind that's changed by medicine. So strongly
Does truth oppose false reasoning and cuts off
The flight of lies in full retreat surrounded,
525 And by a double refutation conquers them.

Another point—we often see how a man
Passes slowly away and limb by limb
Loses the sense of life. First toes grow livid
And then the nails, and then the feet and legs
Die, and then over all his body creep
530 The cold footsteps of death. And so we see
The spirit's divided, and does not depart
All at one time. This shows that it is mortal.
But if perchance you think the spirit can
Pull itself inwards through the limbs, and draw
All of its parts together and in this way
Remove sensation from the limbs, why then
535 The place where all this spirit collects should be
More sensitive, and form a single seat of feeling.
Nowhere does this exist. And so the spirit,
As I have said before, is torn to pieces,
Scattered abroad, and therefore perishes.
540 Moreover, if I were prepared to lie,
And grant you that the spirit could form a mass

Within the body of those who leave the light
Slowly, and slowly die, you must confess
That the spirit is mortal. For whether it dies
Dispersed into the air or drawn together
From all its parts, it matters not at all;   545
Since more and more the senses leave a man
Everywhere, and less and less of life remains.

    The mind has its own place within the body
Fixed, just as eyes and ears are fixed, and noses,
And the other organs of sense that govern life;   550
If they're cut off, they're useless, only fit
For the dustbin. Likewise by itself the mind
Is useless, can't exist without the body,
Which holds it like a jar holds water or   555
Whatever simile you care to choose
Of closeness, since the body clings to it.

    In close conjunction body and mind are strong
With quickened power, enjoying life together.
Nor without body can the mind alone   560
Make living movements, nor deprived of mind
Can body last, and use the senses. Eyes
Torn from their roots can see nothing. Likewise
Mind and spirit alone can do nothing.   565
Yes, mixed through veins and flesh, sinews and bones
Their elements are held in by the body,
Not free to spring apart; and so, shut in,
They act as sense-bringers, which after death   570
They cannot do, ejected from the body
Into the winds of air, held in no more.
For air will be a body and have life
If the spirit can keep itself together, and
Enclose within itself those motions which
It used to make within the limbs and body.

    Wherefore again and yet again I say   576
When all the body's clothing is undone
And the breath of life's thrown out outside, at once
Mind meets its end, and spirit too, since both
Are by one cause united and combined.

580   Again, since body cannot endure division
From spirit without it dies with loathsome stench,
Why do you doubt the cause of this? The spirit
From its deep depths arising has like smoke
Made its thin passage out and spread abroad;
585   The body, changed and crumbling in ruin, collapses.
Why so? Because the body's deep foundations
Have been moved and shaken, while through all its limbs
And winding passages and tiny pores
The spirit has seeped out. So you may learn
That in many ways the spirit was dispersed
When from the limbs it made its exit, and
590   While in the body had been torn apart
Before it emerged outside, you see, and swam
Into the winds of air and so away.

    Let's take another case. Sometimes the spirit
While moving still within the bounds of life
Gets hurt by something (never mind the cause!)
And wants to leave the body and be free.
595   The face grows pale, as at the point of death,
Blood leaves the limbs and all collapse and fall.
This we call fainting. Everyone's distressed,
Wants to hold fast again the chains of life.
600   This happens because the mind and spirit are shaken
And fail, within the fading body. It needs
Only a slightly stronger shock to kill them.
Why then do you doubt that, driven from the body,
Weak, in the open, out of doors, unclothed,
605   Not only not for ever could the spirit
Endure, but not for the smallest length of time?

    For it is evident that no one, dying,
Feels that the soul intact deserts the body
Nor that it rises first to the throat and then
Through the gullet. Instead he feels it fail
610   Seated in some fixed place, just as he feels
His other senses, each in its part, to fail.
But if the mind were immortal, then in dying
It would not complain of being dispersed, but rather
Of going out and shedding its skin, like a snake.

The wisdom and intelligence of mind   615
Never in head or feet or hands are born,
But in one fixed and certain region stay.
This is because fixed places are assigned
To everything that is, in which it must
Be born and grow and have its being. A man   620
Has legs and arms and head and all the rest
And nothing's ever upside down. So sure
One thing follows another. You'll not find
Flames in a river, no, nor frost in fire.

Now, if the mind is immortal and can feel
When parted from the body, we must assume   625
It has the five senses. Only in this way
Can we imagine the spirits of the dead
Go wandering in Hades. Painters and poets
Have always shown us spirits endowed with senses.   630
But what do you think? Can a spirit without body
Have eyes or nose or hand or tongue, and can
The ears hear by themselves without a body?

And since we feel that vital sense inheres   635
In the whole body and that it is the whole
That lives, if suddenly some force
With a swift blow shall cut the body through
So as to sever the two parts asunder,
No doubt the spirit too will be cleft apart,
Divided and cut together with the body.
But what is cut and divided into parts   640
Surely can make no claim to be eternal.
They tell how chariots bearing scythes cut off
A man's limb in the heat of battle. It falls
And quivers on the ground, shorn from the trunk,
But the man feels no pain—the blow's too sudden.   645
A man may lose his left arm and his shield
Torn off amidst the horses by the scythes
Of the chariot wheels and never notice it,   650
Drunk with the fight; or losing his right arm
Press on regardless. Another has lost his leg
And the foot lies on the ground twitching its toes.
The head cut off from the hot and living trunk

655 Stares through its open eyes until what's left
     Of the spirit is given up and passes away.
     Now let's consider a snake, with flickering tongue,
     Long body, and menacing tail. Take your knife
660 And cut it up. You'll see the separate parts
     All writhing while the wound is fresh,
     Spattering the earth with gore. See how its head
     Turns round and back and tries to gnaw its tail,
     Wanting to bite away the burning pain.
     Shall we then say that in each separate piece
665 There is a separate spirit? If we do,
     That means that in one single animal
     There are many spirits spread throughout the body.
     It follows that one single spirit has been
     Divided, just as the body has, so each
     Must be considered mortal, since they both
     Have been alike cut into many parts.

670   Now also, if the spirit is immortal
     And creeps into the body when we are born,
     Why can we not remember time that's past,
     Why do we keep no traces of things done?
     For if the mind has been so greatly changed
675 As to lose all remembrance of past acts,
     That, I think, is not far removed from death.
     Wherefore, you must admit, it follows that
     The spirit that was before has perished and
     The spirit which now is has now been born.

        Moreover, if the body is complete
680 Before the quickened mind can enter it
     When we are born and tread the threshold of life,
     It makes no sense that in our body and limbs
     And in the blood itself it lives and grows;
     Better by far to find a quiet hole
685 For itself, and let the body do the feeling.
     But all experience shows the contrary,
     So interwoven is it with the body
     Through veins, flesh, sinews, even bones, that teeth
     Also have feeling like the rest. We get toothache,
     A twinge from icy water, and grind on grit

That's found in lumps of bread, all hard and rough.   690
Wherefore again and yet again I say
It is unthinkable that spirits have
No beginning or are free from the law of death.
If they come into our bodies from outside
It is unthinkable that they could have
Such close connection with them; and since so close   695
Is this connection, safe and unharmed they can't
Extract themselves from sinews, bones, and joints.
But if by any chance you think that the spirit
Can get into our bodies from outside
And seep through our limbs, then all the more it must,
Fused with the body, perish. What permeates   700
Must also dissolve, and therefore perishes.
Consider food: it goes into our bodies,
Into our limbs, dispersed through many channels,
And perishes; and in so doing supports
Another body. So spirit and mind   705
May enter the body whole, yet permeating
Dissolve, their elements widely dispersed
Into the limbs through the channels of the body,
Those elements of which the mind consists
Which now, in our body born, is lord of it,
Born of that mind which perished when through our limbs   710
It was distributed. Wherefore the spirit
Has both a birthday and a funeral.

   Now here's another question. When the body
Is dead do any seeds of spirit remain in it?
If any do, and stay with it, then clearly
The spirit can't be immortal, since it has gone   715
Away and left some parts of itself behind.
And if it has so completely fled away
That not one particle of itself is left,
How do you explain worms? The body rots
And worms appear. Where from? And the other things   720
Boneless and bloodless that swarm through the limbs,
Where do they come from? Do you really think
That spirits creep into the worms from outside
One by one into a thousand worms—
A thousand spirits where only one has died?   725

Do the spirits go hunting for seeds of the worms
To make a home of them? Or perhaps they creep
Into the bodies of worms already formed?
730 Why should they do this, why take all this trouble?
It's quite a question—worth considering.
For when they are without body they're not plagued
With illnesses or cold or hunger. No,
The body it is that suffers all these ills
And the mind is often sick through contact with it.
735 Suppose, however, that they find it useful
To have a body to enter, there's no way
That they can do this. Spirits therefore do not
Make bodies for themselves. Nor is it possible
That they creep into bodies already made;
For then they'd never make the subtle links
740 They have with body, and the touch of common feeling.

    Another point. Why are lions strong and fierce
And foxes cunning, and deer timid and swift,
And every animal has its character
745 Born in it, when its life begins? It's breed
That does this, the fixed power of mind conjoined
Working with body to establish it.
But if it were immortal and could pass
From body to body, then the behaviour
750 Of animals would be all mixed up. The hound
Would flee before the charging stag's attack,
The hawk would tremble, flying through the air
From the dove pursuing it. Reason, in men
No more, to the wild beasts of the field
Would move her seat. So false it is to say
755 That an immortal spirit can be altered
By a change of body. For that which changes is
Dissolved and therefore perishes, since its parts
Are transposed, and move from their positions.
Wherefore throughout the limbs these parts must be
Capable of being dissolved and in the end
Die when the body dies, along with it.

760   But what if human spirits always go
Into human bodies? Then I still ask why

A foolish spirit can be made of a wise one,
Why children are never wise, and why a foal,
Well trained though it may be, can't match a horse.
No doubt they'll tell you that in a tender body   765
The mind becomes tender. But even if this is so,
The spirit must still be mortal, since being changed
In the body it loses so much life and feeling.
And how could any mind in any body
Grow strong and reach the longed-for flower of life   770
Unless from the beginning it were its consort?
Why does it want to flee from limbs grown old?
Does it fear that a rotting corpse will be its prison
Or that its house worn by the years will fall
And crush it? But the immortal has no dangers.   775

    And really it is ridiculous to imagine
That spirits at the coupling and birth of animals
Stand waiting to get in, immortal spirits
Awaiting mortal bodies, numberless,
Jostling and fighting to get in. Unless, that is,   780
They've made some sort of contract among themselves,
First come first served, that puts an end to squabbling.

    To continue. A tree can't grow in the sky, nor clouds
Float in the sea, nor fish live on dry land,
Nor blood exist in logs nor sap in stones.   785
Everything has its place, certain and fixed,
Where it must live and grow and have its being.
So mind cannot arise without the body
Alone, nor exist apart from blood and sinews.
But if the mind (and this would be much easier)   790
Could be by itself in head or shoulders or heels
And be born in any part, still it would stay
In the same man, the same vessel, enclosed.
And since, within the body, mind and spirit
By a fixed rule and ordinance are given
The place where they may live and grow apart,   795
It is clearly all the more impossible
For them to live and last outside the body.
Wherefore when body has died you must confess
That spirit through body torn has also died.

Really!

It really is quite stupid to suppose
That mortal with immortal can be joined
And feel as one and act upon each other.
What could be more absurd and inconsistent
And contradictory than this: that mortal
805   Linked with immortal could weather furious storms?

Few things there are that last eternally.
First, solid bodies that repel assaults,
And allow nothing to penetrate them
And break apart the close-knit parts within,
810   Such as the atomic particles of matter
The nature of which we have described before;
Next, things which last through all the length of time
Because no blow can hit them; such is the void,
Which stays untouched and nothing can ever strike it;
815   Next, things which have no space around them
Into which they can dissolve and be dispersed;
Such is the eternal sum of the sum of things.
Outside it nowhere any place exists
Into which its elements can spring away,
And nothing exists to impact it or destroy it.

But if you think the spirit is immortal
820   Because it's fortified against all forms of death,
Or nothing ever comes to do it harm
Or, if it does, for some reason turns back
Repulsed before we can see what harm it does,
Yet many ills and dangers harass it.
It sickens when the body itself is sick;
825   But that's not all; for often something comes,
Some doubt about the future that tortures it,
Racks it with fear and wears it out with worry.
Remorse about the past for evil done
Bites it, with madness and forgetfulness,
And lethargy's black waters cover it.

830   Therefore death nothing is to us, nothing
That matters at all, since mind we know is mortal.

Long years ago, when the Phoenicians
Were coming in upon us from all sides,
When the world shook with the tumult of war

And quaked, and shivered to the heights of heaven,   835
When all men doubted where by land and sea
The victory would lie, we were untroubled.
So, when the end shall come, when the close bonds
Of body and spirit that hold us here shall part
And we shall be no more, nothing can harm us   840
Or make us feel, since nothing of us remains,
Though earth be joined with sea and sea with sky.
And if it were true that mind and spirit can still
Have feeling torn from the body, that means to us
Nothing, since the marriage bonds of body and spirit   845
Weld us together in one single whole.
No more, again, if time should after death
Collect our matter and bring it back, and if
The lights of life were given back to us,
Would that concern us, not one whit, when once   850
Our memory of ourselves has passed away.
And nothing now comes back to us from that self
That was before, nor from it now can fear
Or anguish ever touch us.

When you review the whole past length of time   855
Existing measureless, and think how mixed
And various the motions of matter are,
You will easily believe that the same seeds
Of which we now are made, have often before
Been placed in the positions they are now in.
But memory cannot recall it, since in between
A great gulf is fixed, a halt of life, and all   860
The wandering motions have been scattered far
From things we know. If in a future time
A man is to suffer pain and misery,
He must exist, or else he could not feel it.
But death makes this impossible and forbids
The man to exist to whom these ills could come.   865
Therefore we may be certain that in death
There is nothing to fear, that he who does not exist
Cannot feel pain, that it makes no difference
Whether or not a man has been born before,
When death the immortal has taken his mortal life.

870   So when you see a man resent his fate
That after death his body in the tomb
Must rot, or perish in flames or by wild beasts,
You will know that he rings false, that in his heart
Lies deep some hidden sting, though he denies

875   That he believes there's feeling after death.
He does not really accept what he professes,
He does not wholly remove himself from life,
But all unknown to himself he makes something
Of himself to survive and go on living.
For when in life he tells himself his future

880   That after death his body by wild beasts
And birds will be devoured, torn to pieces,
He's pitying himself. For he doesn't separate
Himself from the body lying there, he thinks
It is still himself, and standing by it gives
Some part of his own feeling to it.
Hence he resents that he was born mortal,

885   He does not see that in real death there'll be
No other self that living could bewail
His perished self, or stand by to feel pain
In body torn or burnt. For if in death
It is painful to be mangled by wild beasts,
I do not see how it is not also painful

890   Laid on a pyre to shrivel in hot flames
Or to be packed in honey and stifled, or
To lie stiff with cold upon a marble slab,

893   Or to be crushed under a weight of earth.

912   Men lie at table, goblets in their hands
And garlands on their brows; and in their hearts
They say 'Short is the joy of men,

915   Too soon it is gone and none can e'er recall it.'
As if in death their chief trouble will be
A parching thirst or burning drought, or a desire

918   For something that they crave and cannot get.

894   'No longer now a happy home will greet you
Nor loving wife, nor your sweet children run
To snatch your kisses and to touch your heart
With silent sweet content. Nor shall you prosper
In your life's work, a bulwark to your people.

Unhappy wretch,' they cry, 'one fatal day
Has taken all those sweets of life away.'
But this they do not add, that the desire   900
Of things like these hangs over you no more.
Which if their minds could truly see and words
Follow, why, then from great distress and fear
They'ld free themselves. 'You in the sleep of death
Lie now and will forever lie, removed   905
Far from all pain and grief. But we, who saw
You turned to ashes on a dreadful pyre,
Mourned you in tears insatiable. For ever
No day will lift that sorrow from our hearts.'
Then we must ask, what bitterness is this,
If all things end in sleep and quiet, that   910
A man can waste away in ceaseless grief.   911
For no one feels the want of himself and his life   919
When mind and body alike are quiet in sleep.   920
For all we care, that sleep might have no end.
Free from all yearning for ourselves we lie.
And yet, when a man springs up, startled from sleep
And pulls himself together, through our limbs
Those first beginnings are never far away
From the sense-giving motions of the body.   925
Therefore much less to us must death be thought
To be, if anything can be less than what
We see to be nothing. For matter is thrown apart
More widely after death, and no one wakes
When once death's chilling pause has halted him.   930

   Again, suppose that nature suddenly
Finding a voice upbraided one of us
In words like these: 'What ails you, mortal man,
And makes you wallow in unhealthy grief?
Why do you moan and groan and weep at death?
For if your former life now past has pleased you   935
And if your blessings through a broken jar
Have not run out, all wasted, unenjoyed,
Why don't you, like a man that's wined and dined
Full well on life, bow out, content, and so
Your exit make and rest in peace, you fool?
But if the things you've liked and loved are spent   940

And life's a grievance to you, why then seek
To add more? They will go just like the others,
No joy at all, and all will end in dust.
Better to make an end of life and trouble.
For there is nothing else I can devise

945 To please you. Always everything's the same.
And if your body not yet by the years
Is worn and fails, yet everything remains
The same. There is no change, even if you live
Longer than anyone on earth, and even more
If it should be your fate never to die.'

950 What answer can we give to this, except
That nature's charge is just and that this speech
Makes a good case, from which we're not acquitted?
Consider now an old man who complains
Excessively about his death to come.
Nature would justly cry out louder still
And say in bitter words, 'Away, you rogue,
With all these tears and stop this snivelling.

955 All life's rewards you have reaped and now you're withered,
But since you always want what you have not got
And never are content with that you have,
Your life has been unfulfilled, ungratifying,
And death stands by you unexpectedly

960 Before the feast is finished and you are full.
Come now, remember you're no longer young
And be content to go; thus it must be.'
She would be right, I think, to act like this,
Right to rebuke him and find fault with him.
For the old order always by the new

965 Thrust out gives way; and one thing must from another
Be made afresh; and no one ever falls
Into the deep pit and black Tartarus.
Matter is needed for the seeds to grow
Of future generations. Yes, but all
When life is done will follow you, and all
Before your time have fallen, and will fall.

970 So one thing from another will always come.
And life none have in freehold, all as tenants.

Look back upon the ages of time past

Eternal, before we were born, and see
That they have been nothing to us, nothing at all.
This is the mirror nature holds for us
To show the face of time to come, when we
At last are dead. Is there in this for us   975
Anything horrible? Is there anything sad?
Is it not more free from care than any sleep?

    And all those things, for sure, which fables tell
Exist deep down in Acheron, exist
For us in this our life. No Tantalus   980
Unhappy wretch fears the great rock that hangs
In the air above him, frozen with vain terror.
No. It is in this life that the fear of gods
Oppresses mortals without cause: the fall
They fear is that which chance may bring to them.
No Tityos lying in Acheron is torn
By vultures, nor through all eternity
Dig though they may can they find anything   985
In that vast breast; and though his frame be spread
Immense to cover not nine acres only
But the whole globe of earth with limbs outstretched,
Yet not forever will he suffer pain   990
Nor from his body furnish food always.
Our Tityos is here, lying in love,
And torn by winged cares (anxiety
Consumes him) or tortured by some other craving.
Sisyphus also in this life appears   995
Before our eyes. He seeks the people's votes
Athirst to get the Lictor's rods and axes,
And always loses and retires defeated.
For to seek power that's empty and never got
And always vainly toil and sweat for it
This is to strain to push up the steep hill
The rock that always from the very top   1000
Rolls headlong down again to the plain below.
Another simile! The Danaids.
To be always feeding an ungrateful mind
And fill it with good things, and yet never
To satisfy it (as the seasons do   1005
When they come round bringing their fruits and all

Their manifold delights, and yet we are never
Filled full with all the varied fruits of life),
This I believe is what the story means
Of young and lovely girls that must pour water
Into a leaking urn, and all their pains
1010   Can never fill it. Cerberus and the Furies
Dwell in that land where daylight never comes,
They say, and Tartarus flames belching out;
And none of these exist, nor ever can.
But in this life there is fear of punishment
For evil deeds, fear no less terrible
1015   Than the deeds themselves, and expiation of crime,
Prison, and the dread hurling from the rock,
Stripes, torturers, dungeons, red-hot plates,
Firebrands, and even if all of these be spared
The guilty conscience filled with wild foreboding
Applies the goad and scorches itself with whips,
1020   Seeing no end to all these miseries,
No final limit to its punishment,
And fears that after death there's worse to come.
So fools make for themselves a Hell on earth.

Now here is something you might say to yourself:
1025   'Even good Ancus lost the sight of day,
A better man than you, you rogue, by far.
And many kings and powers after him
Have fallen, rulers of great states and nations.
And he who laid a highway through the sea
1030   And o'er the deep a road for armies made,
Taught them to walk across the briny lake
And spurned the roaring waves with his cavalry,
He also lost the glorious light of day
And dying poured his spirit from his body.
Great Scipio, the thunderbolt of war,
Terror of Carthage, gave to earth his bones
1035   As though he had been the humblest of his slaves.
Add men that found out things of science and beauty
Add all the brotherhood of Helicon,
Whose one and only king throughout the ages
Homer lies now in sleep with all the rest.
Democritus, when a mature old age

Warned him his mind and memory were fading,   1040
Offered his head right willingly to death.
Epicurus himself died when the light of life
Had run its course, he who in genius
Surpassed the race of men, outshone them all
As the sun risen in heaven outshines the stars.
And you, will you doubt and feel aggrieved to die?   1045
Already, while you live and see, your life
Is all but dead. You waste most of your time
In sleep. You snore while wide awake; and dream
Incessantly; and always in your mind
You're plagued with fear that's meaningless, and often
You can't make out what is wrong with you, oppressed,   1050
You drunken wretch, by cares on every side,
And drift on shifting tides of fantasy.'

    If they could see, those men who know they feel
A burden on their minds that wearies them,
If they could also know the causes of it   1055
And whence so great a pile of woe lies on them,
They'ld never live as most of them do now
Each ignorant of what he wants and seeking always
By change of place to lay his burden down.
A man leaves his great house because he's bored   1060
With life at home, and suddenly returns,
Finding himself no happier abroad.
He rushes off to his villa driving like mad,
You'd think he's going to a house on fire,
And yawns before he's put his foot inside,   1065
Or falls asleep and seeks oblivion,
Or even rushes back to town again.
So each man flies from himself (vain hope, because
It clings to him the more closely against his will)
And hates himself because he is sick in mind
And does not know the cause of his disease.   1070
Which if he clearly saw, at once he would
Leave everything, and study first to know
The nature of the world. For what is in question
Is not of one hour but of eternity,
The state in which all mortals after death
Must needs remain for all remaining time.   1075

And what is this great and evil lust of life
That drives and tosses us in doubt and peril?
A certain end of life is fixed for men.
There is no escape from death and we must die.
Again, we live and move and have our being
1080   In the same place always, and no new pleasure
By living longer can be hammered out.
But while we can't get what we want, that seems
Of all things most desirable. Once got,
We must have something else. One constant thirst
Of life besets us ever open-mouthed.
And there is doubt what fortunes later years
1085   And chance may bring us and what end awaits.
Nor by prolonging life, one single second
Do we deduct from the long years of death.
Nor have we strength to make in any way
Our time less long once death has come to us.
1090   Live though you may through all ages that you wish,
No less that eternal death will still await,
And no less long a time will be no more
He who today from light his exit made
Than he who perished months and years ago.

albert Ellis
"It's not the events that
upset us but our judgement
about the events"

BOOK FOUR

A pathless country of the Pierides
I traverse, where no foot has ever trod.
A joy it is to come to virgin springs
And drink, a joy it is to pluck new flowers,
To make a glorious garland for my head
From fields whose blooms the Muses never picked   5
To crown the brows of any man before.
First, since of matters high I make my theme,
Proceeding to set free the minds of men
Bound by the tight knots of religion.
Next, since of things so dark in verse so clear
I write, and touch all things with the Muses' charm.
In this no lack of purpose may be seen.   10
For as with children, when the doctors try
To give them loathsome wormwood, first they smear
Sweet yellow honey on the goblet's rim,
That childhood all unheeding may be deceived
At the lip's edge, and so drink up the juice
Of bitter medicine, tricked but not betrayed,   15
And by such means gain health and strength again,
So now do I: for oft my doctrine seems
Distasteful to those that have not sampled it
And most shrink back from it. My purpose is
With the sweet voices of Pierian song
To expound my doctrine, and as it were to touch it   20
With the delicious honey of the Muses;
So in this way perchance my poetry
Can hold your mind, while you attempt to grasp
The nature of the world, and understand
Its value and its usefulness to men.   25

And since I have shown the nature of the mind,
What it consists of, and how combined with body

It flourishes, and how when torn away
From the body it returns to its first elements,
Now I address a matter of great import
For our enquiries, and I show that there
30 Exist what we call images of things;
Which as it were peeled off from the surfaces
Of objects, fly this way and that through the air;
These same, encountering us in wakeful hours,
Terrify our minds, and also in sleep, as when
35 We see strange shapes and phantoms of the dead
Which often as in slumber sunk we lay
Have roused us in horror; lest perchance we think
That spirits escape from Acheron, or ghosts
Flit among the living, or that after death
Something of us remains when once the body
40 And mind alike together have been destroyed,
And each to its primal atoms has dissolved.

41   I say therefore that likenesses or thin shapes
42 Are sent out from the surfaces of things
43 Which we must call as it were their films or bark
51 Because the image bears the look and shape
52 Of the body from which it came, as it floats in the air.
53 And this the dullest brain can recognize:
44 In the first place, since within the range of vision
55 Many things throw off bodies, some rarefied
As bonfires throw off smoke or fires heat,
And others denser and more closely knit
Like the thin coats cicadas often drop
In summer, and when calves in birth throw off
60 The caul from the body's surface, or when snakes
Slough off their skins on thorns, and so we see
Brambles bedizened with their fluttering spoils.
Since these things happen, thin images also
Must be thrown off from the surface of things;
65 For if those other things fall, there is no reason,
No whisper of one, why these thinnest films
Should not also and all the more fall off;
Especially since on the outer surface of things
Are many minute bodies which can be cast off
In the same order in which they were before

And keep the shape of the objects, and far more quickly,
Since they are so much less able to be impeded   70
Being fewer and placed on the extreme outside.
For many things are thrown off lavishly
Not only from deep within (as we said before)
But from their surfaces, among them colour.
Awnings do this, yellow and red and purple   75
Spread over a great theatre, for all to see,
On posts and beams, flapping and billowing;
For then the great assembly massed below,
The scenes on the stage, the grandees in their boxes,
They dye, and make to glow and flow with colour.   80
And the more the theatre's surrounding walls
Enclose it, the more all things with beauty filled
Laugh when the light of day is thus confined.
Therefore, since canvas throws off colour from its surface,
All other things must equally send out   85
Thin images from the surface everywhere.
And so there are now fixed outlines of shapes
Of finest texture which fly all around
But individually cannot be seen.
Again, the reason why all smell, smoke, heat,   90
And similar things stream out into the air diffused
So widely is that they come up from the depths
And in their tortuous course are split apart,
And there are no straight openings to the paths
Of exit, through which they can push out together.
But on the other hand, when the thin film   95
Of surface colour is thrown off, there is nothing
To tear it up, because it lies exposed
And is located on the outer surface.
Lastly, whatever similitudes we see
In mirrors, water, or any shining surface,
Since they possess the same outward appearance   100
As those objects, it follows that they must
Consist of images thrown off from them.
There are therefore thin shapes and likenesses
Of things which singly no one can perceive   105
Yet being flung back by continual
And instantaneous recoil produce

A vision from the surfaces of mirrors.
Nor is there clearly any other way
In which they could be presented to reproduce
So accurate a likeness of each object.

110   Now I'll explain to you how very thin
Each image is. First since their atoms are
So far below our senses and so much
Smaller than those things which the eyes begin
No longer to see, to confirm this let me explain
In a few words how exceedingly minute
115 The primal elements of all things are.
First, there exist some animals so small
That a third part of them is quite invisible.
What do you think one of their guts is like?
The ball of the heart? or the eyes? or limbs and joints?
120 How small they are! And what too of the atoms
Of which the mind and spirit are composed?
Do you not see how fine and minute they are?
Consider also things that from their bodies
Emit a pungent small—all-heal, rank wormwood,
125 Strong southern-wood, astringent centaury
If you press lightly a leaf of one of them
Between two fingers

[*Some lines missing*]

Rather you may know that many likenesses
Of things are flying about in many ways
And all beneath the power of our perception.

    Now these similitudes cast off from objects
130 Are not the only ones that fly around.
Others there are which of their own accord
Come into being and by themselves are formed
In this part of the sky we call the air,
Which formed in many ways are carried aloft
135 And melting never cease to change their shapes
And form the outlines of things of many kinds.
We see clouds quickly massing in the sky
That mar the clear face of the firmament
Stroking the air as they move. For often giants
Appear to fly above, casting deep shadows,

Sometimes great mountains and rocks torn off from them 140
Seem to confront the sun and pass across it
And then some monster pulling other clouds.
Unceasingly they melt and change their shapes
And take the outlines of forms of every kind.

Now let me tell you how easily and swiftly
These images arise, perpetually
Flowing and falling from things and moving away. 145
For there is always something streaming off
From the surface of things which they eject. And this,
When it meets some things, passes through them, like glass
Especially. But when it meets rough stone
Or solid wood at once it is broken up,
And then it cannot reproduce an image.
But when the object opposed is bright and compact 150
As a mirror is, none of these things occurs;
For it cannot pass through it, as it does through glass,
And also it cannot be broken up, so much
Safety the smoothness never forgets to give.
That is why the images stream back to us.
However suddenly you place a thing 155
In front of a mirror, at once its image appears;
So you may know that from the surface of things
There is a constant and perpetual flow
Of thin shapes and thin tissues everywhere.
Therefore in a short time many images
Come into being, so you may rightly call
The origin of them instantaneous. 160
The sun must send out many beams of light
In a short time, to fill the world with it,
So in one moment many images
Are borne in many ways into all parts. 165
Whichever way we turn a mirror, something
Makes answer to us of like form and colour.

Consider this now: when the weather has been
Most brilliant, suddenly the sky becomes
Gloomy and ugly so that you might think
That all the dark from Acheron had fled 170
And filled the mighty caverns of the sky.

So foul a night of clouds has massed together
And the black face of fear lours from on high;
And the image of these clouds, how small it is,
175   No man can tell or reasonably describe.

I now explain how fast these images move
And what velocity as they swim through the air
Is given them, a brief hour for a mighty space,
Where each with varied impulse makes its course.
180   And this I tell in words both sweet and few.
Better the swan's brief song than that cry of cranes
Spread by the south wind through the clouds on high.
First, you may very often see that things
Light and of minute elements move swiftly.
185   Of such kind are the sun's light and its heat
Because they are made of minute elements
Which are hit, at it were, and cross immediately
The intervening space hit by a blow that follows:
For instantly light follows light, and flash
190   Is triggered off by flash, like a team of oxen.
In much the same way therefore the images
Must be able to run through space incalculable
In a moment of time; first, since a very small impulse
From far behind is enough to set them in motion,
Since with so swift a lightness they rush on.
195   Next, since their texture is so very fine
That they can easily penetrate anything
And ooze as it were through the intervening air.

Consider this too: certain particles
200   Which rise from deep down, like the sun's heat and light,
Are seen at the very instant of daybreak
Through the whole space of heaven to pour themselves
And fly over land and sea and flood the sky;
What then of those already on the surface
205   When they are thrown off and nothing checks their flight?
Faster and further clearly they must go
And cover a distance many times as great
In the same time that it takes the sun
To spread its light abroad across the sky.
This also especially seems to show most truly

The speed at which these images are borne: 210
A smooth surface of water is exposed
To a clear sky at night, at once the stars
And constellations of the firmament
Shining serene make answer in the water.
Now do you see how in an instant the image
Falls from the edge of heaven to the edge of earth? 215
Wherefore again and yet again I say
How marvellously swift the motion is
Of the bodies which strike our eyes and make us see.

   And odours flow perpetually from things,
As cold from rivers, heat from the sun, and spray
From the sea which scours the walls along the shore. 220
And always different sounds fly through the air.
Again, a damp taste of salt enters our mouths
When we walk by the sea; and when we watch wormwood
Being mixed with water we sense its bitterness.
So does from all things always something flow 225
And everywhere into all parts spreads abroad.
And no delay or rest is given this flow
Since we constantly feel it, and all things always
We can see and smell, and hear the sound of them.

   Again, a shape that is handled in the dark 230
Is recognized to be the same we see
In the clear light of day. It follows then
That sight and touch derive from a like cause.
If we touch something square and it stimulates
Our senses in the dark, what can it be
That in the light comes to our sight as square, 235
If not an image of it?
Images therefore clearly are the cause
Of vision, and without them nothing can be seen.
Now these images I speak of are flying around
Everywhere and sprayed about in all directions; 240
But since it is only with our eyes we see them
It follows that only where we turn our sight
There all things strike it with their form and colour.

   Also the image enables us to see
How far away things are, and to distinguish 245

Distances, for when it is sent off
At once it drives and pushes all the air
That is between the object and our eyes,
And this air all passes through our eyeballs
And brushes the pupils as it were in going through.
250   This is the reason why we can see how far
Away things are, and the greater the volume of air
That is driven before it and the longer the stream
That brushes our eyes, the more distant
And far removed the thing is seen to be.
And all this happens extremely rapidly,
You may be sure, so that at the same moment
255   We see both what a thing is and how far away.

    And here is a thing that need not cause surprise—
That objects can be perceived though the images
That strike our eyes cannot themselves be seen.
For when wind blows slowly on us and bitter cold
260   Flows round, we do not feel each particle
Of wind or cold, but rather the whole at once,
And we feel blows falling upon our body, as if
Something were striking it, and giving us the feeling
Of its own body coming from outside.
265   And when we knock a stone with a toe, we touch
Just the outer surface of it and the surface colour,
But we do not feel this by our touch, but rather
The hardness of the stone deep down inside.

    Now I will tell you why the image is seen
Beyond the mirror; for certainly it seems
270   To be far withdrawn and lie deeply within.
We see things in the same way through open doors
When the doorway gives an open view through it
And lets us see many things outside the house.
This vision is caused by a double stream of air.
275   For first the air this side of the doorposts is seen,
Then follow the doorposts themselves both right and left,
And then the light outside and the second stream
Of light brushes the eyes, and finally
The objects which are really seen out of doors.
The same thing happens when a mirrored image

Projects itself on to our sight: on its way to our eyes 280
It drives and pushes all the air between
Itself and our eyes, and makes us feel this first
Before we see the mirror. But when we have seen
The mirror itself also, at once the image
That travels from us to it and is reflected 285
Comes back to our eyes, pushing a stream of air
In front of it, and so this first we sense
Before we see the object in the mirror;
That is why it appears to be so far within it.
Wherefore again and yet again I say
It is by no means right to be surprised
At this appearance of objects reflected
In the surface of a mirror, since they involve 290
A double journey with two streams of air.

Now why is it that the right side of our body
Appears in a mirror on the left? This is because
When the approaching image strikes the mirror
It is not turned round intact, but flung straight back 295
In reverse, as if someone should throw a mask
Of plaster before it is dry against a pillar
So that it bounces straight back keeping the features
Set on its front, but showing them in reverse.
In this case what was the right eye would become 300
The left, and the left eye again the right.
An image may also pass from mirror to mirror
So that five or six reflections are produced.
For things can be out of sight at the back of a house
And yet however far removed they are 305
Through twisting passages can all be brought out
By a number of mirrors, and be seen to be inside.
So does the image shine from mirror to mirror.
And when the left is given it comes back right
And then comes back again turned round to the same position. 310
Moreover, mirrors that have small sides that are curved
In the same degree as our sides send back images
Right to our right and unreversed. Either
Since the image is carried across from mirror to mirror
And then flies to us having been twice reflected,
Or since the image is turned round when it approaches 315

As the curved shape of the mirror turns it towards us.
Sometimes the images march along with us
Keeping step with us and mimicking our gestures.
320 This is because if you move from a part of a mirror
At once the images cannot return from that part.
Nature compels all things that strike a mirror
To be reflected back at equal angles.

Now here is another thing: the eyes avoid
Bright objects and refuse to gaze at them.
325 The sun will blind you if you stare at it.
This is because its power is very great
And from on high through the pure air the images
Travel with great momentum and strike the eyes
And in so doing disrupt the structure of them.
And any strong brightness often burns the eyes
330 For the reason that it contains many seeds of fire
Which cause pain to the eyes by piercing them.

People with jaundice see everything yellow.
This is because many seeds of yellow colour
Stream from their bodies to meet the images of things;
335 And many such seeds are mingled in their eyes
And by their contact paint everything with pallor.

Again, we see in the dark things in the light
Because, when the black air of darkness, being nearer,
Has entered our eyes and taken possession of them
340 There follows immediately a bright clear air
Which purifies them as it were and scatters
The black shades of the first air; for this bright air
Is made of particles much more minute
And much more mobile and more powerful;
As soon as this has filled the paths of the eyes
345 And opened them, which previously were beset
By the black air, at once the images of things
That are in the light follow and make us see them.
But on the contrary, we cannot see
Out of the light things that are in the dark,
350 And this is why: a grosser air of darkness
Follows behind, fills every pore, blockades
The channels of the eyes, so that no images
Thrown off from things in any way can move them.

And when we see the square towers of a city
From far away, they often appear to be round.
This is because every angle when seen at a distance   355
Is blurred, or rather is not seen at all.
Its flow is lost, it does not strike our eyes,
And the air, while the images travel so far through it,
Inflicts many blows upon them and blunts them.
So when every angle has escaped our vision   360
The stone structures appear as though turned on a lathe,
Not like things really round that are seen close to,
But in a shadowy way they mimic them.
Our shadow also appears to move in the sun,
To follow our footsteps, imitate our gestures,   365
If you can conceive that air without light can walk
And follow the movements and gestures of men;
For what we are accustomed to call shadow
Can be nothing else than air deprived of light.
Doubtless because the air in certain places   370
One after another is deprived of the sun's light
Wherever in our movements we obstruct it,
And the point which we have left is filled again;
That is why the successive shadows of our body
Seem to be the same shadow always following us.
For always new rays of light are pouring out   375
And the first are consumed, like wood thrown into a flame.
Thus easily the earth is robbed of light
And is replenished as it washes away
The stain of the black shadows darkening it.

And here we do not concede in any way
That the eyes are deluded. For their task it is
To see in what place light is, and where shadow;   380
But whether one light is the same as another,
Whether the shadow that was here is now moving there,
Or rather what happens is what I have just described,
That the mind's reasoning power must discern.
Eyes cannot understand the nature of things.   385
Do not then blame the eyes for this fault of the mind.

A ship we sail in moves while it seems to stand still.
A ship at anchor seems to be passing by,
And hills and plains appear to fly astern

390   When we drive our vessel past them with flying sails.
The stars in all the vaults of heaven seem fixed
And still, yet all are in constant motion,
Since to their distant setting they return
When with bright bodies they have crossed the sky.
395   The sun and moon likewise seem to stand still
In their places, though the facts show that they move.
In the midst of the ocean mountains rise far off,
Between them lies a channel for a fleet,
And yet they seem to form a single island.
400   When children spinning round have come to a stop
They seem to see halls and pillars whirling round
So vividly that they can scarce believe
That the whole roof will not fall in on them.
And when with flickering fires nature begins
405   To lift her red glow on high, above the hills,
The glowing sun seems to be close upon them
And touching them with its own heat and fire.
Yet scarce two thousand bowshots are they distant
Or even five hundred throws of a javelin;
410   But far between them and the sun there lie
Enormous tracts of ocean spread below
Vast regions of the sky, and many thousands
Of lands lie in between where many men
And varied nations dwell and tribes of beasts.

     A puddle no more than a finger deep
415   Lying between stones on a paved highway
Gives a view downwards below the earth as far
As the expanse of sky that yawns above,
So that you seem to look down upon the clouds
And see the heavenly bodies wonderfully
Deep-buried in a heaven below the earth.

     Again, when in midstream our lively horse
420   Stands fast, and we look down upon the waves
Of the river flowing rapidly, a force
Seems to be carrying his body sideways
And to push it violently against the stream,
And wherever we turn our eyes, everything seems
425   To be rushing and flowing in a similar way.

A colonnade of equal width throughout
Supported by pillars of equal height
If you look down its whole length from one end
It gradually takes the outlines of a cone
Quite joining roof to floor and right to left   430
Until the invisible apex of the cone is reached.

At sea, to sailors from the waves the sun
Appears to rise, then set and hide its light in them.
This is because they see only sea and sky,
Lest you should readily believe the senses   435
Are everywhere confused and undermined.
To landsmen ignorant of the sea a ship
In harbour seems to struggle against the waves
Maimed, its poop broken. For whatever part
Of the oar is raised above the sea is straight
And the rudders above are straight; but the parts submerged 440
Below the water appear all broken back
And wrenched and turned flat upwards and so bent
Right back almost to float upon the surface.

And when at night the winds drive scattered clouds
Across the sky, the shining stars appear
To glide against the clouds and pass above them   445
On a way far different from their actual course.
And if you place a hand below one eye
And press it, then a new sensation comes.
Everything we see is doubled by our vision.
Two lights of lamps a-flowering with flames,   450
Two sets of furniture all through the house,
And men with double faces and two bodies.

When in sweet slumber sleep has bound our limbs
And in deep quiet all the body lies
Yet we seem then to ourselves to be awake   455
And move our limbs, and in the night's blind dark
We think we see the sun and light of day,
That in our narrow room we pass in turn
Over sky and sea, rivers and mountains;
We see ourselves walking across wide plains.
We hear sounds, though the stern silence of night   460
Reigns everywhere; we speak, but still are silent.

And many marvels in this way we see
Which seek as it were to break the credit of our senses,
But all in vain, since the most part of them
465 Deceive because of notions of the mind
Which we ourselves bring to them, so that things
Seem so be seen which senses have not seen.
For nothing is more difficult than to distinguish
And separate plain things from doubtful things
Which all at once are added by the mind.

Now here's another thing: if someone thinks
That nothing is known, he does not even know
470 Whether that can be known, since he declares
That he knows nothing. Therefore I will spare
To argue a case against a man like this
Who has put his head where his feet ought to be.
And yet, if I were to grant that he does know, then
I ask him this: since you could see no truth
In anything before, how do you know
475 What it is to know, and what again not to know?
What gave you the idea of true and false,
What proves to you that there's a difference,
That the doubtful and the certain are not the same?
You will find that it is from the senses
In the first place that the concept of truth has come,
And that the senses cannot be refuted.
480 For some standard must be found of greater credit
Able of itself to refute false things with true.
And what can be held to tell the truth more clearly
Than the senses? or shall reasoning derived
From false senses prevail against those senses
Being itself wholly derived from them?
485 Unless they are true, all reasoning is false.
Will the ear be able to convict the eye?
Or the touch the ear? Or taste refute the touch,
Or nose confound it or eye discredit it?
Not so, I think. For each has its own force
490 And separate power, so it needs must be
That softness and cold or heat and colour each
Is separately perceived and separately
We see whatever is involved in colour.

The taste in our mouth has its separate power, and smells
Have separate birth, and sounds. So it must be   495
That one sense never can refute another
Nor can they possibly convict themselves
Since each must always equally be trusted.
Accordingly whatever at any time
Has seemed to the senses to be true, is true.
And if reason cannot explain the cause   500
Why objects seen as square close to at a distance
Seem round, yet it is better that a man
Lacking reason should give a faulty explanation
Than to let slip from your hands in any way
Your grip upon the obvious, and break
The trust upon which all depends, and tear up   505
All the foundations on which life is built.
For not only would all reason come to ruin,
Life itself also would at once collapse,
Unless you dare to place trust in your senses,
Avoiding precipices and such things
As must be shunned, and follow the contrary.   510
Believe me, all that array of words is vain
That has been massed and deployed against the senses.
Lastly, in a building, if the ruler is crooked
And the square is faulty and misses the straight line
And the level is even slightly unbalanced,   515
The whole house then will of necessity
Be wrongly constructed and be falling over,
Warped, sloping, leaning forward, leaning back,
All out of proportion, so that some parts seem
Ready to collapse, and the whole destined to fall,
A victim to the first false measurements.
So your reasoning about things must be false and warped   520
Whenever it is based upon false senses.

   And now I have no stony path to tread
In showing how the other senses work.

   In the first place, every sound and voice is heard
When it has crept into the ears, and then
Made impact with its body upon the senses.   525
For we must confess that voice and sound also

Have bodies, since they strike upon the senses.
Besides, the voice often scrapes the throat. A shout
530 Roughens the windpipe on its outward course.
For when the voice's atoms massed together
Make their way out through the narrow passage,
As the mouth is filled the gateway is scraped.
There is no doubt therefore that words and voices
Consist of bodily elements, since they can hurt.

535 You see also how much the body is worn,
How much is drawn from man's very thews and sinews
By a speech that lasts from the first gleam of dawn
To the black shades of night, especially
If the words are shouted, at the top of the voice.
540 Therefore the voice must be made of bodily stuff,
Since much speaking diminishes the body.
The roughness of the voice moreover comes
From the roughness of its atoms, and smoothness from smooth.
The atoms that enter the ear are not of the same shape
545 When the horn bellows with deep and hollow roar
And the land re-echoes with its barbarous boom
As when swans from the glens of Helicon
With liquid voice uplift their mournful plaint.

When therefore from deep within our body
550 We force the voices out and send them forth
Straight through the mouth, the quickly moving tongue,
The cunning fashioner of words, joints them
And moulds them, and the shaping of the lips
Plays its due part in giving form to them.
When there is no great distance for the voice
To run, it follows that the words themselves
555 Are clearly heard, each separate syllable.
For the sound keeps its shape and keeps its form.
But if the space between is unduly long,
Words passing through much air must be confused
And the voice distorted as it flies through the air.
560 And that is why, though you can hear the sound,
You cannot grasp the meaning of the words,
The voice is so obstructed and confused.

Often one voice can penetrate the ears
Of a whole crowd, when uttered by a cryer.

Therefore one voice is suddenly dispersed
Into many voices, since it divides itself 565
Into separate ears, stamping on them
The form of the word and its distinctive sound.
But those voices that do not strike the ear
Are carried past, and lost, and all in vain
Are scattered through the air and perish there.
Some, hitting solid objects, give back a sound 570
And at times delude with the image of a word.
And when you clearly see this you'll be able
To give the reason to yourself and others
Why cliffs and rocks standing in lonely places
Give back the sounds in the same shape and order
When straying comrades in thick mountain country 575
We seek and with loud voices call to them.
Six times or even seven I have heard come back
One voice, so skilfully did hill from hill
Repeat the words and throw them back again.
Nymphs and goat-footed satyrs haunt these places, 580
So country-folk make out; and fauns they say
Are there as well, when their night-wandering noises
And merry pranks break the deep silences;
And there are sounds of strings; and sweet laments
The flute pours out pressed by a player's fingers; 585
And everywhere the farm-folk listen, while Pan
Shaking the pine-leaves from his half-wild head
Runs his curved lips along the hollow reeds
And pipes all day his woodland melody.
And other signs and wonders they relate 590
Lest they be thought to live in haunts so wild
That even the gods have left them; or maybe
They have some other reason, for mankind
Is greedy aye for things that please the ear.

Well now, here's something you can well believe: 595
That voices can come and impact on the ears
From places through which eyes can never see.
We hear a conversation through closed doors
Doubtless because the voice can travel safe
Through tortuous paths, while images refuse. 600
For they are split apart unless they swim

Through straight passages, such as glass contains,
Through which all things that can be seen can fly.
The voice is spread about in all directions
Since voices beget voices, when one voice
605 Once spoken has sprung apart into many, as fires
Lit by a spark break out into many fires.
So places are filled with voices, and though withdrawn
And hidden from sight they are stirred and boil with sound.
But images all travel in straight paths
610 When once they have been sent out. And therefore no one
Can see beyond a wall, though he hear voices through it.
Yet the voice itself passing through the walls of a house
Comes blunted and confused into the ears
And we seem to hear a sound rather than words.

615   The tongue now, and the palate, which give us taste
Need no more work of reasoning to explain.
In the first place we sense flavour in the mouth
When we press it out in chewing food, as a sponge
When full of water is pressed and begins to dry.
620 Next, what we press out is distributed
Abroad through all the passages of the palate
And winding channels of the porous tongue.
Therefore when bodies of the oozing juice
Are smooth, they sweetly touch and sweetly stroke
All the wet trickling regions round the tongue.
625 But contrariwise they prick the sense and tear it,
Being pressed out, the more they are filled with roughness.
The pleasure of flavour stops short at the palate.
When it has dropped down through the throat no pleasure
Is given while it disperses through our limbs.
630 It matters not what food is given the body
Provided good digestion waits on it
Letting its virtue spread through all the limbs
And keep intact the moisture of the stomach.

   Now I shall explain why different food
Is sweet and nourishing for different creatures,
And why what is to some unpleasant and bitter
635 Can yet to others seem truly delicious,
Why in these things there is such great difference

That one man's meat is another's deadly poison.
It is like the snake, which touched by human spittle,
Bites itself to death, and perishes.
And hellebore to us is deadly poison   640
But fed to goats and quails it makes them fat.
Now, that you may understand why these things happen
You must first remember what I said before
That things contain seeds mixed in many ways.
In fact all living creatures that take food
As they are different externally   645
And the contour and circumscription of their limbs
Compass each according to its kind,
So they are made of seeds of different shape;
And since the seeds differ, so also must
The intervals and paths, which we call channels,   650
Differ throughout our body, and in our mouth and palate.
Some therefore must be larger and some smaller,
And some triangular and others square,
And many round, and some with many angles,
Disposed in many different arrangements.
For as the order and motions of figures require   655
The channels of the figures must be different
And the paths vary as the texture compels.
Therefore if what is sweet to some is bitter to others,
When it is sweet to one, very small bodies
Must enter the pores of the palate with soothing touch.   660
But if it tastes bitter, that is no doubt because
Rough and hooked atoms penetrate the throat.
Thus it is easy to understand each case.
For when fever grips a man through excess of bile
Or disease is excited in some other way,   665
Then the whole body is thrown into confusion
And all the positions of its atoms are upset,
So that all the bodies which conformed with the senses
Conform no longer, and others come more apt
To penetrate and produce a bitter taste.   670
Indeed in honey both these tastes are mixed,
A thing which I have explained to you before.

   I now examine how the impact of smell
Affects the nose. First of necessity

675　There must be many things from all of which
　　　Flows rolling out a varied stream of odours
　　　Which flow and are sped and scattered everywhere.
　　　But different scents suit different animals
　　　Because of their different shapes. Bees are attracted
　　　Over great distances by the smell of honey,
680　Vultures by carcasses. A pack of hounds
　　　Leads where the cloven hoof of game has gone.
　　　And from afar the scent of man is caught
　　　By the white goose that saved Rome's citadel.
　　　So different scent is given to different creatures
　　　And leads each to its food, and forces it
685　To leap back from loathsome poison; and in this way
　　　The generations of wild beasts are preserved.

　　　　Take all the smells then that assail the nostrils:
　　　One may be carried farther than another
　　　But yet no smell can ever travel as far
690　As sound or voice or (and I need not add)
　　　Those things which strike the eye and give us sight.
　　　It wanders slowly coming and dies first
　　　Gradually dispersed into the winds of air.
　　　There are two reasons for this; first because
695　It comes with difficulty from the depths of things:
　　　Things have a stronger smell when broken up,
　　　Or crushed, or melted down by fire; this means
　　　That scent flows out released from deep within.
　　　Second, it may be seen that smell is made
　　　Of larger elements than voice, since through stone walls
700　It cannot pass as voice and sounds may do.
　　　Wherefore also you will see that it is not so easy
　　　To trace out where scent is coming from,
　　　For the flow grows cold as it dawdles through the air
　　　And no messenger runs hot-foot to the sense.
　　　This is why in the chase we often see
705　Hounds are at fault and cast about for scent.

　　　　Nor yet is this confined to smells and tastes:
　　　The look of things also and their various colours
　　　Do not all suit the senses in the same way
　　　But to some they come much sharper than to others.

The cock, that claps the night out with his wings   710
And with clear voice is wont to call the dawn,
Before him ravening lions cannot stand
Or stare, so instantly flight fills their minds,
Doubtless since in the cock's body certain seeds
There are which when sent into the lion's eyes   715
Dig holes in the pupils and cause stinging pain
Which fierce though they may be they cannot endure.
And yet these cannot hurt our sight at all,
Either because they do not penetrate
Or if they do they find a ready exit
From the eyes and so do not by lingering   720
Damage the light of the eyes in any part.

  Now I shall tell you what things move the mind,
And whence those things which come into the mind
Do come, in a few words I shall explain.
First I say this, that images of things
Many in many modes wander about
In all directions, thin, and easily   725
Unite when they meet in the air, like spiders' webs
Or leaf of gold, of texture much more thin
Than those which strike the eyes and provoke vision.
For they penetrate the chinks of the body, and stir
The thin substance of the mind and provoke sensation.   730
Centaurs and mermaids in this way we see
And dogs with many heads like Cerberus,
And images of men when after death
Their bones lie in the cold embrace of earth.
For images of every kind fly everywhere;   735
Some of their own accord form in the air,
Some are thrown off from many different things,
Others combine together from these shapes.
For sure no image of a Centaur came from life
Since no such animal did ever exist.
But when the images of man and horse   740
Happen to meet, they easily adhere
Immediately, as I said before,
Because of their subtle nature and thin texture.
All things of this kind are made in this way.
And since being very light they are so mobile,   745

As I showed before, any one of these fine images
By a single touch can easily move the mind,
For the mind is thin and marvellously mobile.

That these things happen as I say, you may know
Quite easily from what I now shall tell you.
750 Since this is like that—what in the mind we see
Like what we see with our eyes—it needs must be
That both are caused by similar processes.
Now therefore since I have shown that I see a lion
By means of images which strike the eyes,
It is clear that in like way the mind is moved.
755 It sees the lion and everything else by images
No less than the eyes, though what it sees is thinner.
Nor is there any other reason why,
When sleep has laid out the limbs, the mind is awake,
Than this, that these same images assail
The mind as when we are awake. Indeed
760 We seem to see a man who has left this life
And death and earth have mastered him. So great
Is the power of nature. All our senses
Lie quiet throughout the body and are blocked,
Unable to refute the false by the true.
765 And memory faints in sleep, and languishes,
And when the mind thinks it sees the man alive
It does not dissent, and say that long ago
The man was dead and in death's mighty power.
And it is not wonderful that images move
And sway their arms and other limbs in rhythm—
770 For the image does seem to do this in our sleep.
The fact is that when the first one perishes
And a new one is born and takes its place,
The former seems to have changed its attitude.
All this of course takes place extremely swiftly,
So great is the velocity and so great the store
Of them, so great the quantity of atoms
775 In any single moment of sensation
Always available to keep up the supply.

And many are the questions to be asked
About these things, and many explanations given
If we desire to make the matter clear.

The first question is, why is it that the mind,
As soon as it fancies something, thinks of it?   780
Is there an image that waits upon our will
And as soon as we wish presents itself to us,
Of sea or land, as we may choose, or sky?
Assemblies of men, processions, banquets, battles,
Does nature create them at a word and prepare them for us?   785
And all the while, at the same place and time,
Other minds are thinking of quite different things.
And what when we see in dreams the images
Moving in time and swaying supple limbs,
Swinging one supple arm after the other   790
In fluid gestures and repeating the movement
Foot meeting foot, as eyes direct? Ah, steeped in art,
Well trained the wandering images must be
That in the night have learned such games to play!
Or will this rather be the reason? that
In one instant of time that we perceive and one voice
Is uttered, many units of time are there   795
All unperceived, though reason knows of them,
And at any moment all these images
Are present ready to hand in every place.
And because they are thin the mind cannot clearly see   802
Any except those which it strains to perceive;
The rest all perish, and only those survive
Such as it has prepared itself to see:
And it does prepare itself, and hopes to see   805
What follows on each thing; and it does see it.
Do you not know that when even our eyes begin
To look at thin things they strain and prepare themselves
And otherwise we could not clearly see them.   810
And even in things plainly visible
You will find that unless you apply your mind to them
They might just as well be far removed from you.
What wonder is it then, if the mind misses
Everything except what it is itself intent on?
So from small signs we draw great inferences   815
And lead ourselves into error and delusion.

  It sometimes happens also that the image
Which follows is of a different kind: a woman

820 Seems in our grasp to have become a man.
And different shapes and different ages follow.
But sleep and oblivion cause us not to wonder.

Now here's a fault you must most keenly avoid,
An error from which with great care you must flee:
825 Do not suppose that the clear light of the eyes
Was made that we might see our way before us,
Or that the ends of thighs and calves were jointed
And set on the foundation of the feet
To help us with great strides to march along,
Or that our arms were fitted to stout shoulders
830 With ministering hands on either side
To enable us to do what life requires.
Every interpretation of this kind
Is quite perverse, turns reason upside down,
Since nothing is born in our body that we may use it,
835 But what is born itself creates the use.
There was no sight before the eyes were born
Or speech of words before the tongue was made,
But long before speech is the tongue's origin,
840 Long before sound was heard our ears were made,
And all our limbs existed, as I think,
Before their use. It cannot therefore be
That they could have grown for the sake of being used.
No. But fighting hand to hand in battle,
Tearing of limbs and fouling bodies with blood
845 Came long before bright shafts of weapons flew;
And nature taught men to avoid a wound
Before through art the left arm opposed a shield.
And sure to give the wearied body rest
Is much more ancient than soft mattresses.
850 Men quenched their thirst long before cups were made.
These things which men found out from life and need
Were doubtless fashioned for the sake of use.
Quite different are those things which came into being
Before any conception of their usefulness;
855 And first in this class are the senses and the limbs.
Wherefore again and yet again I say
Banish from your mind the possibility
That they could have been made for the sake of usefulness.

Nor is there any reason to be surprised
That by the very nature of its body
Every animal seeks food. I have shown you that
Many atoms in many ways are thrown off from things,   860
But most must come from animals. Always these are
In motion, and many atoms are pressed out
From deep down in sweat and many through the mouth
As they pant in exhaustion, so the body is rarefied   865
And its nature undermined; and pain results.
So food is taken, to prop up the body,
And working inside renews the strength and stops
Through veins and limbs the gaping desire to eat.
And fluid also goes into all those parts   870
That need it, and the massed particles of heat
That set our stomach in a blaze are scattered
By the fluid entering, and quenched like fire,
So the parching heat no longer burns our frame.
Thus then your panting thirst is swilled away
Out of the body, thus your famished craving   875
Is satisfied, the body's needs fulfilled.

Now I will tell you how it is that we walk
And can stride forward when we wish, and how
We are able to move our limbs in various ways,
And what it is that is wont to push along
Our body's heavy weight. Please mark my words.   880
I say that in the first place images
Of walking come in contact with the mind
And strike the mind, as I have said before.
Hence follows will: for no one ever begins
Anything unless the mind has first foreseen
What it wills to do (and what the mind foresees
Is the image of the thing). Therefore the mind   885
When it conceives the wish of walking forward
Immediately strikes the mass of spirit
Dispersed through all the body and the limbs
(And this is easy for it, since it lives
In such close combination with the spirit).
The spirit then strikes the body, and so the whole mass   890
Is gradually pushed forward into movement.
The body then also expands its pores, and air,

As is natural with something always mobile,
Pours into the opened passages and penetrates them,
895   Thus reaching the very smallest parts of the body.
So thus by two things acting in two ways
The body is moved, like a ship by sails and wind.
Nor is there anything surprising here
That elements so small can turn so large
900   A body and twist our whole weight around.
The wind, that is so subtle and so fine,
Drives on a mighty ship with mighty power,
And one hand rules it whatever its speed may be,
One rudder steers it whither you may will;
905   And many a heavy weight by blocks and pulleys
A derrick can move and lift with little effort.

Next, in what way sleep floods the limbs with peace
And from the heart lets free the mind's disquiet
I shall declare in verses sweet though few.
910   Better the swan's brief song than that cry of cranes
Spread by the south wind through the clouds on high.
Give me keen ears and understanding mind
Lest you deny that what I say can be,
And shrink back, your heart repelling words of truth
915   Though you are in fault yourself and cannot see it.
In the first place, sleep comes when the power of the spirit
Is drawn apart through the body, and part of it
Cast forth has gone away, and part retreats
Into the depths compacted and compressed.
For only then the limbs relax and lie.
920   For there is no doubt that by the work of the spirit
Sensation comes, and when sleep deadens it
We must suppose that the spirit has been disordered
And quite cast out; not all of it; for then the body
Would lie steeped in the eternal chill of death.
925   Since if no part of the spirit remained hidden
In our body, as fire lies covered deep in ashes,
Whence could our feeling suddenly through the limbs
Rekindle, as flame leaps from hidden fire?

But by what cause this new state comes to pass
And whence the spirit can be disordered, and how

The body made to languish, I will explain.
Please see that my words are not wasted on the winds.   930
First it must be that since the body is touched
By the motions of the air surrounding it
Its outer part by frequent blows of air
Is thumped and buffeted; and that is why
Nearly all things that live and grow are covered   935
By skin or even shells or rind or bark.
The body's inside also when we breathe
This same air strikes, drawn in and out. And so
Since the body is beaten outside and in, and since
The blows through tiny channels penetrate
The primary parts and primal elements,   940
Slowly, collapse (as it were) occurs in the limbs.
The atoms of mind and body are dislodged
From their positions. Next part of the spirit
Is ejected out, and part withdraws within,
And part also is scattered through the body   945
And so cannot unite and combine in motion.
For nature blocks the paths and meeting places,
So feeling sinks down deep when the motions are changed.
And since there is nothing to prop up the limbs,
The body becomes weak, the limbs grow faint,   950
Arms and eyelids fall, and as we lie down
The knees give way and all their strength is gone.
Again sleep follows food, since it acts like air
When it has dissolved through all the veins.
And much the deepest sleep is that which comes   955
From satiety or weariness, for then
The greatest number of atoms is disordered,
Bruised by much labour. Of the spirit too
In the same way a part is thrown together
At a greater depth, and the part ejected is greater,   960
And the separations and divisions magnified.

And those pursuits which most we love to follow,
The things in which just now we have been engaged,
The mind being thus the more intent upon them,
These are most oft the substance of our dreams.   965
Lawyers argue their cases and make laws,
Generals fight battles, leading troops to war,

Sailors pursue their struggles with the wind,
And I ply my own task and seek the nature of things
970 Always, and tell them in our native tongue.
All other pursuits and arts seem thus in dreams
To hold the minds of men with their illusions.
When men have been to games and theatres
For many days, we usually see,
975 When they have ceased to observe these with their senses,
That paths are left still open in the mind
By which the images of these things can enter.
For many days then these same things are moving
Before their eyes, so that even while awake
980 They seem to see dancers swaying supple limbs,
And the lyre's liquid notes and speaking strings
Enter their ears, and the same audience
They see and the varied glories of the stage.
So great is the effect of interest and pleasure
985 And of things which form the habits of men's lives,
Not only of men, but of all animals.
You will see horses, when they lie in sleep,
Break out in sweat and panting hard and fast
As if straining every nerve to win a race,
990 Or plunging from the opened starting gates.
And often hounds lying in gentle sleep
Suddenly throw up their legs and all at once
Give tongue and keenly sniff the air, as if
They have found and held the scent of some wild beast.
995 And even when awake they often chase
Phantoms of stags as though they saw them in flight
Until, the error spent, they come to their senses.
A litter of soft puppies, household pets,
1000 Will shake themselves and jump up, just as if
They saw the forms and faces of strangers coming in.
And the fiercer the breed, the wilder it is in its dreams.
And birds fly up and suddenly at night
With whirring wings disturb the gods' dark groves,
If in their quiet sleep dreams come to them
1010 Of hawks stooping to the fray in hot pursuit.
And mighty men do mighty deeds in dreams.
Kings conquer, and are captured, and give battle,

And scream with the assassin's dagger at their throats,
All without moving from the spot. Men fight   1015
And groan in pain and fill the air with cries
As if in the jaws of a panther or a lion.
And men in sleep things of great moment tell
And by their words themselves betray their guilt.
Many meet death. And many from high cliffs   1020
Feeling themselves falling are beside themselves
And start from sleep almost out of their minds, and hardly
Recover from the torment of their body.
A thirsty man oft sits beside a river
Or pleasant spring and nearly drinks it up.   1025
And often boys held fast in sleep believe
They are standing by a privy or chamber pot
Lifting their clothes, and pour out all the fluid
That has filtered through their body and drench the sheets
And splendid Babylonian coverlets.
And others, when the seed first penetrates   1030
The racing tides of youth, as time matures it,
Meet with a wandering image from some body
That tells of lovely face and rosy cheeks,
And this excites the parts swelling with seed,
And so, as if the act were being performed,   1035
They pour a great flood out and stain their clothes.

   This seed I speak of is stirred up in us
As soon as manhood in our limbs grows strong.
And different things respond to different forces.
But only man from man draws human seed.   1040
As soon as seed comes out from its retreats,
It travels through every member of the body
And gathers in a fixed place in the loins
And arouses straight away the genital parts.
The parts swell with the seed, then comes desire   1045
To eject it where the dire craving pulls
And the body seeks that which has wounded the mind with love.
For men in battle fall towards a wound
And the blood spurts out in the direction of the blow   1050
And if he is close the foe is drenched in blood.
So therefore when the shafts of Venus strike,
Whether a boy with girlish limbs has thrown it

Or a woman from her whole body launches love,
1055 He leans towards the blow, desires to unite,
And cast the fluid from body into body;
His speechless yearning tells of bliss to come.

    This is our Venus; hence the name of love;
Hence into the heart distilled the drop
1060 Of Venus' sweetness, and numbing heartache followed.
For if what you love is absent, none the less
Its images are there, and the sweet name
Sounds in your ears. Ah, cursed images!
Flee them you must and all the food of love
Reject, and turn the mind away, and throw
1065 The pent-up fluid into other bodies,
And let it go, not with one single love
Straitjacketed, not storing in your heart
The certainty of endless cares and pain.
For feeding quickens the sore and strengthens it,
And day by day the madness grows and woe
1070 Is heaped on woe, unless the first wounds by new blows
Are deadened and while the wound's still fresh you cure it
By wandering with Venus of the streets,
Or to some newer purpose turn your mind.

    And by avoiding love you need not miss
The fruits that Venus offers, but instead
You may take the goods without the penalty.
1075 For sure from this a purer pleasure comes
To the healthy than to the lovesick. Yes, for in
The moment of possession lovers' minds
Are all at sea storm-tossed, confused, and can't
Decide what first to enjoy with eye or hand,
They hurt the body they love, so close they press,
1080 They kiss so fiercely that teeth enter lips,
All this because the pleasure is not pure,
And hidden stings there are which make them harm
Whatever it be from which the frenzy comes.
But in their loving Venus lightly lifts
1085 The penalties she inflicts, and soothing pleasure
Holds back the sting; for there is hope in it
That the same body whence the frenzy came

May have the power also to quench the fire—
And that does nature totally reject.
This is the only thing for which the more we have
The more the heart burns with fell desire for it. 1090
For food and drink are taken into the body
And since they can enter their appointed places
Easily the desire for water and bread is met.
But from a pretty face or rosy cheeks
Nothing comes into the body to enjoy 1095
But images, thin images, fond hopes,
For often they are scattered to the winds.
As when in dreams a thirsty man seeks water
And none is given to quench the fire within
But he seeks the image of the water all in vain
And standing in a river thirsts while he drinks, 1100
So in love Venus mocks lovers with images.
They cannot satisfy their eyes with looking,
Nor with hands wandering aimless o'er the body
Can they glean anything from tender limbs;
And when at last with body clasped to body 1105
They pluck the flower of youth, when body knows
The bliss to come and Venus is ready, poised
To sow the fields of love, they cling together
Mouth pressed to watering mouth and lips to lips
Drawing deep breaths as body calls to body.
In vain. For they can rub nothing off from it, 1110
Neither can body be absorbed in body.
For that sometimes they seem to want and strive for,
So ardently in Venus' toils they cling
Their limbs with rapture liquefied and melted.
At last when all the pent-up lust is spent 1115
There comes a brief pause in the raging fever;
But then the fit returns, madness comes back,
They ask themselves what it is they are craving for,
They can find no device to cure their ill,
Bewildered and confused they waste away,
The hapless victims of an unseen wound. 1120

And add this also, they consume their strength,
The effort kills them; and their days are passed
Obeying another's whim. Wealth vanishes

Turned into Babylonian coverlets.
Duties neglected, reputation falls.
1125 For her, soft lovely slippers from Sicyon
Shine on her feet, great emeralds set in gold
Glow with green light, the sea-blue dress well worn
In constant use absorbs the sweat of Venus.
The family's wealth, hard earned, binds up her hair
1130 Turned into a tiara or becomes
A gown of silk from Elis or from Ceos.
Banquets with shining tables and rich fare,
Wines, dancers, ointments, garlands, ribbons—
All useless; since from the very fount of joy
Something bitter comes, and midst the flowers
1135 Brings torment. Perchance a guilty conscience bites
With rue for years of idleness and vice,
Perchance she's spoken some doubtful word which sticks
And burns like fire in his yearning heart;
Or else he thinks she moves her eyes too much,
Too many glances at another man,
1140 And in her face a hint of mockery.

    These evils can be found in love that prospers
And goes well; but in a love that's starved and wretched
Though your eyes be closed they are there all plain to see,
Innumerable; so be on your guard,
1145 Take my advice and keep your fancy free.
For to avoid being captured in the snares of love
Is not so difficult as to escape
Once in, and break the powerful knots of Venus.
And yet, although entangled and ensnared,
1150 You can escape this danger unless you stand
In your own way, and overlook the faults
In the body and the mind of her you love,
For this is what men blinded with desire
So often do, attributing to them
Virtues with which in truth they are not endowed.
1155 So ugly and mis-shapen women are called
Sweet charmers and are held in highest honour.
A lover derides another, and urges him
To propitiate Venus since his love's so foul,
But cannot see his own disastrous plight.

The dark girl is a nut-brown maid, the rank
And filthy is a sweet disorder. Is she green-eyed?   1160
Then she's grey-eyed Athene. Stringy and wooden?
Then she's a gazelle. Is she a dwarf? Why then
She's one of the Graces, the very soul of wit.
A giantess? She's full of dignity.
If she stammers, she has a lisp. If dumb, she's modest.
If she's a fiery hateful chatterbox,   1165
She's a little squib. If she's too thin to live,
She's svelte and willowy. If she's half dead
With coughing, then she's delicate, you see.
Is she swollen, with enormous breasts? She's Ceres
Suckling Iacchus. She's a faun or satyr
If she's snub-nosed. If she's thick-lipped she's 'Kissie'.
I will not weary you with all the rest.   1170
But let her have the finest face of all,
Let Venus radiate from all her body,
Still there are others; still we have lived so far
Without this woman; still, as well we know,
She does things which the plainest women do.
She fumigates herself, poor wretch, with odours   1175
So foul and evil-smelling that her maids
Keep well away and laugh behind her back.
The lover, shut out, weeping, heaps the threshold
With flowers, anoints the proud doorposts with perfumes,
And plants his love-sick kisses on the door.
But, once admitted, one whiff would promptly make him   1180
Seek some polite excuse to take his leave;
His fond complaint, deep-seated, long-rehearsed,
Would turn to nothing, he'ld damn his stupid folly
In placing her above all mortal women.

　　Our Venuses know this; hence the pains they take   1185
To hide all that goes on behind the scenes
From those they wish to hold in chains of love.
In vain; for in your mind as clear as day
You can see it, and all those other absurdities.
And if you like her mind and she's good-tempered,
Why then you in your turn can overlook   1190
And make allowances for human frailty.

Not always is a woman feigning love
When she sighs and clings to a man in close embrace
And body pressed to body, lips to lips,
Moistens his mouth with hers to prolong his kisses.

1195 Often she does it from the heart, and seeking
Shared mutual delights she rouses him
To run with her through all the lists of love.
And in no wise could birds and beasts and sheep
And mares and cattle to the male submit
But that their nature burns for it, and with joy

1200 Receives the seed from the covering animal.
Do you not see how pairs whom mutual pleasure
Has bound are tortured in their common chains?
Dogs at a crossroads often you may see,
Wanting to part, pull hard with all their might
In different directions, while all the time
By the strong couplings of Venus they are held fast.

1205 This they would never do unless both felt
Pleasures which lead them astray and hold them bound.
Wherefore again and again, I say, the pleasure is mutual.

And in the mingling of seed it sometimes happens
That the woman by a sudden move overcomes

1210 The force of the man and takes control of it;
From the mother's seed then children like the mother
Are born; as from the father's children like the father.
But those you see with figures like to each
And faces like both parents', these have sprung
From the father's body and the mother's blood

1215 When under the goads of Venus through the limbs
The coursing seeds are driven, and dashed together
By two hearts breathing as one in mutual passion,
And neither masters the other nor is mastered.

It sometimes also happens that the children
May look like their grandparents or great-grandparents,
Since parents in their bodies oft conceal

1220 Many first elements mixed in many ways,
And these deriving from ancestral stock
Fathers transmit to fathers. From these Venus
With varying lot makes shapes and reproduces
The look, the voice, the hair of ancestors;

Since from a fixed seed all these features come 1225
No less than our faces and our limbs and bodies.
And female children spring from fathers' seed
And male are made out of the mother's substance;
For always birth derives from seeds of both.
Whichever parent the child most resembles, 1230
Of that it has more than half; which you can see
Whether the progeny be male or female.

　　And it is not the power of gods that blocks
The generating seed in any man
So that no darling children call him father
And he drags out his years in barren love, 1235
Which many think, and with much blood in tears
Sprinkle the altars, honour them with gifts,
To make their wives pregnant with abundant seed.
In vain do they importune gods and fates.
They are barren, some because the seed's too thick, 1240
Others because it is too watery and thin.
The thin, because it can't stick in its place,
At once runs out and so returns aborted.
The thick comes out too closely clotted, and either
Cannot fly forward with far-reaching blow, 1245
Or cannot penetrate the place, or else, once in,
Does not mix easily with the woman's seed.
For sure love's harmonies do greatly differ.
Some men more easily impregnate some women,
Some women more readily receive a man
And grow big from him. Many women barren 1250
In earlier marriages have later found
A source from which they could bear little children
And with sweet progeny enrich themselves.
And often men whose fruitful wives have been
Unable to bear a child, for these also
A woman of matching nature has been found 1255
To fortify their ageing years with children.
So much it matters that seeds can with seeds
Suited for generation be commingled,
Thick meeting watery, watery meeting thick.
It matters too what food supports the life, 1260
For some foods make the seeds thicken in the body

And others make them thin and waste away.
What matters most of all is the position
In which the soothing pleasure itself is taken;
For in the manner of four-footed beasts,
1265 It is generally thought that women best conceive,
Breast down and loins uplifted, so the seeds
Can take more easily their proper places.
Wives have no need at all of wanton movements.
For a woman avoids conception and fights against it,
1270 If in delight she holds his penis close
Between her buttocks, and all her body limp,
Flows with the waves and sways with every tide.
She turns the furrow from its rightful course
Under the ploughshare, makes the seed fall wide.
Whores do this for their private purposes
1275 Lest they be filled too often and lie pregnant,
And to make their loves more pleasing to their men.
Clearly our wives can find no use for this.

And not from power divine or Venus' shafts
It sometimes happens that a wench is loved,
No beauty she; for sometimes she herself
1280 By what she does, by person neat and clean,
And gentle pleasing ways can easily
Accustom you to share your life with her.
And for the rest—by custom love is bred.
Something which feels a blow, however light,
1285 But frequently, must in the end give way.
Do you not see how even a drop of water
1287 By constant dripping wears away a stone?

BOOK FIVE

Who has the genius to build a song
Worthy of nature's majesty, and worthy
Of these discoveries? Who can find fit words
To praise the man who left us such great treasures
Born from his breast and searched out by his mind?   5
No one, I think, from mortal body sprung.
If I must speak, my noble Memmius,
As nature's majesty now known demands,
He was a god, a god indeed, who first
Found out that rule and principle of life
Which bears the name of Wisdom, and by his skill   10
Brought life out from such mighty waves and darkness
And placed it in such calm and light so clear.

Only compare the things that others found
In ancient time, and earned the name divine.
Ceres they say brought crops to mortal men
And Bacchus the vine-born liquor of the grape;
But life without these things could still abide,   15
As even now they say some nations live.
But good life needs a heart that's pure and clean.
So he more rightly earns the name of god
From whom even now through mighty nations spread   20
Sweet solace comes to soothe the minds of men.

And if you think the deeds of Hercules
Can stand in rivalry with his, why then
You'll stray much further from true reasoning.
What harm now could Nemean lion do
With gaping jaws, or bristling Arcadian boar?   25
What harm the Cretan bull or Lerna's pest,
The Hydra fenced about with poisonous snakes?
What threefold Geryon with his tripled breast?

What matter now Stymphalus' horrid birds
And Diomed's Thracian horses breathing fire
In lands by Bistony and Ismara?
The golden apples of the Hesperides,
The snake that guards them with unsleeping eye,
Enormous body coiled around the tree,
What mischief by the wild Atlantic shore
Could it now do, where no one ever comes
From lands we know, and natives fear to tread?
And all the other monsters of this kind,
All dead; but if they had not been slain, and still
Were living, why, what mischief could they do?
None as I think, seeing that even now
Earth teems with wild beasts and is filled with fear
Through forests and great mountains and deep thickets;
Though as a rule it lies within our power
To shun these places, and leave them unvisited.

But unless the mind is purged, what battles then
And perils must enter it against our will!
How great then the sharp cares with which lust rends
The troubled man, how great likewise the fears!
And what of pride and filth and wantonness?
What ruin they bring! and luxury and sloth?
He therefore who has mastered all these vices
And cast them from the mind by words, not arms,
Will it not then be right to find him worthy
To be counted in the number of the gods?
Especially since in words from heaven inspired
He used to teach about the gods themselves,
And all the nature of the world make plain.

In his footsteps I tread and his great doctrines
I follow, and in my poem I teach how all things
Must stay within the law of their creation
And cannot annul the strong statutes of time.
And herein first of all we have found that mind
Consists of body that first itself had birth
And cannot last intact through endless years,
But images in dreams deceive the mind
When we seem to see a man whom life has left.

Next at this point the order of my theme
Leads me to show that all the whole wide world
Came into birth and in the end must die; 65
And in what ways that mass of matter founded
The earth and sky and sea and stars and sun
And the moon's orb; and then what animals
Arose from the earth, and what were never born; 70
And how men first made use of varied speech
Among themselves by finding names for things;
And how into their minds that fear of gods
Crept in, which over all the world keeps holy
Shrines, pools, groves, altars, and images of gods; 75
And by what force the courses of the sun
And the moon's movements pilot nature steers,
I shall explain, lest haply we believe
That these between the earth and sky are free
Of their own will to make their yearly courses,
Meet for the growth of crops and animals, 80
Or think they are turned by some design of gods.
For men who have been well taught about the gods
That they live free from care may wonder still
By what design the world goes on, not least
Those things they see in heaven above their heads; 85
And then to the old religions back they turn,
And cleave to cruel masters whom they think,
Unhappy fools, to be all-powerful,
Not knowing what can be and what cannot,
Not knowing in a word how everything
Has finite power and deep-set boundary stone. 90

To proceed, and make no more delay with promises,
First please observe the earth and sea and sky;
These three, a threefold nature, Memmius,
Three forms so unalike, so interwoven,
One day will give to destruction; all the mass 95
And mighty engine of the world, upheld
For many centuries, will crash in ruin.
Nor do I fail to see how strange and new
This ruin of heaven and earth must strike the mind,
How hard it is to prove by words of mine;
As happens when some unaccustomed thing 100

Comes to the ears, something eyes cannot grasp
Nor hands lay hold of, hands the surest way
To bring belief to hearts and minds of men.
Yet I'll speak out. Perhaps the facts themselves
Will bring belief and in a little time
105 The earth with mighty movements torn apart
You will see, and all the world convulsed with shocks.
This far from us may pilot fortune steer,
And reason rather than the event declare
The fearful crash that brings the world's collapse.

110   And now, before I utter oracles
More holy and more surely true than those
The Pythia speaks from Phoebus' laurelled tripod,
With words of wisdom I shall comfort you;
Lest bridled by religion you may think
115 That earth and sun and sky, sea, stars, and moon
Must last for ever, their bodies being divine;
Lest you should think that for a monstrous crime
Men should, like giants, suffer punishment
Whose reason shakes the ramparts of the world,
120 Willing to quench the shining sun in heaven
And stain immortal things with mortal speech.
So far these things are from divinity,
So little worthy to be counted gods,
That we should rather find in them the pattern
125 Of things possessing neither life nor sense.

    For clearly not in any and every body
Can mind and can intelligence exist.
There can be no trees in the sky, no clouds
In the salt sea, nor fish live in the fields,
130 Nor blood exist in logs nor sap in stones.
Everything has its place, certain and fixed,
Where it must live and grow and have its being.
So the mind cannot arise without the body,
Alone, nor exist apart from blood and sinews.
But if it could, then much more easily
It would place itself in head or shoulders, or right down
In heels, or indeed in any part, provided
135 It were in the same man, the same vessel, enclosed;

And since, within the body, mind and spirit
By a fixed rule and ordinance are given
The place where they can live and grow apart,
All the more strongly then must we deny
That wholly outside body or animal form 140
In crumbling clods of earth or the sun's fire
They can live, or in water or the high shores of sky.
These things therefore for sure are not endowed
With consciousness divine, since they are unable
To be animated with the breath of life. 145
Another thing you cannot believe is this:
That holy dwelling places of the gods
Exist in any regions of this world.
For the nature of the gods is thin, and far removed
From our senses, and is hardly perceived by the mind.
We cannot touch it with our hands; therefore 150
It cannot touch anything that we can touch.
For that cannot touch which cannot itself be touched.
Wherefore their dwelling places also must differ
From ours, being thin, like the thinness of their bodies.
This I will prove to you later at some length. 155

   Also, to say that for the sake of men
The gods willed the creation of the world
With all its brilliant fabric, and therefore
We ought to praise their most praiseworthy work
And think it everlasting and immortal,
And that a thing by the gods' ancient rule 160
Founded for all time for the race of men
May not by any force at any time
Be shaken, or be challenged by argument,
And turned right upside down—and to invent
Similar fictions, all this, Memmius,
Is nonsense. For what meed of gratitude
On gods immortal, blest, could we bestow 165
That for our sakes they should do anything?
And what new thing after so long a time
Could tempt them in their blest tranquillity
To wish to change their old life for a new?
For to take pleasure in new things befits 170
A man the old have hurt; but when past years

Have brought no ill, and life is sweet, what then
Could kindle a desire for novelty?
What ill had it been for us had we not been made?
175 Did our life lie in darkness and in grief
Until creation's light first shone abroad?
A man once born must wish to stay in life
So long as soothing pleasure keeps him there.
But he who has never tasted love of life
Or ever been enrolled among the living,
180 How does it hurt him not to have been made?

     Another point. The pattern of creation,
The very concept of mankind, how did it come
Into the minds of gods, that they should know
What they wanted to make, and grasp it with their minds?
How was the power of atoms ever known,
185 What they could do by changes of position,
Had nature herself not given a model for creation?
So many atoms in so many ways
Smitten with blows through infinite time, and massed
By their own weights together, have combined
190 In every way, tried every variation,
Of things that by them ever could be made.
No wonder then if into those positions
And into those movements they came, by which
Though always new this world is kept in being.

     But even if I had no knowledge of atoms,
195 This from the order of the heavens itself
And many other facts I would assert—
That in no way for us the power of gods
Fashioned the world and brought it into being;
So great the fault with which it stands endowed.

200   In the first place, of all that lies beneath
The mighty sweep of sky, a greedy part
Mountains possess and forests full of wild beasts.
Rocks hold it, and vast marshes, and the sea
Which widely separates the shores of lands.
Nearly two thirds are kept from mortal use
205 By burning heat and constant fall of frost;
What land is left, nature by her own power

Would choke with brambles did not man resist,
Man, for the sake of life well used to groan
Over strong mattock and cleave earth with plough.
Unless the ploughshare turn the fruitful clods   210
And we, working the soil, bring them to birth,
No plants can ever of their own accord
Spring up into the melting air above.
And even sometimes when with great labour won
They fill the smiling earth with leaf and flower,
Either the sun in heaven scorches them   215
Or sudden rains destroy them, or chilling frosts,
And storms with violent whirlwinds harass them.

Consider now the wild beasts' fearsome breed,
Enemies of mankind by land and sea,
Why does nature feed them? Why do the seasons bring   220
Diseases? Why does death untimely stalk abroad?

And then the child, like sailor cast ashore
By cruel waves, lies naked on the ground,
Sans speech, sans all the aids that life requires,
When nature first into the shores of light
In throes has cast him from his mother's womb,   225
And fills the place with cries—as well he might
Seeing that so great ills await his life.

But flocks and herds and wild beasts live and grow
Without the aid of rattles; they don't want
The baby talk of nurses petting them   230
Nor change of clothing with the changing year,
Nor have they need of arms or lofty walls
To guard their goods, since earth all things to all
Brings forth in bounty and nature's skill supplies.

Well now, in the first place since earth and water   235
And the light breaths of air and burning heat,
From which we see this sum of things is made—
Since these have bodies which are born and die,
Of the whole world we must believe the same.
For things of which we see that their parts and limbs 240
Consist of matter which is born and dies,
We know that these same things are certainly
Subject to birth and death. So when I see

The mighty members of the world consumed
And born again, why, then I may be sure
That heaven and earth likewise had their beginning
And in destruction too will have their end.

Please do not think that I have begged the question
When I assume that earth and fire are mortal
And do not doubt that air and water perish,
And say that they are born and grow again.

Take the earth first. A large part of it, burnt
By constant sun and beaten by myriad feet,
Breathes out a cloud of dust and flying mists
Which strong winds scatter abroad all through the air.
Part of the soil also is washed away
By rain, and rivers scrape away their banks;
Besides, whatever the earth throws up returns
In due proportion; and since beyond doubt we see
The mother of all to be their common grave,
Therefore, my friend, you see the earth is diminished
And then in turn increased and grows again.

And next, there is no need of words to say
How sea, rivers, and springs are always full
With waters new and streams forever flow:
The mighty fall of waters everywhere
Makes this quite plain. But the front part of the flood
Is lifted off and drawn away, and so
In total there is no excess of water;
Partly because strong winds sweeping its surface
Diminish it, and the sun's high rays unravel it,
Partly because it seeps through the earth below,
The brine is filtered off, and the mass of water
Oozes back and joins the rivers at their source,
And thence, in a column of sweet water,
Over the ground it flows along the path
Cut once by liquid foot to guide the waters.

Air next I'll speak of, which throughout its body
Changes innumerably hour by hour.
Always whatever flows off from things is carried
Into the great ocean of the air; unless in turn
The air gave matter back to things again

And in their flux created them anew,
All would by now be dissolved and changed into air.
Therefore forever air is born from things
And falls back into things, since it is certain
That all things are continually in flux.   280

The eternal sun, rich fountain of clear light,
Forever floods the sky with radiance new,
Swiftly supplying new light in place of old.
For the first flash of light that comes is lost,
Wherever it falls. As you may learn from this: 285
As soon as clouds begin to front the sun
And as it were break in between its rays,
The lower part of them at once is lost,
And the earth is in shadow, wherever the clouds move;
So you may see things always need new light,   290
That every burst of radiance perishes,
That in no other way could things be seen
In sunlight, did the fount of light itself
Cease ever to maintain a fresh supply.

And lights that shine at night on earth, these too—
Your hanging lamps and torches flaming bright,   295
Flaring and flashing through the pitchy smoke—
In the same way, fed by the fire, they haste
To bring up new supplies of light, and on
And on they press, alive with flickering flames,
Seeming to pour an unbroken stream of light;
So speedily is its extinction hid   300
By the swift birth of flame from all the fires.

So you must think that sun and moon and stars
Send out quick bursts of light one after another,
And always the first flash of flame is lost;
And none of these is indestructible.   305

And stones—these too you see that time subdues,
And lofty towers fall, their masonry
All crumbling, and the shrines and images
Of gods, wearied by time, are cracked and fall.
Nor can their holy power extend the bounds
Of fate, nor struggle against nature's laws.   310
The monuments of men collapsed we see,

Should we look there for immortality;
And rocks roll down, from lofty mountains torn,
Unable to endure the strong force of time,
315   Of finite time. For certainly no shock
Could make them suddenly break off and fall,
If from time infinite they had withstood
Intact the assault and torment of the years.

Look last at that which above and all around
Holds the whole earth in its embrace.
320   If it is this, as some declare, that makes
All things from itself and takes them back again
When their time is finished, it must all consist
Of matter subject to both birth and death.
For that which from itself feeds other things
And nourishes them, must be diminished,
And made anew when it receives them back.

Now here's another point. If earth and sky
325   Had no beginning or no time of birth
But have been always everlasting, why
Before the Theban war and doom of Troy
Have other poets not sung other things?
Where have so many deeds of men so many times
Fallen from sight and mind, and nowhere flower
Implanted on eternal monuments?
330   In truth I think the world is young and new
And in quite recent time its life began.
See even now some arts are being refined
And others springing up and growing; in ships
Many new things have now been done, and lately
Musicians found out tuneful harmonies.
335   Yes, and the nature and order of this world
In recent time has been discovered, and this
I now myself the very first am found
Able to tell it in our native tongue.

But if perchance it may be your belief
That all these things existed once before,
But that mankind perished in burning fire
340   Or cities fell in some great upheaval of the world,
Or tearing rivers fed by endless rains

Flooding the country overwhelmed the towns,
Why, all the more then you must be convinced
That earth and sky themselves will be destroyed.
For when such great afflictions, such great perils,   345
Once shook the world, then if some more potent cause
More terrible had come upon it, there must have followed
Widespread destruction and a mighty fall.
And there's no surer proof of our mortality
Than this, that we sicken of the same diseases
As those whom nature has recalled from life.   350

    Few things there are that last eternally.
First, solid bodies that repel assaults,
And allow nothing to penetrate them
And break apart the close-knit parts within,
Such as the atomic particles of matter
The nature of which we have described before;   355
Next, things which last through all the length of time
Because no blow can hit them; such is the void,
Which stays untouched and nothing can ever strike it;
Next, things which have no space around them
Into which they can dissolve and be dispersed;   360
Such is the eternal sum of the sum of things.
Outside it nowhere any place exists
Into which its elements can spring away,
And nothing exists to impact it or destroy it.   363
But, as I have shown, the world is not composed
Of solid body, since void is mixed with things.   365
Nor is it like the void. Nor are there lacking
Bodies which from the infinite spring forth
And rack this world with violent hurricanes
Or bring some other danger and disaster;
Nor is there lacking in the depths of space   370
Room for the world's walls fallen to fly apart;
Or they may perish struck by other force.
Therefore the door of death is never closed
To sky and sun and earth and sea's deep waters.
No. It stands open, and with vast gaping mouth   375
It waits for them.
Wherefore you must confess that these same things
Have had their birth; for nothing of mortal build

Could ever through infinite ages until now
Have scorned the mighty power of endless time.

380　　Again, since the mighty members of the world
So furiously fight among themselves
In most unrighteous war, do you not see
Some end to their long struggles may be given?
Perhaps the sun and universal heat
Will overcome, and drink the waters dry,
385　　Which is their aim, though not so far achieved,
So much the rivers supply and threaten in turn
To flood the world from ocean's deep abyss.
In vain. Since winds that sweep across its surface
Diminish it, and the sun's high rays unravel it,
390　　Confident that they can dry up everything
Before the waters can achieve their end.
Such war they breathe in equal combat locked
Seeking decision in a mighty cause.
Though once meanwhile fire won the victory,
395　　And once, so legend tells, water reigned in the fields.

　　For fire was lord, and burnt up all around,
When far from his course the Sun's fierce horses hurled
Phaethon through the heavens and o'er the earth.
But the almighty sire to anger moved
400　　With sudden thunderbolt the aspiring youth
Struck from his chariot down to earth. The Sun
Meeting his fall, caught up the eternal lamp
That lights the world, brought back the scattered horses,
Reined them in, trembling, then to their proper courses
Guiding them back restored the world again.
405　　At least that's what the old Greek poets sang,
And that is very far removed from truth.
For fire can triumph when from the infinite
The atoms of its matter issue forth
In greater mass than usual. And then
Either subdued somehow its force declines,
410　　Or the world dies, burnt up by scorching blasts.

　　Water likewise began once to prevail,
Massing its floods, so legend tells, and many
Races of men were overwhelmed; but then

That which had massed from out the infinite
Turned back, by some compelling force withdrawn,
The rains stopped, and the rivers checked their flow.   415

   Next in due order I'll set out the ways
In which by assembly of matter were established
The earth, the sky, and the vast depths profound
Of sea, and courses of the sun and moon.
For sure, not by design or intelligence
Did primal atoms place themselves in order,   420
Nor did they make contracts, you may be certain,
As to what movements each of them should make.
But many primal atoms in many ways
Moving through infinite time up to the present,
Clashing among themselves and carried by their own weight,
Have come together in every possible way,
Tried every combination that could be made;   425
And so advancing through vast lengths of time,
Exploring every union and motion,
At length those of them came together
Which by a sudden conjunction interfused
Often become the beginnings of great things—   430
Of earth and sea and sky and living creatures.

   Then not the sun's great wheel with bounteous light
Soaring aloft was seen, nor stars of heaven,
Nor sea nor sky nor earth at all nor air
Nor aught like things that in our world we know,   435
But a strange storm and surging mighty mass
Of atoms of all kinds in conflict locked
Created turmoil, in their intervals
Connections, courses, weights, blows, meetings, motions,
Because by reason of their different shapes and patterns
They could not all when joined together remain so,   440
Nor make the movements needed for their union.
Then parts began to separate, like things
Joining with like, and parcel out the world,
Fashion its limbs, set out its mighty parts—
That is, to set apart high heaven from earth,   445
And the sea apart, spreading its separate waters,
And apart too the pure and separate fires of ether.

In the first place, all the particles of earth,
450 Being heavy and entangled, came together
In the middle, and took the lowest positions.
And the more closely mixed they came together
The more they pressed out elements that could make
Sea, stars, sun, and moon, and the world's great walls.
For all of these consist of elements
455 More round and smooth and smaller far than those
Of earth. First therefore through its porous crust
Ether broke out and raised itself aloft,
Ether the fire-bringer, and many fires
460 It lightly drew with it. As oft we see
With blush of morn the golden sun's new beams
Colour the meadow grasses pearled with dew,
And lakes and living streams breathe out a mist,
And earth itself appears sometimes to smoke;
465 And then the vapours forming high above
Thicken, and weave a web across the sky,
So in this way then ether light and thin
Thickened, and bent round curving everywhere
Expanding everywhere in all directions,
470 And thus fenced in the rest with keen embrace.

Next the beginnings came of sun and moon,
Whose globes revolve in middle course on high.
Them neither earth nor mighty ether claimed,
Being not so heavy as to sink and lie
475 Nor light enough to rise through highest heaven,
But in between they turn as living bodies
And take their place as parts of all the world;
As in our bodies too some limbs may stay
At rest, while others yet are moving.

480 And now, when these two orbs had been drawn off,
Earth suddenly into the wide blue sea
Sank down, and filled the ditches with salt floods;
And day by day the more the tides of ether
And sun's rays all around beat on the earth,
485 And to its farthest bounds with many blows
Compressed it, so that forced towards its centre
It became solid, so much then the more

The salt sweat pressed out oozing from its body
Increased the sea, increased the swimming plains,
So much the more slipped out and flew away
Those many bodies of heat and air, and far from earth 490
Uplifted filled the shining vault of heaven.
The plains subsided and the mountains grew,
High mountains, since the rocks could not sink down,
Nor all things everywhere sink equally.

   So in this way earth with its solid weight 495
Stood, and the mud as it were of all the world
Flowing down together in a heavy mass
Sank to the bottom like the lees of wine.
Then sea, then air, then ether fire-bearer
All were left pure, of liquid atoms made,
Some lighter than others. Liquidest of all, 500
And lightest, ether flows above the air,
Nor is its liquid essence e'er disturbed
By whirling winds. It lets all things below
Be tossed by violent tempests, racked by storms;
Itself with motion undisturbed and sure
Bearing its own fires keeps its onward way. 505
For that a gentle flow in one direction
Is possible for ether, Pontus shows, a sea
That flows with an unchanging current, keeping
One tide forever moving in its waters.

   The causes of the motions of the stars
Let us now sing. First, if the great orb of heaven
Turns round, we must say that air presses on each pole, 510
And holds it from outside and shuts it in;
Then, that another air flows above and moves
On the same course as roll the signs of heaven
And shining stars of the everlasting world;
Or else some other air flowing beneath
In the opposite direction drives it from below, 515
As we see rivers turning wheels and buckets.

   It may be also that the whole of heaven
Remains at rest, and yet the bright stars move;
Whether because swift tides of ether shut in
Seeking escape whirl round in circles, and roll 520

Their fires through all the thundering realms of heaven;
Or some air flowing from some place outside
Turns and drives fires; or perhaps of their own accord
They wind where food invites them, fiery bodies
525   Grazing the starry pastures of the sky.

Which of these causes operates in this world
It is difficult to say beyond all doubt;
But what can and does happen in the universe
In various worlds created in various ways
That do I teach, and set out several causes
530   That may apply to the movements of the stars
Throughout the universe; and one of these
Must certainly within this world of ours
Excite the movements of the constellations;
But to lay down which it is, is not for one
With stumbling footsteps moving slowly forward.

Now earth rests in the centre of the world.
535   This is because its mass slowly reduces
And vanishes, and underneath is joined
Another substance, joined when its life began,
Fitted and grafted into the regions of air
In which it lives, and for that very reason
It is no burden and does not depress the air.
540   A man's limbs have no weight that he can feel,
The head's no burden to the neck, nor body
For all its size weighs heavy on our feet.
But heavy things striking us from outside
Cause injury, though they be very much smaller.
545   So much it matters what each thing can do.
In the same way, earth was not suddenly
Imposed on air as something alien,
Or from outside thrust in on alien air,
But from the first beginning of the world
It was conceived and grew together with it,
A fixed part of it, as limbs are of our body.

550   Besides, when earth by sudden mighty thunder
Is struck, it shakes all the air that lies above.
This it could never do, were it not bound
To the world's airy regions and to the sky.

By common roots united and conjoined,
Joined when their lives began, they cling together.   555

    See also how a most thin essence of spirit
Sustains our body, despite its heavy weight
Because it is so conjoined and united with it.
And what can lift the body in a leap
If not the force of spirit that guides the limbs?   560
Now do you see how great the power can be
Of a thin substance joined with heavy body,
As air is joined with earth, and mind with us?

    The sun's heat and its size can hardly be
Much greater or less than is perceived by our senses.   565
Though great the distances through which its fires
Throw light, and breathe warm air upon our limbs,
The heat is not lessened by these intervals
Nor is the fire made smaller to our vision;
Therefore since the sun's heat and light outpoured   570
Reach to our senses and shine everywhere,
The shape and size of the sun can so truly be seen
That nothing need be added or taken away.

    The moon too, whether it shines with borrowed light   575
Illumining the world, or whether it sends
Its own light from its own body, whichever it is,
Its size, as it moves through the heavens, is no larger
Than it appears to our eyes as we see it.
For all things which we see at a great distance
Through large expanse of air have outlines blurred   580
Before the bulk is lessened. Therefore the moon,
Since it displays a clear face and firm outline,
Must, as we see it move on high, possess
The same shape and same size as what we see.

    Lastly, all the fires of ether which we see—   585
Since all the fires that we see here on earth,
So long as their flickering is clear and blaze perceived,
Appear sometimes to change extremely little
In size, however distant they may be—
You may be sure that only by a fraction
Or by a small and trifling difference,   590
Can they be smaller or larger than what we see.

And here's another thing that need not cause surprise.
How does so small a sun so great a light
Send out that floods the seas and lands and sky,
595   And fills them and bathes them in its glowing heat?
Perhaps from there one spring of all the world
Wells forth in bounteous flood and pours out light,
Because elements of heat so mass together,
600   Coming from everywhere through all the world,
That heat flows out here from one single source.
Do you not see how widely a small spring
Can water the meadows and flood across the fields?
Or it may be that no great heat of sun
605   Can set the air on fire, if it may chance
That air is present of a kind that can
Be kindled by a small amount of heat,
As sometimes we see standing corn or stubble
Caught by a single spark blaze everywhere.
610   Perhaps also the sun with rosy lamp
Shining on high possesses hidden fires
Invisible, all round it, with no radiance marked,
And in this way the mighty heat-bearer
Increases the force and impact of its rays.

Nor does a straight and simple path lie open
615   To tell us how the sun from its summer heights
Sinks down to Capricorn in winter, then coming back
Turns to its goal again of Cancer's solstice;
Nor how the moon traverses month by month
The space which the sun takes a full year to travel.
620   These things, I say, can be given no single cause.

One of the most likely explanations
Is that put forward by Democritus,
Divine philosopher. In his opinion
The nearer the heavenly bodies are to earth
The less the whirling of the sky can move them;
625   For its violent and rapid force grows less
And fades away lower down, and so the sun
Together with the signs that follow it
Is gradually left behind, because its path
Is so much lower than that of the burning stars.

And still more so the moon: its course is lower,
And the further it is from the sky and the nearer to earth 630
So much the less it can keep up with the signs.
And as the whirling movement carrying it
Is weaker, since it is lower than the sun,
So much the sooner do the constellations
Catch up with it all round and pass it by.
It seems to travel back more quickly to them 635
Because in fact they catch up faster on it.

It is possible also that two currents of air
Blow across the world in opposite directions,
Alternately, each at fixed intervals;
One driving the sun down from its summer signs
To the winter turning point of frost and ice, 640
One throwing it back out of the cold and dark
To regions of heat and to the burning stars.
In the same way we must think that the moon
And the stars which turn for great years in great orbits
May be driven by alternate currents of air. 645
You see how clouds driven by opposing winds
Move in opposite directions, one above another.
Why should the stars not through the mighty orbits
Of ether be carried by opposing tides?

Night with vast darkness overwhelms the earth 650
Either because the sun on its long course
Has reached the farthest limits of the sky,
And faint and weary has breathed out its fires
Worn by the journey and weakened by much air,
Or else it is driven to turn beneath the earth
By the same force that carried it above. 655

At a fixed time also Matuta spreads
Her rosy dawn abroad through ether's shores
And flings wide the light of day; either because
The sun returning from beneath the earth
Comes up and tries to set the sky on fire,
Or because fires and many seeds of heat 660
At a fixed time combine and mass together
And make each day a newborn sun to shine.
So it is said from Ida's mountain peaks

At daybreak in the East strange fires are seen
Scattered along the morning's rim, which mass

665   As it were into a ball and form an orb.
Nor is it anything miraculous
That at so fixed a time these seeds of fire
Combine to make anew the sun's bright rays.
For we see many things that come to pass
At a fixed time everywhere. At a fixed time

670   Trees bloom, at a fixed time flowers fall,
At a fixed time no less does age command
The teeth to fall, brings the soft growth of down
On face of ripening youth and bids the beard
Come down in equal length on manly cheek.

675   And lightning too and snow, rains, clouds, and winds,
These mostly come at fixed times of the year.
For since the causes from the first beginning
Were of this nature, and from the world's origin
Things happened in this way, in sequence then
And order fixed they even now recur.

680   Days may grow longer and nights melt away
And daylight lessen as the nights increase
For various reasons. It may be that the sun
Running below and then above the earth
Moves through the ether in unequal curves
Dividing its orbit into unequal parts,

685   And what from one point it has taken away
It adds to the other on its journey back,
Until it comes to that great sign in heaven
Where the two knotted circles of the year
Equate the shades of night with light of day.
For in mid-course between the mighty blasts
Of North wind and of South the sky maintains

690   Its turning points at equal distances,
Obeying the pattern of the zodiac
Through which the sun creeps on its yearly course
Shining obliquely upon earth and sky.
So they declare who have mapped out all the parts
Of heaven and marked the signs in their due places.

695   Or perhaps the air is thicker in certain parts
So that below the earth the trembling gleam

Of fire delays and cannot easily
Pass through and so come forth into its rising.
And therefore the long winter nights drag on
Until the radiant banner of day appears. 700
Or again, the truth may lie with those who say
That in alternate seasons of the year
Slower or quicker flow together the fires
That cause the sun to rise in its due place.

Let us now consider the moon. Perhaps it shines 705
Because the sun's rays strike it, day by day
Turning a larger light into our eyes
As it moves further from the sun, until
Rising on high it sees its setting, and then
Right opposite the sun the moon shines full.
Then gradually it must needs hide its light 710
Behind it, as it glides nearer to the sun
From the opposite region through the zodiac.
So they make out that say the moon's like a ball
Moving in an orbit below the sun.
Perhaps also the moon has its own light 715
And with it displays its bright shapes as they change.
For there may be some other moving body
That glides along with it, obstructing it
And blocking it in all sorts of ways,
Which cannot be seen because it has no light.
Or it may be that it rotates like a ball 720
One half of which is filled with brilliant light
And as it turns displays a changing shape
Until it brings round to our gazing eyes
All of the part that is enriched with fire.
Then gradually as it turns it bears away 725
The luminous surface of its rounded globe.
This do the Babylonian Chaldees
Maintain, refuting the astronomers,
And trying to prove their art is all in vain.
As if each of these contentions might not be true,
Or there were any reason why you should dare
To embrace one of them rather than another. 730

Lastly, why should not a new moon every day
Be created, with fixed phases and fixed shapes,

And every single day the new creation
Perish, and a new one take its place?
That is difficult to explain by reasoning
735   And prove by words, seeing that many things
Are created in so fixed and sure an order.
Spring comes, and Venus, and Venus' harbinger
Winged Cupid runs in front, in Zephyr's steps,
And mother Flora strews the path before them
740   With choicest scents and colours everywhere.
Next follows parching heat and hand in hand
Ceres his dusty friend, and Aquilo
That blows in summertime across the sea;
Next autumn comes and Bacchus' revel rout;
Then follow other seasons, other winds,
745   Volturnus thunderer and Auster armed with lightning.
Last winter brings his snows and freezing frost,
And cold comes after him with chattering teeth.
No marvel then, if at fixed times the moon
Is born and at fixed times again destroyed,
Seeing that in this world so many things
750   Come into being at so fixed a time.

The sun's eclipses and the moon's retreats
Likewise you must suppose have several causes.
For if the moon can cut the sun's light off
From earth, with head on high obstructing it,
755   Blocking its burning rays with its dark orb,
Why should we not think that some other body
Gliding always without light could do the same?
And why should not the sun at a fixed time
Be able fainting to lay down its fires
And then renew its light, when it has passed
760   Through regions of air hostile to its flames
Which can extinguish and destroy its fires?
And if the earth in turn can rob the moon
Of light and keep the sun subdued below
While moon glides monthly through the cone of shadow,
765   Why should not some other body at the same time
Be able to travel underneath the moon
Or glide above the sun's great orb, and so
Block and cut off its rays and light outpoured?

And if the moon shines with its own bright light,
Why should it not in a fixed part of the heavens
Grow faint as it passes through regions hostile to it?   770

Well now, since the blue firmament on high
Has been my theme, and I have explained its working,
So that the varying courses of the sun
And wanderings of the moon, what force and cause   775
Impels them we can better understand,
And in what way their light dies in eclipse
And darkness brings o'er unexpecting earth
As first they blink and then with open eyes
View all again shining with brilliant light,
I now return to the childhood of the world   780
And the soft fields of earth, and tell what first
Into the shores of light they chose to bring
Newborn, and offer to the fickle winds.

In the beginning earth gave birth to plants
After their kind, and ringed with shining green
The hills and plains. The flowering meadows shone   785
With verdure. Then between the various trees
A mighty race began, all galloping
To be the first to shoot up into the sky.
As feathers, hair, and bristles sprout from bodies
Of animals four-footed and from birds
Strong on the wing, so then the newborn earth
First thrust forth herbs and shrubs, and then created   790
The mortal creatures in their generations,
Of many kinds from many sources sprung.
For animals cannot have fallen from the sky
Nor creatures of the land come from salt pools.

So it remains that earth does well deserve
The name of mother which we give to her,
Since from the earth all things have been created.   795
Even now many animals come up from earth
Formed by the rains and warm heat of the sun,
So it's no wonder if many and larger ones
Sprang and grew up when earth and air were young.   800
First the winged things, the varied race of birds,
Were hatched from eggs in springtime, just as now

In summer cicadas from their smooth round shells
Crawl out in search of sustenance and life.
805 For earth then first gave birth to mortal creatures.
In the fields were warmth and moisture everywhere
And so wherever a suitable place occurred
Wombs would grow, held by roots into the soil;
These in maturing time young offspring broke
810 Fleeing from moisture now and seeking air;
Then nature opened there the pores of earth
And made it from its veins pour out a juice
Like milk, as now when a woman has borne a child
Her breasts fill with sweet milk since all the force
815 Of nourishment in her flows into the breasts.
Earth furnished food for the children, warmth for their clothes,
And herbs for bed all covered in soft down.
The world when young knew neither freezing cold
Nor scorching heat nor furious blasts of wind,
For at the same pace all things equally
820 Increase and reach their peak of strength together.

Wherefore again and again does earth deserve
The name of mother given to her, for she
Herself alone created the human race
And at an appointed time herself produced
All animals that range the mountains wide
825 And fowls of the air in all their varied forms.

But since an end must come to all her bearing
She ceased, like a woman worn out by old age.
For time doth change the nature of the world;
One state of things must pass into another;
830 Nothing remains the same. All things move on.
All things does nature turn, transform, and change.
One thing decays, grows faint and weak with age;
Another grows, and is despised no more.
So therefore time the whole nature of the world
835 Changes, and one state of the earth yields place to another,
So that what it bore before it cannot bear,
But can bear what it did not bear before.

And many monsters in those days did earth
Try to create, most strange in form and aspect,

Hermaphrodites, halfway 'twixt man and woman
Yet being neither, and cut off from both;
And creatures without feet, or bereft of hands,
Some dumb and mouthless, some eyeless and blind,   840
Some crippled, all their limbs stuck to their bodies,
Unable to do anything, go anywhere,
Nor avoid ill nor take what they might need.
And other monsters of like kind earth made,   845
In vain, since nature scared away their growth,
Nor could they reach the longed-for flower of age,
Nor find food nor be joined in acts of Venus.
For any things we see must needs combine
Before by procreation living beings   850
Can hammer out the pattern of their kind.
First they need food, then the life-bringing seed
From limbs lying limp must find a way to flow;
And male and female cannot join together
Unless they have means to make their shared delights.

In those days many breeds of animals   855
Must have died out, unable by procreation
To hammer out a chain of progeny.
All those that you see drawing the breath of life
Either by guile or courage or by speed
From the beginning of time have been preserved.
And there are many which their usefulness   860
Has commended to us, entrusted to our protection.
Courage has kept the savage lion safe,
Cunning the fox and speed the fleeing stag.
The dog, our faithful watchman of the night,
And beasts of burden of all kinds, and sheep   865
With woolly fleeces also, and horned cattle,
All these have man's protection, Memmius.
Gladly they fled the beasts of prey and sought
Peace and good victuals without labour won
Which we supply them in reward for service.   870
But those on which nature no such qualities
Bestowed, no means to fend for themselves, no use
That might persuade us to give them sustenance
To live in safety under our protection,
All these to prey or profit victims lay,   875

Bound by the shackles of their destiny
Till nature brought destruction to their kind.

Centaurs never existed, nor at any time
Can there be creatures of a double nature
880   Composed of alien limbs and twofold body
Such that the two parts live in balance together.
And here is proof the dullest brain can grasp.
First, the horse reaches its vigorous prime
At about three years; by no means so the boy.
For even at that age oft he will in sleep
885   Seek the soft comfort of his mother's breasts.
And later, when the horse's strong limbs fail
Wearied by age, and faint as life recedes,
Then long-delayed the flower of boyhood comes,
And youth begins, and clothes his cheeks with down.
890   Think not therefore that Centaurs can be formed
From seed of man and horse that bears the rider,
Or Scyllas, half-fish, girt with rabid dogs,
And all the other monsters of that kind
Composed of members incompatible;
895   Which neither reach their flower and prime of life
Together, nor fail as old age weakens them,
Nor burn with Venus equally, nor join
In the same habits, nor the same pleasures feel.
In fact you may see that often bearded goats
900   Grow fat on hemlock which to man is poison.
Again, since fire burns lions' tawny bodies
No less than all things made of flesh and blood,
How could the Chimaera, three bodies joined in one,
905   Lion in front, serpent behind, goat in the middle,
Belch from its body blasts of burning flame?

Wherefore, if anyone pretends that beasts
Of such a kind could have been brought to birth
And made, when earth was young and heaven new,
Relying on that empty concept 'new',
910   Let him continue with his nonsense,
Let him believe that rivers ran with gold,
That trees bore jewels for blossom, that a man
Was born with such a mighty stretch of limbs

That he could set his stride across the sea
And turn the whole sky round him with his hands.   915
Though many seeds of things were in the soil
At the time when earth first brought forth animals,
That is no proof that beasts of compound form
Could have been made, from alien bodies joined.
Things which now spring abundantly from earth,   920
All breeds of plants, and crops, and smiling woodlands
Cannot be interbred and woven together,
But each proceeds on its appointed way
And by fixed laws of nature stays distinct.

And in those days the men that roamed the earth   925
Were hardier by far, as was most fitting,
Since hard earth made them. Larger bones they had
And solider, with stronger sinews fitted;
And neither heat nor cold could readily
Subdue them, nor strange food, nor ills of body.   930
Through many lustres of the circling sun
They led their lives, wide-wandering like wild beasts.
No sturdy arm then steered the curving plough,
No one knew how to work the fields with iron,
Or to set cuttings into the soil, or use   935
The hook to cut dead branches from the trees.
What sun and rain had given them, what earth
Created for them of her own accord,
That was a gift enough to bring content.
Mostly amid the oaks they stayed their hunger
With acorns; and the berries which now you see   940
In winter on arbutus ripening red
Earth then bore larger and more plentiful.
And many other foods young flowering earth
Then bore for them, hard foods, but food enough
To meet poor mortals' needs.

Rivers and springs called them to quench their thirst,   945
As now in the high hills the waterfalls
Call from afar the thirsting tribes of beasts.
They made their homes amid the woodland realms
Of nymphs, known to them in their wanderings,
Where well they knew the living waters still

950 Washed the wet rocks in their abundant flow,
Wet rocks, and dripped down o'er the verdant moss,
Or bubbling up broke out across the plain.
Nor yet they knew how to work things with fire
Nor skins for clothes, the spoils of animals,
955 But woods and forests and the mountain caves
They made their homes, and hid their uncouth limbs
Beneath the bushes, when they must needs
Seek shelter from the lash of wind and rain.
They could not look to any common good
Nor guide their lives by custom or by law.
960 What nature gave a man for prey, he kept,
Taught that his own will gave him strength to live.
And Venus coupled lovers in the woods;
Mutual desire attracted them, or else
The strength of man and overpowering lust
Forced her, or else he won her by a bribe
965 Of acorns or arbutus or choice pears.
And with their marvellous powers of hand and foot
They hunted the beasts that roamed the woods and plains,
With stones for missiles or with heavy clubs.
Many they killed; from few they hid themselves.

970 When night came o'er them, naked on the ground
Like bristling hogs they laid their woodland limbs
And made a coverlet of leaves and branches.
Nor, wandering frightened in the shades of night,
Sought they with wailing loud the sun and day,
975 But buried in sleep they waited quietly
Until the sun with rosy torch again
Spread his new morning light across the sky.
For since from childhood always to their sight
Darkness and light returned alternately,
This brought no wonder to their minds, no cause
980 To tremble lest the earth be held in night
Perpetual, the sun's bright light withdrawn.
Much more they worried that the hours of rest
Brought danger from marauding animals.
Driven from home, they fled their rocky shelters
985 At the approach of foaming boar, or lion,

And at dead of night they'ld yield their leaf-strewn beds
In terror to their savage visitors.

Nor did poor mortals much more then than now
Leave the sweet light of life with sad lament.
More often then one single man might die
Caught by wild beasts and torn, devoured alive,
Filling the woods and hills with screams, seeing
His living flesh buried in a living tomb.
And those whom flight had saved with mangled bodies
Pressed trembling palms over their ghastly sores,
Calling on Orcus with heart-rending cries
Till cruel torments put an end to life,
With none to help, not knowing what wounds need.
But many thousands on the battlefield
One day did not destroy, nor did rough seas
Dash ships and men together on the rocks.
Then all in vain, all useless, all for nothing,
The sea would rise and roar and then again
Lightly lay down her empty threats. No one
By quiet seas' deceitful blandishments
And laughing waves was e'er enticed to ruin.
The wicked art of seamanship lay hid.
Then lack of food brought fainting limbs to death,
Today, by contrast, plenty 'tis that kills.
Then men unknowing poured poison for themselves,
Today with greater skill they poison others.

And then, when huts and skins and fire they had got themselves,
And woman joined with man had made a home,
And laws of married life were known to them,
And they saw loving children born to them,
Then first the human race began to soften.
Through fire their chilly limbs became less able
To bear the cold with sky for covering;
Venus sapped their strength; and children easily
With winning smiles could break their parents' will.
And neighbours then began to join in friendship,
Wishing to do no ill nor suffer harm,
And sought protection for their womankind
And children, with stammering voice and gesture showing

990
995
1000
1005
1010
1015
1020

That pity for the weak is right for all.
Not everywhere could harmony be born,
1025   But the most part kept faithful to their bonds,
Or else the human race had quite been lost
In the old days, nor could its progeny
Have passed till now through all the generations.

   As for the various sounds of speech, 'twas nature
That made men utter them, and convenience
1030   Found names for things, rather as we see children
Driven to make gestures by their lack of speech
And point with finger at things in front of them.
For every creature feels the purposes
For which he can use the power that lies in him.
Before the budding horns sprout from its forehead
1035   A calf will use them, butting angrily,
And cubs of panthers and lions fight and scratch
With feet and claws, and use their mouths to bite
When teeth and claws have scarcely yet been formed.
And birds of every kind we see place trust
1040   In their wings and seek unsteady aid from them.

   Therefore to think that someone then allotted
Names to things, and that men learnt words from him,
Is folly. Why should we think that this man had the power
To mark all things with voices and to utter
The various sounds of speech, and not believe
That others had the power to do the same?
1045   Besides, if others had not used these sounds,
Whence was the concept of this usefulness
Implanted in him, whence first came the power
To picture in his mind what he should do?
1050   And one man could not compel many and force them
That they should wish to learn the names of things.
One cannot easily in any way
Teach deaf men what to do. And to have sounds
Unheard before all meaningless in vain
1055   Dinned into their ears, that they could not endure.

   Lastly, what is so very wonderful
If the human race, with vigorous voice and tongue
Endowed, should mark things out with voices

Differing according to their different feelings?
Dumb cattle and wild beasts of every kind
Make noises quite distinct and different   1060
When they are gripped by fear or pain, or joy
Wells up within them. And the evidence
For this lies in plain facts well known to all.
Angry Molossian hounds, when first they draw back
Their flabby jowls and bare their teeth and growl   1065
With rage suppressed, make sounds quite different
From when they bark and fill the place with din.
And when they lick their pups with loving tongue
And toss them with their paws and nibbling them
Pretend to make sweet tender mouthfuls of them,
Far different then the playful yelps they make   1070
From when they howl abandoned in the house
Or whimper cringing from the master's whip.
In neighing too, there is a difference
When a young stallion in the prime of life
Pricked by the spurs of winged love runs wild   1075
Among the mares, and from his flaring nostrils
Snorts out his challenge to arms, and when he's weak
At other times and neighs with quaking limbs.
Lastly, among the different types of birds,
Ospreys, sea hawks, and gulls amid the waves
Seeking their life and living from the sea,   1080
At other times make very different cries
From when they are fishing and struggling with their prey.
And some birds change their voices with the weather,
As ancient ravens do and flocks of rooks,
Or so they say, when they cry out for rain
To bring them water, or summon wind and storm.   1085
Therefore if animals are caused by different feelings,
Dumb though they be, to utter different sounds,
So much the more and with compelling reason
Must we suppose that men could in those days
Mark different things by different sounds of speech.   1090

    Now here's an answer to another question.
Fire was first brought to earth for mortal men
By lightning. From this every flame has spread.
For fire from on high fills many things, and makes them   1095

Blaze, when a stroke from heaven has kindled them.
But also when a branching tree struck by the wind
Swaying and surging leans against another,
Fire is pressed out by the strong force of friction
Until sometimes the gleam of flame springs forth
1100　As bough rubs bough and trunk rubs trunk together.
Fire may have come to men from either cause.
Then, to cook food and soften it by heat
It was the sun that taught them, since they saw,
Roaming the fields, how many things were softened
By its strong rays and vanquished by the heat.

1105　　　And as the days passed, more and more they learnt
To change their former life and way of living
By new inventions and by fire, well taught
By those pre-eminent in heart and mind.
Kings founded cities and built citadels,
Safeguard and refuge of their royal power.
1110　Cattle and lands they divided, giving to each
According to his talent and strength and beauty.
For beauty then was prized and strength had power.
Next property was established and gold was found,
And all the honour given to strength and beauty
1115　Was quickly lost, for 'tis the general rule,
Where riches call, the strong and handsome follow.
But if a man should guide his life by wisdom,
His greatest riches are a frugal life
And quiet mind. In that little there's no poverty.
1120　But men instead sought after fame and power
To make a firm foundation for their fortune
And live in wealth a life of quiet content—
In vain. Since as they strove to reach the heights
They made a lonely path beset with danger,
1125　And from the summit like a thunderbolt,
Envy struck them down to a Hell of shame.
For envy as a rule like thunderbolts
Is wont to strike the summits, scorching all
That stand above the common range of things.
Far better therefore is it in obedience
1130　To live a life of quiet than lust for kingdom
And fell desire to hold the world subdued.

So let them sweat blood, wearied by fruitless toil,
Struggling along ambition's narrow path.
Since all their wisdom comes from others' lips
And they strive for things relying on what they hear
From others, and ignore the evidence
Of their own senses, it profits no more now,
Nor ever will do, than it did before.   1135

Therefore the kings were killed, and in the dust
The ancient majesty of thrones and sceptres proud
Lay overthrown. The sovereign head's great crown
Bloodstained beneath the rabble's trampling feet,
All honour lost, bewailed its high estate.
For men do eagerly tread underfoot
What they have feared too much in former time.   1140
So things fell back to utter dregs and turmoil
As every man sought power for himself.
Then some men taught them to appoint magistrates
With rights established and the rule of law;
For mankind worn by a life of violence   1145
And weakened by its feuds, was ready now
To yield to rules of law and binding statutes.
For men in anger would avenge themselves
More savagely than just laws now would suffer;
And for this reason a life of violence
Was viewed with utter weariness and loathing.   1150

Hence comes the fear of punishment that stains
The prizes of life. For violence and wrong
Enmesh a man and oft recoil upon him;
Nor easily with calm and quiet mind
Can he abide who violates the bonds
Of peace established for the common good.   1155
Though he should keep it hid from gods and men,
Yet he must wonder how his sin can stay
Secret for ever, seeing that many men
Talking in dreams or raving in disease
Are said to have betrayed themselves, and brought
Long-hidden crimes into the light of day.   1160

Let us now think why reverence for gods
Has spread through mighty nations and filled cities

With altars, and established solemn rites,
Rites that now flourish in great states and places;
Whence even now implanted in men's hearts
1165 Comes that dread awe which over all the world
Raises new temples to the gods, and summons
The crowds that throng them on great festal days.
These matters are quite easy to explain.
The truth is then that in those early days
Men in their waking hours and still more in sleep
1170 Had visions of gods, conspicuous in beauty,
Of form surpassing and of wondrous stature.
These they endowed with senses, since they seemed
To move their limbs, and speak proud words, befitting
Their splendid beauty and their mighty strength;
1175 And they gave them eternal life, because always
The figures were renewed with form unchanged,
And they thought indeed that figures of such strength
Could hardly be by any force subdued.
Therefore they thought them past all measure blest
1180 Since none was troubled by the fear of death,
And because also in their dreams they saw
These wondrous beings do many miracles
All without labour wrought or weariness.
And men observed the order of the heavens
And seasons of the year on their fixed course
1185 Turning, and could not tell the reason why.
Therefore for refuge everything they gave
To gods, their nod controlling everything.
And in the sky they placed the gods' abodes
Since night and moon are seen to cross the sky,
1190 Moon, day, and night, and the stern signs of night,
Night-wandering torches of heaven, flying flames,
Clouds, sun, rain, snow, winds, lightnings, hail,
And thunderclaps and mighty murmurings.

Ah, wretched race of men, that to the gods
1195 Ascribe such things, and add fierce bursts of wrath!
What groans they made for themselves, what wounds for us,
What tears for generations still to come!
It is no piety to show oneself

Bowing with veiled head towards a stone,
Nor to be seen frequenting every altar,
Nor to fall prostrate on the ground, with palms outspread   1200
Before the shrines of gods, nor deluge altars
With streams of blood from beasts, vow piled on vow.
True piety is for a man to have the power
To contemplate the world with quiet mind.

When we look upward to the heavenly realms
Of the great firmament, and see the sky
Bedecked with sparkling stars, and when we think   1205
Of the sure courses of the sun and moon,
Then in our hearts already worn with woes
A new anxiety lifts up its head,
Whether some power beyond all reckoning
Hangs over us perchance, of gods, that make
The bright stars in their varied courses move.   1210
The doubting mind is racked by ignorance
Whether the world had a beginning, whether
Some final end is set for it, when all
The mighty bastions of the world no longer
Can bear the forces of its restless motion,
Or whether by power divine forever sure   1215
They glide eternal through the course of ages
And scorn the power of time immeasurable.

And what man does not quail with fear of gods,
With shrinking mind and flesh creeping with terror,
When the parched earth struck by a thunderbolt   1220
Trembles, and thunder rolls across the sky.
Nations and people tremble and proud kings
Shiver, limbs shaken by the fear of gods,
Lest for some foul deed or contemptuous word
The solemn hour of punishment be near.   1225
And when at sea a mighty wind and storm
Sweeps o'er the waters some high admiral
With all his legions and his elephants,
What vows he makes to gods to send him peace,
What prayers for gentle winds and favouring breezes!   1230
In vain, since oft the violent hurricane
Drives him no less upon the reefs of death.

So true it is that by some hidden power
Human affairs are ground to dust, a power
That seems to trample on the splendid rods
1235 And cruel axes, and hold them in derision.
Then, when the whole world reels beneath their feet,
And cities shaken fall or threaten ruin,
What wonder if mortal men despise themselves
And all the great and wondrous powers relinquish
1240 To gods, as governors of all the world?

I now discuss how metals first were found.
Copper and iron and gold and heavy silver
And serviceable lead, these were discovered
When fire upon high mountains had consumed
Vast forests, or a bolt from heaven had struck,
1245 Or because tribesmen in some forest war
Had fired the woods to scare their enemies,
Or because seeing the bounty of the soil
They wished to clear fat fields for pasturage,
Or else they wished to kill the forest beasts
And profit by their spoils, for pits and fire
1250 Were found of use for hunting before they learnt
To fence a wood with nets and drive with dogs.
Whatever the reason was that flaming heat
With hideous roar burnt all the forest down
Deep to its roots and baked the earth with fire,
1255 Through melted veins into hollows in the earth
Would trickle a stream of silver and of gold
And copper and lead, collecting; and when they saw
These hardened and glowing with colour on the earth
They would pick them up, charmed by their bright smooth beauty,
1260 And see that each was formed into a shape
Printed like that of the hollow in the earth.
Then the thought came to them that these things melted
By heat could run into any shape or form,
And into sharpest point or thinnest edge
1265 Be drawn by hammering, and so make tools
To cut down woods and rough-hew timber, and plane
Smooth planks, and bore and pierce and perforate.
And they tried to make these things of gold and silver

At first, no less than of bronze so tough and strong— 1270
In vain, since all their strength gave way defeated,
Unable to bear so well the heavy labour.
Then bronze was valued higher and gold sank low,
Thought useless since its edge was quickly blunted.
Now bronze lies low in the esteem of men,
And gold has mounted to the highest honour. 1275
So with the rolling years times change for things.
What once was valued has no honour now.
Next follows something else, no longer scorned,
Which day by day more keenly sought once found
Is crowned with praise and honoured beyond belief. 1280

   Now it is easy for you, Memmius,
To understand by yourself the way in which
The properties of iron were discovered.
The ancient weapons were hands and nails and teeth
And stones and branches torn from trees
And flame and fire, as soon as they were known. 1285
Later the power of iron and bronze was found.
The use of bronze was known before that of iron,
Being worked more easily and more plentiful.
With bronze they tilled the soil, with bronze they roused
The waves of war, and sowed the withering seeds 1290
Of wounds, and made a spoil of flocks and fields.
For all things naked and unarmed must yield,
An easy prey, to men equipped with arms.
Then gradually the sword of iron came forth
And, the bronze sickle's curving blade despised,
With iron they began to cleave the earth. 1295
And in the dark uncertain fates of war
Things were made equal on the battlefield.

   To mount a horse in arms, controlling it
With reins and bit, the right hand freed for action,
Came earlier than in a two-horsed chariot
To chance the hazards of war; and the two-horsed car
Came earlier than harnessing two pairs, 1300
And before armed men mounted scythed chariots.
Next elephants with turrets on their backs,
Snake-handed hideous beasts, the men of Carthage

Taught to endure the dreadful wounds of war
And all the mighty hosts of Mars embroil.
1305 Thus Discord bred one foul thing after another
To bring new terror to the battlefield
And day by day increased the horrors of war.

Bulls too were pressed into the service of war,
And they tried to send boars against the enemy,
1310 And sometimes they sent lions in front of them
With trainers armed and cruel keepers, skilled
To master them and hold them on the leash—
In vain, since heated by the general slaughter
Raging uncontrolled they threw the squadrons into turmoil
1315 Tossing their dread manes everywhere. The riders
Quite lacked the power to calm the terrified horses
And rear them round against the enemy.
The lionesses hurled their frenzied bodies
In all directions, leaping at men's throats,
1320 Or snatching unsuspecting victims from behind,
Dragging them mortally wounded to the ground
Held fast by their strong teeth and curving claws.
Bulls tossed their masters and trod them underfoot
And gored the flanks and bellies of the horses,
1325 Striking upwards with their horns, and in their fury
Tore up the earth. And boars with their strong tusks
Savaged their allies, and bathing in their own blood
The weapons broken in their reeking bodies
To horse and foot alike dealt out destruction.
Horses would shy and swerve to avoid the tusks'
1330 Fierce onset, or rear up and paw the air—
In vain, since they were hamstrung and collapsed
And fell, and spread their bodies on the ground.
Even the animals that seemed tame at home
1335 They saw boil over in the heat of action—
Wounds, shouting, flight and terror and tumult—
And none of them would answer the recall.
For all the different wild beasts fled away,
As elephants often at the present time
Will run amok when wounded by the steel,
1340 After they have turned their fury on their keepers.

If in fact they did do this. For I
Can scarce believe that in their minds no vision
Or apprehension came that this would happen
Before the foul and evil event occurred.
Indeed it would be wiser to maintain
That this happened somewhere in the universe,
Somewhere among the many different worlds
Created in so many different ways,
Than to credit it to any particular globe.   1345
They did this not in hope of victory
But to dismay their enemies (and perish themselves),
Mistrustful of their numbers and lacking in arms.

The plaited garment came before woven cloth.   1350
And cloth comes after iron, since iron is needed
To make the loom: only iron can give the smoothness
Needed for treadles and spindles and shuttles and clattering leash-rods.
Nature ordained that this should be men's work
Before it was women's (for the male sex as a whole
Is much more skilled than women and more clever)
Until the farm-folk called it a disgrace.   1355
So men preferred to leave it to women's hands
And join themselves with others in hard toil
And by hard labour hardened limbs and hands.   1360

A model for sowing and for grafting plants
Nature herself the great creatress formed.
Berries and acorns fallen beneath the trees
Sent up in season due a swarm of shoots.
From this they learnt too to graft slips in branches   1365
And plant young tender saplings in the fields.
Next, different types of husbandry they tried
One after another in their cherished plots,
And saw wild fruits grow tame in the sweet soil
With loving care and gentle humouring.
And day by day they made the woods retreat   1370
Ever higher up the hills, surrendering
The place below to tilth, to make for them
Meadows and crops, pools, streams, and smiling vineyards
O'er hills and plains, and running in between
The grey-green olives marking out the land,

1375 O'er hills and valleys and across the plains;
As now we see the countryside laid out
In charming patterns, studded and adorned
With luscious orchards everywhere, and full
Of fertile woods and groves enclosing them.

To imitate the liquid notes of birds
1380 With mouth and lips came long before men learnt
To charm the ears by singing tuneful songs.
And zephyrs whistling through the hollow reeds
First taught the country-folk to blow through pipes.
Then gradually they learnt the sweet laments
1385 The flute pours out pressed by a player's fingers,
Through pathless woods and glades and forests sounding
And shepherds' lonely haunts beneath the sky.

1390 These melodies would soothe and cheer their hearts
When they had had their fill of food; for then
All things go well and please the minds of men.
So often, lying in company together
On the soft grass beside a flowing stream
Beneath a tall tree's shade, at little cost
1395 They found sweet rustic pleasure; most of all
When weather smiled and the season of the year
Painted the meadows and green lanes with flowers.
Then jests and talk and happy bursts of laughter
Were there, and the rustic muse was in her prime.
1400 And then in joyful sport their heads and shoulders
They crowned with garlands, of leaves and flowers woven,
And danced, all out of step, with clumsy limbs,
And stamped with clumsy feet on mother earth.
What mirth was there, what peals of happy laughter!
For these things then were new and wonderful
And flourished in the charm of novelty.
1405 And when at night they watched, bereft of sleep,
Their solace was to raise the tuneful voice
In song, with many a varied melody,
And run the curving lip along the reeds;
So watchmen now this old tradition keep,
1410 Learning to play in tune; and not one whit
Of greater pleasure do they get from it
Than those old earth-born woodland people got.

For what we have, unless we have seen before
Something more lovely, pleases most of all,
And seems the best; till afterwards some new
And better thing is found which spoils and mars
What was before, and blunts the taste for it.   1415
So acorns fell from favour. So the beds
Of piled up leaves and herbage were abandoned.
So wild beasts' skins for clothing were despised.
And yet this form of dress when first discovered
Was I think so much envied that the wearer   1420
Was murdered for it, and then the coat of skins
Was torn to pieces by men fighting for it
And stained with blood and lost, no use at all.
So skins in those days, gold and purple now,
Distract men's lives and weary them with war.
And blame for this I think lies in ourselves.   1425
For lacking skins the naked sons of earth
Were tortured by the cold; but we no harm
Can suffer from a lack of purple robes
With stars of gold emblazoned, so we have
Some commonplace attire to cover us.
Therefore always in vain and uselessly   1430
Men labour, and waste their days in empty cares,
Because they fail to see what bounds are set
To getting, and what limits to true pleasure.
And gradually this evil discontent
Has carried life quite out to sea, and from
The depths has roused the mighty tides of war.   1435

But sun and moon the watchmen of the world
Circling with light the vast rotating vault
Have taught men well that seasons of the year
Revolve, and that in all things is established
A pattern and order fixed which governs them.

Men lived already fenced in with strong towers,   1440
And a land split up and parcelled out,
And ships with flying sails bedecked the sea,
And they had friends and allies bound by treaties,
And poets began to celebrate in verse
The mighty deeds of old; but letters then

1445   Had been not long discovered. Therefore our age
        Cannot look back to see those early things
        Except where reason may point out the traces.

        Seafaring and farming, city walls, and laws
        And arms, roads, clothing, and all such other things,
1450   All the rewards, all the delights of life,
        Songs, pictures, statues curiously wrought,
        All these they learnt by practice gradually
        And by experiments of eager minds
        As step by step they made their forward way.
        So each thing in its turn by slow degrees
        Time doth bring forward to the lives of men,
1455   And reason lifts it to the light of day.
        For as one concept followed on another
        Men saw it form and brighten in their minds
1457   Till by their arts they scaled the highest peak.

BOOK SIX

Athens of glorious name in former days
First brought corn-bearing crops to suffering mortals,
Brought them new life, established laws for them,
And Athens first sweet solace gave to life
When she brought forth a man of genius   5
Who from his lips revealed the truth of things.
His glory, though he be dead, from ancient times
For his divine discoveries so far renowned,
Is even now exalted to the skies.

For when he saw that nearly all those things
Which need demands for living were enjoyed   10
By mortal men, their life established safe
So far as might be, and when he saw them flourish
With all that wealth and praise and honour bring,
And glorying in the fair fame of their sons,
And saw no less that deep in every home
Were aching hearts and torments of the mind
All hapless, self-inflicted without pause,   15
And sorrows breeding furious laments,
He understood then that the vessel itself
Produced the flaw, and by this flaw corrupted
All that came into it however lovely.
He saw that it must leak, being riddled with holes,   20
And so could not by any means be filled.
He saw that, as it were with a noisome flavour,
It tainted everything that entered it.
Therefore with words of truth he purged men's hearts
And set a limit to desire and fear.
He showed the nature of that highest good   25
For which all mankind strives, and showed the way,
The strait and narrow path which leads to it
If we go forward with unswerving steps.

30   He showed the evil in the lives of men
Flying far and wide, caused either by natural chance
Or else by force, as nature so ordained.
He showed the sally-ports within the walls
From which each different attack could best be met.
He proved that mankind mostly without cause
Stirred up sad waves of care within their breasts.
For we, like children frightened of the dark,
35   Are sometimes frightened in the light—of things
No more to be feared than fears that in the dark
Distress a child, thinking they may come true.
Therefore this terror and darkness of the mind
Not by the sun's rays, nor the bright shafts of day,
Must be dispersed, as is most necessary,
But by the face of nature and her laws.
40   So all the more I press on to complete
The woven fabric of my argument.

    I have shown that all the realms of the universe
Are mortal, and that the substance of the heavens
Had birth; and I have explained most of those things
45   That in the heavens occur and must occur.
Please listen now to what remains to tell.
Since I have dared to mount the Muses' glorious chariot,
I will now tell how storms of wind arise,
And then are calmed again, so that all things
Return to what they were, all fury spent;
50   And all those other things in earth and sky
Which men observe, and tremble, wondering,
Their hearts laid low through fear of gods, oppressed,
Crushed down to earth, because their ignorance
Of causes makes them yield to power divine
55   Kingdom and Empire over all that is.
For men who have been well taught about the gods
That they live free from care, may wonder still
60   By what design the world goes on, not least
Those things they see in heaven above their heads;
And then to the old religions back they turn,
And cleave to cruel masters whom they think,
Unhappy fools, to be all-powerful,
65   Not knowing what can be and what cannot,

Not knowing in a word how everything
Has finite power and deep-set boundary stone.
So all the more by blindness of the mind
They are driven astray, and wander in the dark.

  Unless you spew these notions from your mind
And banish far away from you all thoughts
Unworthy of the gods and alien to their peace,
These holy powers, objects of your insults,
Will often do you mischief. Not because   70
The majesty of the eternal gods
Can suffer injury, so that in wrath they seek
To wreak revenge. No. You yourself will picture
Those quiet beings in their untroubled peace
As tossed by violent waves of wrath, and be unable
To come before their shrines with quiet mind;   75
And those sweet images which to men's hearts
Are borne from holy bodies, messengers
Of form divine, these images no more
Will come to you, your heart at peace and tranquil.
What kind of life must follow is plain enough.

  That such a life by truest reasoning   80
May be banished far from us, though many words
I have uttered, much remains to tell, adorned
In polished verse. The order of the heavens
And visage of the sky must be my theme
And storm and lightning flash must be my song,
Both what they do and from what cause they spring;   85
Lest senselessly you tremble at the sky
Divided into parts and speculate
Which one the flying fire came from or to which other
It went, and in what way it penetrated
Through walls of buildings, and having worked its will
Inside, made its way out again and so away.
                                                           90

  Calliope, most skilful of the Muses,
Solace of men, delight of gods, do you
Now go before me as the last lap I run
And point the way to the white winning post
Marked out for me, that led by you renown
May greet me as I win the victor's crown.

                                                           95

First, thunder shakes the blue expanse of sky
Because clouds flying high across the ether
Are dashed together by conflicting winds.
For no sound comes from a clear sky, but where
100 The clouds in close formation are deployed
Often the mighty crash of thunder rolls.
Besides, the substance of the clouds can't be
As thick as that of stones or logs, nor yet
As thin as that of mist or flying smoke.
105 For either they must fall, by their dead weight
Dragged down, like stones, or like smoke they'ld be too thin
To contain freezing snow or showers of hail.
Above the levels of the world outspread
They make a noise like that of awnings stretched
110 Across the beams of some great theatre
That flap and crack under the riotous winds
And split and break and make the crackling sound
Of tearing paper (for that kind of sound
Also you can detect in thunderstorms).
Or as when clothing hanging on a line
Or sheets of paper whirling in the wind
115 Are slapped and beaten by the sudden gusts.
Sometimes it happens also that the clouds
Cannot meet front to front, but scrape each other
Along the sides, moving in opposite directions,
And then that dry sound comes which on the ears
Grates, long drawn out, until they make their exit
120 Out of close quarters and move free in the sky.
      Another way by which a thunderstorm
Has seemed to make the whole earth quake and tremble,
By which in sudden shock the mighty walls
Of the embracing firmament have seemed
To leap apart, is when a sudden gale
Of strong winds massed together has thrust its way
125 Into the clouds, and there enclosed in them
With whirling motion everywhere has scooped out
An ever-growing hollow, with a shell
Of cloud all round compacted more and more;
Then when the force and impulse of the wind
Has weakened it, the cloud is torn, and splits,

Exploding with a terrifying crash.
No wonder: since a small bladder full of air   130
Makes such a loud noise when it suddenly bursts.
   Another way that clouds produce a noise
Is when winds blow through them. We often see
Clouds branching out in many ways and tattered
Driven through the sky, just as, we may be sure,   135
When the strong blasts of the north-west wind
Blow through a wood, leaves rustle and branches crack.
Sometimes also a furious force of wind
Shears through a cloud head on and splits it up.
For what the blast can do there, we can tell
From our own experience, seeing that here on earth,
Where it is gentler, none the less tall trees   140
It overturns and tears up from the roots.
And there are waves among the clouds, which make
A kind of low roar as they break, as happens
Likewise in deep rivers and when the sea
Breaks with its rolling tide upon the shore.
   Thunder comes also when a flaming stroke   145
Of lightning falls from a cloud upon a cloud.
If the receiving cloud is full of water
It makes a great noise quenching it at once,
As red-hot iron taken from the furnace
Hisses when plunged into a tank of water.
And if a drier cloud receives the fire   150
It lights at once and burns with mighty roar,
As on the mountains crowned with laurel came
A flame that driven by a whirling wind
Burnt all the woodlands with its rushing fire.
No other thing than Phoebus' Delphic laurel
Burns with such fearful sound and crackling flame.   155
Lastly, the crack of ice and fall of hail
Oft makes a noise in the great clouds on high.
For the great mountains of the thunderclouds
Are broken, pressed together by the wind,
And crushed into a narrow space, and mixed with hail.

   Lightning occurs likewise when clouds colliding   160
Have struck out many seeds of fire, as stone

Strikes stone or iron; then also light leaps out
When stone is struck and scatters sparks of fire.

Our ears receive the sound of thunder later
165   Than our eyes see the lightning, for this reason;
Things always come more slowly to the ears
Than to the eyes; as this example shows:
If in the distance you observe a man
Felling a tall tree with twin-bladed axe
You see the stroke before the sound of it
170   Reaches your ears; so also we see lightning
Before we hear the thunder, which is produced
At the same time as the fire, and by the same cause,
Born of the same collision of the clouds.

Here is another way in which the clouds
Bathe all the landscape in a fleeting light
As the storm flashes with its quivering stroke.
175   When wind has entered a cloud and whirling round
Has made the cloud condense around the hollow,
As I explained before, it becomes hot
With its own motion, as you see everything
Grows burning hot with motion; leaden bullets
Melt as they spin in a long flight through the air.
180   So when the black cloud by the burning wind
Has been split up, the sudden violent pressure
Makes it shoot out the seeds of heat, and these
Produce the winking flashes of bright flame.
Then the sound follows, coming to the ears
More slowly than the light comes to our eyes.
185   This happens, you must understand, when clouds are thick
And are piled high, one cloud upon another,
By an amazing force. Don't be misled
Because observing from below we see
More easily their wide expanse spread out
Than the great mighty mass piled high above.
Take note then, when you see clouds like mountains
190   Carried before the winds across the sky,
Or when you see them on the mountain tops
Piled high, one on another, pressing down
And lying still, with all the winds at rest,

Then you will recognize their mighty mass,
And see great caverns fashioned in them   195
With beetling crags, and when a storm builds up
Winds fill them, and imprisoned in the clouds
They vent their indignation with a roar,
And growl like angry beasts shut up in cages;
This way and that they fill the clouds with din,
And circle round and round trying to escape;   200
They roll the seeds of fire out of the clouds
And mass them together, and in the hollow furnace
They spin a circling flame, until at last
They burst the cloud, and blaze into the sky.

And also there's another reason why
That rushing golden gleam of liquid fire   205
Darts down to earth. It is that the clouds themselves
Must contain very many seeds of fire.
For when they are entirely free of moisture
Mostly their colour is flaming and shining bright.
Indeed from the sun's light they must receive
Many such seeds, so with good cause they blush   210
And pour out fires. These therefore, when the wind
Has driven them together and compressed them,
Squeeze out and then eject the seeds of fire
Which make the colours of the lightning-flash.
Lightning occurs also when in the sky
The clouds are thinning out, for when the wind   215
Gently disperses them as they move on
And dissolves them, then the seeds that make the lightning
Must fall perforce; but then the lightning comes
Noiseless, and without the hideous crash and terror.

I now discuss the nature of thunderbolts.
This the strokes show, and branding marks of heat,   220
And the holes breathing noxious fumes of sulphur.
These are the marks of fire, not wind or rain.
Besides, they often set roofs alight, and flame
Gains quick dominion all inside the houses.
This fire, my friend, the thinnest of all fires,   225
Nature has made of atoms so small and swift
That nothing in the world can stand against it.

The thunderbolt passes through walls of buildings
As sounds and voices do, through stone, through bronze,
230 And in an instant melts both bronze and gold.
And wine inside a vessel suddenly
It makes evaporate, though the jar remains intact;
Doubtless because, as the heat reaches it,
It loosens the fabric of the earthenware
And makes it porous, then entering the jar
235 It quickly dissolves the atoms of wine and scatters them.
And this we see the sun can never do
In an age, however strong its flashing heat.
So much more mobile and more masterful
Is the strong power of the thunderbolt.

     And now, how they are made and have such power
240 That with a stroke they can split towers asunder,
Overturn houses, tear out beams and rafters,
Move monuments of men, struck down and shattered,
Rob human beings of life and slaughter cattle,
And all else of this kind, by what strange power
245 They work, I'll tell, and delay you no more with promises.
We must believe that thunderbolts are made
From thick clouds piled up high; they never strike
From a clear sky or thin layer of cloud.
The facts themselves make clear without a doubt
250 That at a time of thunderstorms clouds mass together
Everywhere through the air, so that we think
That all the darkness out of Acheron
Has filled the mighty caverns of the sky.
So dark, beneath the hideous night of cloud,
The face of fear hangs over us above,
255 When storm begins to forge the thunderbolts.
And very often too across the sea
A black cloud falls, like pitch poured from the sky,
Loaded with darkness from afar, and draws with it
A black storm big with thunderbolts and blasts
260 Filled to the brim itself with wind and fire,
So that on land also men shiver and seek shelter.
From this we must infer that thunderstorms
Stretch high above our heads. For so much blackness
Could never overwhelm the earth unless

A multitude of clouds piled high on clouds
Built up above us, blotting out the sun.   265
Nor could there fall that torrent of the rain
That makes the rivers flood and drowns the fields
If ether were not full of clouds piled high.
So everything is full of winds and fires
And thunderclaps and lightning everywhere.   270
For indeed I have shown above that hollow clouds
Must contain very many seeds of fire
And must receive many from the sun's hot rays.
Therefore, when the same wind that has driven them
Into one place together, has squeezed out
Many seeds of fires, and in so doing itself   275
Has intermingled with the fire, the whirlwind
Finds its way in, whirls round in the narrow space
And in the hot furnace sharpens the thunderbolt.
For the wind is kindled in two ways: by the heat   280
Of its own motion, and by contact with the fire.
Next when the wind has reached a mighty heat
And the strong impulse of the fire has entered,
The thunderbolt, now as it were ripe, cleaves through
The cloud by a sudden blow, and the heat, shot out,
Lights all the place beneath with flashing flames.
A deep roar follows, such that the vault of heaven   285
Seems to be sundered apart and falling on us.
A violent tremor now assails the earth
And murmurs roll about the sky; for then
Almost the whole storm quivers with the shock
And roars and crashes. Rain then, heavy and full,   290
Follows the shock, so that the whole ether
Seems to be turned to rain, and teeming down
Recalls again the universal Flood.
So much the bursting cloud and raging wind
Pour out when the sound flies from the flaming stroke.

   Sometimes also a powerful wind outside   295
Falls on a cloud pregnant with a ripe thunderbolt.
It bursts it, and at once that fiery whirlwind falls
Which we name thunderbolt in our native tongue.
And this can strike in various directions,
Depending on the impulse given to it.

300 Sometimes also a wind that has no fire
     Kindles nevertheless on its long flight through space;
     It loses on its course a number of bodies
     Too large to keep up with it through the air,
     And scrapes together from the air itself
     And carries with it other tiny bodies
305 That mixed with it make fire as it flies,
     In much the same way as a leaden bullet
     Often grows hot in flight, when throwing off
     The seeds of cold it catches fire in the air.

     Sometimes also a blow produces fire,
310 When a cold wind launched without fire has struck.
     Doubtless because when it has struck a violent blow
     Elements of heat can flow together
     Both from the wind itself and at the same time
     From the object receiving the blow, as fire flies out
315 When stone is struck with iron, and the fire comes
     No whit the less because the iron is cold.
     So also a thing must take fire from a thunderbolt
     If it be fit and suitable for flame.
     And no wind ever can be utterly
320 And absolutely cold, if from above
     So powerful a force has driven it.
     If it has not caught fire on its course,
     When it arrives it must be warm and mixed with heat.

     The speed and violent stroke of thunderbolts
     And the swift fall with which they cleave the sky
325 Have this as their cause: a force within the clouds,
     First everywhere aroused, accumulating
     Takes on a mighty energy of movement.
     Then when the cloud cannot hold the growing impetus
     The force explodes, and flies with wondrous speed
     Like missiles hurled from powerful catapults.

330 Moreover, it consists of elements
     Both small and smooth, so that it is not easy
     For anything to counter such a substance.
     For it flies in between and penetrates
     Through narrow passages, therefore few obstacles

Can check it or delay it as it comes;
And this is why it falls with flight so swift.

    Again, while all weights naturally possess
A downward momentum, when a blow is added   335
The speed is doubled, and the first impulse
Grows heavier, so that with greater speed and strength
It shatters whatever delays it on its course.
Again, the momentum of its lengthy flight
Must give it ever-growing speed, increasing   340
As it falls, and this augments its mighty power
And strengthens the blow. It causes all its atoms
To move straight forward to a single point
And throws them together as they flow into that path.
It may perhaps draw from the air itself   345
In the course of its flight certain particles
Which by their impact set its speed ablaze.

    It passes through things without harming them,
And leaves many things intact after its transit,
Because the fluid fire goes through the pores.
And many it transfixes, when its atoms   350
Strike upon other atoms that form a joint.
It readily dissolves bronze and in an instant
Melts gold, because the atoms of which it is made
Are small and smooth and therefore easily
Make their way in, and having got in, at once
Untie all knots and loosen every bond.   355

    In autumn thunder shakes the house of heaven,
Studded with shining stars, more often, and shakes the earth,
And also when springtime opens with its flowers.
For in the cold fires are few, and in the heat   360
The winds fail and clouds are not so thick.
So when the season stands between the two
Then all the various causes of thunderbolts
Combine and flow together in the sky.
For then the year's rough straits mix cold and heat
(And a cloud needs both to make a thunderbolt),   365
So discord comes and with a mighty tumult
And fire and wind the heavens rage and swell.
For the first time of heat is the last of cold,

That is the spring. So battle must be joined
370   With fray embroiled between things unalike.
And when the last heat mixed with early cold
Comes round, to which we give the name of autumn,
Here also bitter winter fights with summer.
Therefore these must be named the straits of the year,
375   And it's no wonder if these seasons produce
Thunderbolts in abundance, and a whirling storm
Forms in the sky, since war everywhere
Rocks it on two fronts, on the one side flames
And on the other wind and water mixed.

Thus the true nature of the thunderbolt
380   Can now be understood, and how it works;
Not by unrolling scrolls of Tuscan charms
To search in vain the hidden minds of gods
And ask them whence the flying fire has come
Or to what other quarter of the sky
It went, and in what way it penetrated
385   Through walls of buildings, and having worked its will
Inside, made its way out again, or ask what harm
The stroke of a thunderbolt from heaven can do.

If Jupiter and other gods, my friend,
Shake with appalling din the realms of heaven,
And shoot their fire where each one wants to aim,
390   Why do they not arrange that when a man
Is guilty of some abominable crime
He's struck, and from his breast transfixed breathes out
Hot flames, a bitter lesson to mankind?
Why is a man of conscience free from stain
Engulfed in flames, all innocent, suddenly
395   Seized by a fiery whirlwind from the sky?
Why do they waste their pains shooting at deserts?
Or are they merely practising their aim
And strengthening their muscles? Why do they allow
The Father's bolt to be blunted on the ground?
Why does he allow this himself, and not keep it
For his enemies? And why does Jupiter
400   Never when the sky is cloudless everywhere
Launch bolts upon the earth and sound his thunder?

Or does he wait until the clouds have formed
And then himself descend down into them
To aim his weapon from a shorter range?
What is his object when he strikes the sea?
Has he some grudge against the waves and all
The liquid mass of water and swimming plains?   405
And if he wants us to beware the stroke
Why is he loth to let us see it coming?
But if he wants to crush us unawares
Why does he thunder from the same direction
And put us on our guard? Why does he first
Summon the darkness, with its roars and growls?   410
And can you possibly believe he shoots
In many directions simultaneously?
Or would you dare to say this never happens,
Never many strikes at the same time?
In fact this often occurs, and it must be
That just as rain-showers fall in many places
So at one time fall many thunderbolts.   415

    Lastly, why does he wreck the holy shrines of gods
And his own glorious habitations
With hostile thunderbolt? Why does he smash
The noble images of gods, and dishonour
His own fine statues with a violent wound?   420
Why does he mostly strike high ground, why do we see
The signs of fire most often on the mountain tops?

    From what has been said, it is easy to understand
Those whirlwinds which the Greeks name from their nature
Presters, and how they come from above into the sea.   425
It sometimes happens that a kind of column
Is let down from the sky into the sea.
The waters boil round it, lashed by furious winds,
And any ships caught in this mighty tumult
Find themselves storm-tossed, in the greatest danger.   430
This happens when sometimes a powerful wind
Starts to break up a cloud, but cannot do it;
It then depresses it, and it becomes
Like a column let down from the sky into the sea,
Slowly, as though a fist thrust by an arm

435 Were pushing something down, and spreading it
Into the waves; then when the wind has burst it
It rushes out upon the sea, and makes
A wondrous boiling in the waves below.
For the whirlwind turns as it comes down, and brings
The cloud down with it, a soft and yielding body.
440 But as soon as it has thrust the teeming cloud
Down to the ocean's surface, then at once
The whirlwind plunges into the water and stirs up
The sea all round and makes it boil and roar.
Sometimes a whirlwind wraps itself in a cloud
Scraping together seeds of cloud from the air,
445 And behaves like a prester let down from the sky.
When this has reached the earth and broken up
It vomits out a monstrous violence
Of mighty whirling wind and rushing storm.
But since this occurs quite rarely, and on land
The view of it must often be blocked by mountains,
It is seen most frequently upon the sea
450 With its wide prospect and its open sky.

   Clouds form when in the expanse of sky above
Many flying atoms come together
All at once, and these are rougher, and so although
They tangle together lightly, that is enough
To hold them firmly fixed and joined together.
455 From these at first small clouds are formed; these then
Take hold of one another and band together,
Then join and grow, and the winds drive them on
Until in time a furious storm builds up.

   Now let us look at clouds on mountain tops.
The closer the crests are neighbours to the heavens,
460 The more from their exalted seats they smoke
With the thick darkness of the tawny cloud.
This is because when first the clouds are formed,
Before the eye can see them, so thin they are,
Winds drive and lift them to the mountain tops.
465 At length then, massed together and condensing,
They become visible, and appear to rise
From the mountains' very top into the ether.

For our own senses and the facts themselves
Make evident to us when we climb high mountains
That these lofty places are open to the winds.

And nature makes a constant stream of atoms
To rise up from the surface of the sea,   470
As is shown by clothes that hung out on the shore
Grow damp and sticky. This suggests that clouds
Also can grow by receiving many atoms
That rise up from the ocean's briny swell,
For these possess a similar kind of moisture.   475

Besides, from all rivers and from the earth itself
We see mists and vapours rise, which, drawn up from them
Like breath, move upwards and fill all the sky
With gloom, and gradually as they come together
Bring up supplies to the high clouds above.   480
For the heat also of the starry ether
Presses down on them from above, condensing them,
And weaves a curtain of cloud beneath the blue.

Lastly, those atoms which make clouds and storm-rack
Sometimes come into our sky from outside.
For I have proved that their number is innumerable,   485
And that the sum of space is infinite,
And I have shown the great velocity
With which the atoms fly, and how in an instant
They cover distances beyond all telling.
No wonder is it then if storm and darkness   490
Often so swiftly, with great thunderclouds
Poised overhanging, cover land and sea,
Since everywhere through the channels of the ether
And as it were through all the breathing-holes
Of the great world around, the atoms are free
To make their exits and their entrances.

Now let me demonstrate how rainy moisture   495
Condenses in clouds high above, and falls
In a shower of rain upon the earth beneath.
First you will concede that many atoms of water
Rise up together with the clouds themselves
From things of every kind, and in this way

500   Both grow together, the clouds and whatever water
      Is in the clouds, just as our bodies grow
      Concurrently with the blood and sweat and whatever
      Moisture there may in fact be in the limbs.
      Also the clouds often take up a quantity
      Of sea water, like hanging fleeces of wool,
505   When the winds drive them above the mighty ocean.
      In a similar way moisture rises to the clouds
      From every river. And when into the clouds
      Many atoms of water have in many ways
      Joined up together, increasing everywhere,
      The clouds stuffed full strive to discharge the moisture;
510   For two reasons: the wind compresses them,
      And the clouds themselves, collecting into a mass
      Larger than usual bear down and press
      Down from above and make the showers flow out.
      Besides, when clouds are thinned out by the wind
      And dissipated by the sun's heat from above,
515   They send out rainy moisture, and drip, as wax
      Over a hot fire melts and liquefies.

      A downpour comes when clouds are strongly pressed
      By both these forces: by their own mass piled up
      And by the strong power of the rushing winds.
520   Long and persistent rain occurs when atoms of water
      Are set in motion in great multitude
      And clouds on clouds are carried streaming down
      In universal rainfall everywhere
      And all the earth smokes and breathes back the moisture.
      And when the sun amidst the gloomy storm
      Shines with its rays upon the falling drops
525   From black clouds opposite, then there stand out
      Amid the clouds the colours of the rainbow.

      And all those other things that grow above
      And are created above and collect in the clouds,
      All, absolutely all of these, snow, wind,
      Hail, freezing front, and ice's mighty power,
530   Great hardener of waters, impediment
      That everywhere reins back the eager rivers—
      To find these out and picture in your mind

How they are all produced and why they are made
Is very easy, once you have fully grasped
The different natures of their elements.

Come now, and learn the causes of earthquakes. 535
First, you must get into your mind that the earth
Below us, as above, is everywhere
Full of windy caves; and many lakes and pools
She bears in her bosom, and rocks and beetling cliffs,
And many hidden rivers beneath earth's back 540
Roll their rough currents over sunken rocks.
For the facts themselves require that everywhere
Earth should be like herself, above and below.

With these things therefore joined to it below
And placed beneath it, earth trembles with the shock
Of vast collapse and ruin when age and time 545
Have undermined the mighty caves below.
Whole mountains fall, and from the mighty shock
Tremors spread abroad in an instant far and wide;
Quite naturally, since buildings by the roadside
Tremble with the shock of waggons passing by
Of no great weight, and jump when the iron-shod wheels 550
On either side jolt over stones or potholes.

And sometimes also when some enormous lump
Weakened by time rolls forward from the earth
Into some huge wide pool, the earth itself
Sways shaken by the wave of water, as a jar
Sometimes cannot stand still unless the water 555
Inside has stopped from moving to and fro.

Besides, when through the hollows below the earth
A wind collects, and thrusting in one direction
Bears down and drives into the lofty caverns,
The earth leans under the impact of the wind.
The houses that are built up on the earth, 560
And all the more the more they tower to heaven,
Lean dangerously, bulging and pushing forward
In the same direction, and the beams askew
Hang in the air projecting, ready to go.
And yet men fear to believe that the great world 565
Has waiting for it some disastrous hour

Of ruin and destruction, though they see
So great and mighty a mass of earth lean over!

And yet unless the winds abate, no power
Could curb the world's rush to ruin and hold it back.
570 But since in fact the winds alternately
Abate and gather strength, and as it were
Collect their forces and rally, and then retreat
Repulsed again, more often for this reason
Earth threatens to fall than it actually does fall.
For it leans forward and then again springs back,
And after falling forward it recovers
Its proper place and stands in balance again.
575 This is how all buildings totter, the top
More than the middle, the middle more than the base;
The base itself is hardly moved at all.

These mighty tremors have another cause.
When wind and some great sudden force of air
Either from outside or within the earth itself
580 Has hurled itself into earth's hollow places
And there, inside the mighty caverns, first it roars
Tumultuously and rushes whirling round,
Then with its violence intensified
And agitated, out it bursts, and cleaves
Earth to its depths and makes a mighty chasm.
585 This is what happened at Sidon in Syria
And Aegeum in the Peloponnese. Both cities
Were rocked and torn by such an issue of air,
And demolished by the earthquake that took place.
And many another city wall has fallen
By mighty movements of the earth, and many
Cities of men with all their citizens
590 Have sunk down to the bottom of the sea.

But if no burst occurs, yet the strong wind
And violent force of air is disturbed
Through all the many passages of the earth,
Like a shudder, and this creates the tremor,
Just as when cold comes deep into our limbs
595 It shakes them and makes them tremble against their will.
So in their cities men are disquieted

By twofold terror: they fear the houses above,
They dread the caverns beneath, lest suddenly
Earth fling them open, or splitting wide apart
With gaping jaws create a mighty chasm
And fill it with the ruins it has made. 600

Therefore let them believe, however they please,
That earth and sky are incorruptible
And stand destined to everlasting life,
Yet sometimes comes a very present danger
To stab them with the fear that suddenly
Earth may withdraw beneath their feet and fall 605
Into the abyss, and all the sum of things
Follow in total collapse, and then may come
The ruin and confusion of the world.

Some people wonder that nature does not cause
The sea to increase in size, since into it
Runs down so great a flow of water, and since the rivers
All flow into it from every part of the globe.
And add the wandering showers and flying storms 610
That spatter and water every land and sea;
Add too the sea's own springs; yet all of these
Compared to the sea's great mass will scarcely equal
The addition to it of a single drop.
This makes it then the less a matter for wonder
That the great sea does not grow greater still. 615

The sun's heat also draws a great part off.
For certainly we see clothes dripping with water
Dried by the strong rays of the burning sun.
But seas are many, and spread wide below;
Therefore, however small a part the sun 620
May sip from off the surface of the sea
In any single place, yet from that vast expanse
Abundant store of water is drawn off.

Also much water may be taken up
By winds that sweep the surface of the sea,
Since very often in a single night 625
We see the roads dry out and the soft mud
Form into hard crusts all along the way.
Besides, I have shown that clouds also lift off

A mass of moisture from the ocean's surface
Which on the whole world everywhere they sprinkle
630   When rains fall on the earth and wind drives the clouds.

Last, since the earth is of a porous texture,
And everywhere, joined closely to the sea,
Encompasses its shores on every side,
Then, just as water comes from land to sea,
So it must ooze from the salt sea into the earth.
635   The brine is filtered off, and the mass of water
Oozes back and joins the rivers at their source,
And thence in a column of sweet water
Over the ground it flows, along the path
Once cut by liquid foot to guide the waters.

And now the fires that from Mount Etna's throat
640   Breathe out at times in such a furious storm
I shall explain. No ordinary disaster
The flaming tempest wrought that reigned supreme
Over the fields of Sicily, and neighbouring nations
Looked on it with amaze, as all the heavens
Filled with black smoke and flashing flames of fire
645   They saw, and trembled, wondering in fear
What new things nature might be forging for the world.

These things, my friend, with vision wide and deep
Must be surveyed, and in every part descried.
You must remember that the sum of things
650   Is deep beyond all telling. You must see
How small a part, how infinitesimal,
Our world is of the total universe,
A part less large than just one single man
Is of the whole great earth on which he lives.
If you will keep this firmly in your mind,
And clearly comprehend and clearly see it,
There are many things at which you'll cease to wonder.

655   For is there anyone that feels surprise
If fever rising with its burning fire
Attacks the limbs, or if some other pain
Afflicts the body, caused by some disease?
The foot swells suddenly; sometimes a stab of pain
Shoots into the teeth or even into the eyes.

The fiery rash breaks out, creeping over the body,   660
And burns whatever part it seizes on,
Crawling relentlessly across the limbs.
All this is caused by the multitude of atoms;
For sure this earth and sky of ours contain
Sufficient store of noxious disease
To spawn a growth of ills immeasurable.
In this way we must think that heaven and earth   665
Are from the infinite supplied with all that's needed
For earth to move and quake in sudden shock
And the swift whirlwind scour the land and sea,
The fires of Etna flow, the sky to flame.
For this does happen, and the realms of heaven   670
Are set on fire; and a heavier fall
Of rain storms down, when by some chance the atoms
Of water have been massed and concentrated.

   'But surely this tumultuous conflagration
Is much too huge for such an origin.'
Well, any river may appear immense
To a man who has never seen a greater one;   675
So does a tree or a man; and everything,
When a man has seen no larger, he thinks vast.
But all these things, with earth and sea and sky
Added together, are as nothing compared
With the sum total of the universe.

   Now, none the less, I shall explain the ways   680
In which the flame excited suddenly
Blasts out from Etna's mighty furnaces.
First, the whole mountain is hollow underneath,
Supported mostly on caverns in the rock.
In all the caves there is both air and wind;
For air makes wind when strongly agitated.   685
Now when the wind has grown extremely hot,
And heated in fury all the rocks around
Wherever it touches, and also the earth,
And struck from them hot fires and rushing flames,
It rises, and straight through the mountain's throat
Hurls itself upward in a mighty blast.
Then far and wide the heat is spread, and wide   690

The fall of ashes; and in darkness thick
It rolls its smoke, and all the while throws out
Rocks of amazing weight. Beyond a doubt
This is the work of wind most turbulent.

Besides, for a space of many miles the sea
695 Breaks on the mountain's roots, sucks back its waves,
And from this sea caves spread out underneath
Right to the deep throat of the mountain, and through these
It cannot be doubted that wind mixed with water
Comes in from the open sea and penetrates it
Deeply within, thus causing an explosion
And upward blast of flame, throwing out rocks
700 And raising everywhere great clouds of sand.
For on the topmost summit there are craters,
The 'mixing bowls' as the Sicilians call them,
To which we give the name of throats or mouths.

There is also a number of things for which
It is not enough to state one cause; we must
Consider many, and one of them is right.
For example, if from a distance you should see
705 The lifeless body of some man, then all
The causes of death you might think well to mention,
So that the one true cause of it be named.
For though you could not prove that steel or cold
Had caused his death, or disease perhaps, or poison,
710 We know quite well that what has happened to him
Is something of this kind. And so we shall
In many cases argue in this way.

The Nile, the river of all Egypt, swells
And flows across the fields in summertime,
Unique among the rivers of the world.
It waters Egypt through midsummer heats,
715 Either because North winds oppose its mouth
In summer, which blowing at that time of year
Are called Etesian, or 'seasonal';
These blowing against the stream arrest its flow,
And piling up the water fill its banks
And hold up its advance; for there's no doubt
720 That these blasts coming from the Pole's cold star

Do blow against the current of the river.
For the great Nile comes from the land of heat,
The south, where deep among the race of men
Burnt black by sun it rises from the noonday.

    It may be also that a great sandbar
Is heaped against the river's mouths, confronting the flow   725
When the sea driven strongly by the winds
Rolls the sand shorewards. In this way the river
Has less freedom of exit, and the current
Has a less easy downflow to the sea.

    Or it may be perhaps that heavier rains
Fall on its source at the season of the year
When the Etesian breezes of the north
Drive all the clouds into those parts together.   730
You may be sure that when they have massed together
Driven out towards the region of the noonday
There they at length beating against high mountains
Are crushed and with great violence compressed.

    Or deep within the Ethiopian highlands   735
Perhaps the river grows, when the hot sun
Traversing all things with his burning rays
Makes the white snows run down into the plains.

    I shall now explain the nature of the lakes
And other places that are called Avernian.
Firstly, the name Avernian is given
Because no birds can live within these places.   740
For any birds that fly directly above them,
Their wings' oars all forgotten and the sails
Let loose, and neck all limp and lifeless,
Down they fall headlong to the ground,
If it so happens that earth lies below,   745
Or into the water, if perchance a lake
Of Avernus lies outspread. There is near Cumae
A place like this, where the hills filled with sulphur
Give off a pungent smoke fed by hot springs.

    There is another within the walls of Athens
Right at the summit of the citadel
Hard by the temple of Tritonian Pallas,
Where the crows never wing their raucous way,   750

Not even when altars smoke with offerings;
Such care they take to flee, not from the anger
Of Pallas, as the Greek poets have sung,
Because of that fateful vigil; but the nature
755 Of the place itself produces this effect.

In Syria also there's another place
Like this, they say, where as soon as quadrupeds
Have set foot on it, its natural potency
Makes them to fall down flat, as if suddenly
Slaughtered in sacrifice to the gods below.

760 But all these things have a natural origin
And the causes that produce them are quite clear.
Do not believe that in these regions lie
The gates of Hell, and that the gods below
Down to the shores of Acheron draw thence
765 The souls of men, as the light-footed stags
By the breath of their nostrils are often thought to draw
The tribes of creeping creatures from their holes.
How far removed all that is from the truth
Learn now; for of the true facts I try to speak.

Firstly I say, as I have often said before,
770 That in the earth are atoms of every kind.
Many that are in food bring life; and many
Can strike us with disease and hasten death.
And I have shown before that substances
Vary in their power to support life
In different animals, because of their different natures
775 And different textures and atomic shapes.
For many noxious elements make their way
Through the ears, and many through the nostrils
Slip in that are injurious and prickly,
And not a few touch tells us to avoid
780 And sight to shun, or taste proclaims them bitter.

Next it is plain to see how many things
Are violently hostile to the senses,
Noisome and dangerous. First certain trees
Have shade so dangerous that it brings headache
785 If you should lie outstretched on the grass beneath.
And on the great high hills of Helicon

There grows a tree whose flower can kill a man
By the vile nature of its loathsome scent.
And all these things, for sure, rise from the soil
Since many seeds of many things Earth holds
Mixed up in many ways, then separates and delivers them.   790
A lamp at night is extinguished, and its wick
Sends out a pungent smell. If this assails
The nostrils of some epileptic, prone
To fits and foaming, at once it stupefies him.
The heavy scent of beaver musk brings sleep
To a woman; she falls back, the dainty work   795
Drops from her tender hands, if she has smelt it
During the period of her monthly courses.
And many other things there are that melt
And loosen languid limbs throughout the body,
And shake the spirit in its seat within.
Again, if you stay too long in a hot bath   800
After a heavy meal, how easily
You collapse on the seat amidst the steaming water!
How easily the heavy fumes of charcoal
Pass into the brain, unless we have taken water before!
When burning fever has possessed the limbs,   805
The scent of wine is like a deadly blow.
You can see that earth itself produces sulphur
And lumps of asphalt, with its filthy smell.
And when men follow veins of gold and silver
Searching with picks the secrets of the earth,
What smells Scaptensula breathes out from under!   810
What evil noxious fumes come up from gold mines!
What do they make men look like, and what colours!
Have you not seen or heard how speedily
Men die and how their vital forces fail
Whom the strong power of necessity
Forces to labour at such work as this?
And so we see earth throws out all these vapours   815
And breathes them into the open and ready sky.

   In this way also must Avernian places
Send up to birds a deadly effluence
Which rises from the earth into the air
And poisons some part of the space of heaven;   820

At once then, when a bird has winged its way there,
The unseen poison seizes it and checks it,
And it falls straight down to the place that sends up vapours.
And when it has fallen, the power of this same vapour
825 Takes from its body what remains of life.
The vapour seems in fact to produce at first
Some form of giddiness, then later when they have fallen
Into the very fountain of the poison
They must needs spew out life itself, enveloped
All round about them by a mass of evil.

830   Sometimes also this vapour of Avernus
Dispels the air between the birds and earth
So that an almost empty space is left there.
And when the birds come flying into this
At once the thrust of pinions all is lamed
And voided, and the effort of their wings
835 On either side undone. When they can find
Nothing for wings to press on or support them
Nature for sure compels them by their weight
To drop, and through the almost empty space
Lying, their souls breathe out through all the body's pores.

840   Water in wells grows colder in the summer
Because the earth is rarefied by heat
And sends out into the air such seeds of heat
As it itself contains. The more therefore
The earth is drained of heat, the colder grows
The water which lies hidden in the earth.
845 And when in turn earth pressed by cold congeals
And grows together as it were, then by congealing
It presses out of course into the walls
Such heat as it may have within itself.

   Near to the shrine of Ammon there's a spring
That's cold by day and hot at night, they say.
850 Men wonder at this spring too much. Some think
It boils because the sun goes underground,
When night has shrouded earth in dreadful dark,
But this is very far removed from truth.
Though the sun beat on water's naked body,
855 It cannot even heat the surface of it,

Hot though its blazing light above may burn;
How then from under so much solid earth
Could it boil water, fill it with its heat?
Why, even through a house's shuttered walls
It scarce can pass, for all its burning rays.   860

What is the reason then? No doubt because
The ground around the spring remains more porous
Than the rest of the earth, and there are many seeds
Of fire adjacent to the body of water;
And when night's dewy shades have covered the earth,
At once the soil grows cold all through and contracts;   865
And in this way, as if squeezed in the hand,
It presses out whatever seeds of fire
It may possess into the spring, and these
Make the water warm to the touch and steaming.
Next when the risen sun has loosened the earth
And made it porous as the heat penetrates it,   870
Back to their ancient seats the seeds of fire
Return, and all the warmth that's in the water
Goes back into the earth; and for this reason
The spring is cold during the light of day.
Besides, the sun's rays work upon the water,
And when the light comes with the quivering heat   875
They make it porous, therefore it throws off
The seeds of fire inside it, as often water
Throws off the frost contained within itself
And melts the ice and loosens all its knots.

There is also a cold spring over which
If tow be placed it often throws out flame   880
And catches fire at once. Likewise a torch
Is kindled and shines out amidst its waters
Wherever as it floats the breezes blow it.
No doubt because there are present in the water
A great many atoms of heat, and from deep down
In the earth itself bodies of fire must rise   885
All through the spring, and breathing out abroad
Come up into the air; though not so many
As to heat the water of the spring itself.
Besides, dispersed as they are, some force impels them

To burst out suddenly through the water, and then
Unite and gather together on the surface.

890 We may compare the spring at Aradus
Which wells up with sweet water through the sea
And cleaves a passage through the briny waves.
In many other regions does the sea
Give thirsty mariners a timely service,
Gushing sweet waters out amid the salt.

895 In this way therefore through that other spring
The seeds of fire break out and swarm abroad.
And when they come together on the tow
Or cling fast to the body of the torch,
At once they ignite, since tow and floating torch
Also contain many seeds of hidden fire.

900 And if you bring a newly extinguished wick
To a lamp that burns at night, have you not seen
It catches fire before it touches the flame,
And that the same thing happens with a torch?
And many other things blaze up at a distance
By mere contact with heat, before the fire
Comes close and swallows them. So this we must

905 Believe to happen also in this spring.

  Now I propose to discuss what law of nature
Makes iron to be attracted by that stone
Which the Greeks call magnet, naming it from its home,
Since it is found within the Magnetes' land.

910 Men find this stone amazing, since it can make
A chain of little rings that hang from it.
Five you may see sometimes or more hanging down
In succession, swayed by a gentle breeze,
Where one hangs from another, clinging beneath,

915 And each from each learns the stone's binding power;
So deep the penetrating force prevails.

  In matters of this kind you cannot grasp
The real explanation unless first
Much is established; the approach must be
Extremely lengthy, winding, roundabout.

920 So all the more I crave attentive ears and mind.

  In the first place, from all things that we see

A constant stream of particles must flow
And be discharged and scattered through the air
That strike upon the eyes and provoke vision.
Odours flow constantly from certain things,
As cold from rivers, heat from the sun, and spray
From waves that eat away the strong sea walls.　925
And always different sounds fly through the air.
And a damp taste of salt enters our mouths
When we walk by the sea; and when we watch wormwood
Being mixed with water we sense its bitterness.　930
So does from all things always something flow
And everywhere into all parts spreads abroad.
And no delay nor rest is given this flow
Since we constantly feel it, and all things always
We can see and smell and hear the sound of them.　935

　I now repeat, what my first book made quite clear,
That the structure of all objects is most porous.
To understand this fact is relevant
To many studies, but in none more than this
On which I now embark, it is most necessary　940
To establish that all objects which we see
Consist of nothing but atoms mixed with void.
In the first place, in caves the rocky roofs
Sweat moisture out and drip with oozing drops.
Sweat likewise oozes out from all our body,
The beard grows, and hair on every limb and member.　945
Food is diffused all through the veins, increasing
And nourishing the body's furthest parts
Even to the nails. Cold also and warming heat
We feel to pass through bronze, we feel them pass
Through gold and silver, when we hold full cups.　950
And through the stone dividing walls of houses
Voices fly and smells, and cold, and the heat
Of fire that even iron penetrates.
Again, where the great corselet of the heavens
Embraces us, the seeds of clouds fly in,
And of disease that comes in from outside.　955
And storms arising from the earth and sky
Fall duly back into the sky and earth,
Since nothing exists without a porous texture.

We add to this that not all particles
Thrown off from objects have the same effect
960 Upon the senses, and not all are suited
In the same way to influence other things.
First, the sun bakes the earth and makes it dry;
But ice it melts, and snow upon high mountains
Lying deep piled is thawed by its strong rays.
965 And wax placed in its heat is liquefied.
Fire likewise makes bronze melt, turns gold to liquid,
But skins and flesh it shrivels and contracts.
Water hardens iron taken from the fire
But skins and flesh it softens when hardened by heat.
970 The bearded goats find the wild olive sweet
As if it were truly ambrosia and steeped in nectar,
Yet no leaf grows to human taste more bitter.
Pigs detest oil of marjoram and fear
All kinds of ointments, for to the bristly pig
975 What seems to us refreshing is rank poison.
But on the other hand, what is to us
Most loathsome filth, why, pigs delight in it
And love to roll their bodies in the mud.

This still remains, which it seems should be said
980 Before I approach the subject of my theme.
Since various different things have many pores
They must then be endowed with different natures
Each having its nature and its passages.
For instance, living beings have different senses
985 And each perceives the object proper to it;
By one sense sound comes in, and by another
Taste comes from flavour, and to another comes
The smell of odours wafting on the air.
Besides, one thing is seen to seep through stone,
Another through wood, another to pass through gold,
Another makes its way through glass or silver.
For images pass through glass and heat through silver,
And one thing passes through more quickly than another.
It is the nature of the passageways
995 That makes this happen, varying as it does
In many ways, as I have just explained,
For each thing has a different nature and texture.

And now, when all these things have been established,
And well laid down, prepared and ready for us,
It is easy to move on and state the reason   1000
And make plain the cause why iron is attracted.

Firstly, there must needs flow out from this stone
A multitude of atoms, like a stream,
That strikes and cleaves asunder all the air
That lies beneath the iron and the stone.
Now when this space is emptied, and a large   1005
Tract in the middle is left void, at once
The atoms of the iron gliding forward
Fall in a mass into the vacuum.
So the ring follows, its whole form moving forward.
And nothing has its primal elements
More closely intertwined and woven together,   1010
More strongly knit, than iron strong and cold.
No wonder then if all those atoms of iron
Flowing into the void must cause the ring to follow.
And this it does, and follows, until it comes   1015
Right to the stone and clings with hidden ties.
The same thing happens in all directions. Wherever
An empty space is made, the adjacent atoms
Whether they are at the sides or are above
At once are driven into the vacuum.
For they are struck by blows from other quarters   1020
And cannot rise into the air of their own accord.

Moreover, to facilitate the process,
Another thing occurs to aid the movement:
As soon as the air in front of the ring grows thinner,
And the space between becomes more void and empty,   1025
At once then all the air at the back of the ring
Pushes and drives it forward from behind.
For the surrounding air continually
Beats on things, but in this case the iron
Is driven forward because in one direction
There is a vacuum ready to receive it.   1030
This air of which I speak creeps subtly in
Through all the many pores within the iron
And reaching to its tiny particles

Propels it on, as wind drives sails and ship.
Moreover, every object must contain air
1035   Within its body since the structure is porous,
And air encompasses and bounds them all.
Therefore the air which deep within the iron
Lies hid, surges continually, and thus
Beats on the ring and drives it from within.
1040   For certainly the ring is carried forward
On the course on which it has once launched itself
By its first plunge into the vacuum.

It also happens at times that iron moves
Away from this stone, having the tendency
To flee and then pursue again in turns.
I have even seen Samothracian irons jump,
1045   And iron filings in a copper bowl
Go mad with this magnet stone placed underneath,
So frantic seem they to escape the stone.
That so much discord is created by the copper
Set in between is doubtless for this reason:
The stream of atoms flowing from the copper
1050   Comes first, and occupies the open paths
And passageways that lie inside the iron;
Later the stream comes from the stone and finds
The iron already quite filled up, and thus
No way to swim through as it did before.
It is compelled therefore to beat and push
The texture of the iron with its waves.
So it repels the iron from itself,
And working through the copper drives away
1055   What otherwise it normally attracts.

In this connection do not be surprised
That the stream from this stone has not the power
To influence other things as well as iron.
Some things stand firm by reason of their weight;
Gold is like this, but others being of substance
So porous that the stream flies through intact
1060   Cannot be set in motion anywhere.
Wood is a good example of this kind.
Between the two there lies the nature of iron;

When certain atoms of copper have entered it
The magnet stones repel it with their flow.

   These properties are not so different   1065
From others that I could not readily
Produce a number of examples showing
Things which possess unique affinities.
First, only mortar can hold stone together.
Bulls' glue joins wood so fast that frequently
The grain of planks gapes with a natural fault   1070
Before the bonds of glue can loose their grip.
The juices of the vine will mix with water
When heavy pitch and light olive oil refuse.
The dye of the sea-purple from the shell
Combined with wool can never be parted from it,   1075
Not though with Neptune's mighty flood you labour
To make it new, not though the whole wide sea
Should wish with all its waves to wash it out.
And gold to gold one thing alone can bond,
And bronze to bronze only by tin is joined.
How many things like this are to be found!   1080
But to what purpose? Ways so roundabout
You do not need, nor ways so long; nor I
Ought to spend so much labour on this point,
But briefly in few words sum up my theme:
When things have mutually opposing textures
So that the hollows in the one conform
To the projections of the other, and   1085
The converse too holds good, then union is most perfect.
And some things also may be held in union
Linked as it were by hooks and rings; and this
It rather seems is what occurs between iron and magnet.

   Now I'll explain the nature of diseases,   1090
And the source from which the power of pestilence
With sudden onset blasts a storm of death
Upon the race of men, and flocks and herds.
First, I have shown above that there are atoms
Of many things needful to support our life,
And, in contrast, many must fly around   1095
That bring disease and death. When these some chance

Has massed together, and the atmosphere
Has been disordered by them, the air becomes diseased.
And all this power of pestilence and plague
Either comes in from without, down from above,
1100 Like clouds and mists, or often forms and springs
From the earth itself, when damp has made it rot,
Struck by unseasonable rains and sun.
You can see also that unaccustomed climates
And waters make their mark on travellers
1105 Far from home and country, because things are so different.
How different the climate of the Britons
Must be from Egypt, where the world's great pole
Leans sideways; and how different from Pontus
The clime must be of Cadiz, and right on
To lands where black men live, burnt black by sun!
1110 And as we see four separate climes distinguished
By the four winds and quarters of the heavens,
So do the colours and the looks of men
Differ most widely, and diseases fall
After their kind upon the varying nations.
There is the elephant disease which by the Nile
1115 Is bred, in middle-Egypt and nowhere else.
In Attica the feet are attacked, and in Achaea
The eyes. To other members other places
Are hostile, due to the variations of the air.
So when an atmosphere that's alien to us
1120 Comes on, and baleful air begins to creep,
Like mist and cloud it spreads, wherever it goes
Carrying disorder and compelling change.
And when it reaches our region of the sky
It corrupts it, making it like itself, and hostile.
1125 So therefore this new plague and pestilence
Without warning either falls upon the waters
Or else remains suspended in the air,
And when the breath of air is mixed with it
We must likewise absorb it in our body.
1130 In similar manner the plague often comes
To cattle, and a murrain to bleating sheep.
Nor does it matter whether we travel abroad
To unhealthy places, changing the cloak of sky

That covers us, or whether Nature herself
Brings an infected atmosphere to us,   1135
Or something else to which we are unaccustomed,
Which by its newness has the power to attack.

    In days of old such manner of disease
And tide of death fell on the realms of Cecrops,
Laid waste the fields, turned highways into deserts,
And drained the city of its citizens.   1140
Deep in the land of Egypt was its source,
And traversing a wide expanse of air
And swimming plains, it came at length to fall
And lie on all the people of Pandion.
And then in companies and in battalions
They made surrender to disease and death.
First were their heads inflamed with burning heat   1145
And the two eyes all glowing red and bloodshot.
Then throats turned black inside sweated with blood,
And swelling ulcers blocked the voice's path,
And then the tongue, the mind's interpreter,
Weakened by pain oozed blood, and scarce could move,
Lying heavy within the mouth and rough to touch.   1150
Next, when disease had passed down through the throat
And filled the chest, and poured its flood of ill
Right to the victim's sorrowing heart, why then,
Then truly all the barriers of life
Collapsed. The breath rolled out a noisome stench
Like that of rotting corpses lying unburied;   1155
And all the power of mind and all the body
Began to faint, being on death's very threshold.
Constant companion of these intolerable woes
Was torment of anxiety, and laments
Were mixed with groans as mind and body suffered.
And night and day incessant retching shook them   1160
Convulsing limbs and muscles, and exhausting
Bodies already wearied by disease.
You could not observe the surface of the body
To be burning with excessive heat, but rather
It gave a warm sensation to the hand,   1165
And at the same time all of it was red
With ulcers as if burnt into it, as when

The accursed fire spreads out across the limbs.
But in their inward parts men burnt to the bones;
A flame burnt in the stomach as in a furnace;
1170   And there was nothing however light or thin
That could help their bodies, but only wind and cold.
Some cast their burning limbs into cold streams,
Throwing their bodies naked into the water.
Many hurled themselves headlong into wells, their mouths
1175   Gaping to reach the water as they fell.
Dry thirst unquenchable, drenching their bodies,
Made streams of water no better than a trickle.
Nor was there any respite to their pain;
Their bodies lay exhausted; medicine
Muttered beside the bed in silent fear,
1180   As all the while they rolled their staring eyes,
Sleepless, and burning with the fell disease.
Then many signs of death began to appear.
A mind disquieted with fear and sorrow,
A gloomy brow, a furious frenzied face,
1185   Ears troubled and full of noises, breath confused
And either panting fast or deep and laboured.
The neck all sodden with a shining sweat;
A small thin spittle, yellowish and salt,
Drawn by hoarse coughing hardly through the throat.
1190   Then hands began to twitch and limbs to tremble,
And upwards from the feet by slow degrees
Cold crept on. Then at the final hour
Nostrils were pinched, the nose drawn to a point,
Eyes sunken, temples hollow, cold the skin
1195   And hand, mouth grinning, forehead tensed.
No long time after, limbs lay stiff in death.
On the eighth shining of the sun did most,
Or with the ninth day's lamp, give up their lives.

      If a man chanced to escape the ruin of death
1200   Yet later from foul ulcers and black flux
From the bowels, a lingering death awaited him.
Or else a copious stream of putrid blood
With violent headache flowed out through the nostrils,
And all his body's strength flowed into it.
1205   And if a man survived this savage flux

Of noisome blood, yet into his limbs and sinews
And even the genital parts the plague went on.
Some in their grievous fear of death's dark gates
Severed their manly parts to save their lives;
And some without their hands or feet yet still   1210
Clung on to life, and others lost their eyes,
So strongly had the fear of death assailed them.
And some oblivion of everything
Took hold of, that they knew not who they were.

And although bodies piled on bodies lay   1215
In multitudes unburied, birds and beasts
Avoided them, warned by the piercing stench,
Or, having tasted, died a speedy death.
In truth in those dark days scarce any bird
Was to be seen, nor from the forests came   1220
Wild beasts in search of prey; for nearly all
Were sickening with the deadly plague and dying.
Among the first, man's faithful friends the dogs
Lay stretched in every street, fighting in vain
For life the pestilence wrenched out of them.
The lonely funerals, one racing with another,   1225
Were rushed without a mourner to the grave.
There was no sure and general remedy.
For what had given to one the power to draw
The breath of life into his lips, and see
The realms of heaven, this to another was
Destruction and a minister of death.

One thing most woeful and most pitiful   1230
Was this: that when a man saw himself
Caught by the plague, as if condemned to death
Losing all heart he lay in misery,
And so expecting death died where he lay.
Unceasing the contagion of the plague   1235
Seized in its grasp first one man then another,
Like flocks of fleecy sheep or horned cattle.
This was the chief cause of death piled on death.
And if from greed for life and fear of death
Men shunned the sick-beds of those dear to them,
In no long time avenging negligence   1240

Brought punishment, a foul and evil death,
Bereft of help, deserted, all alone.
But those that stood to help the plague destroyed,
And toil, which honour drove them to endure,
Hearing the pleading voices of the weary,
1245 Listening to the sad voice of complaint.
In this way all the noblest met their death.

[*The text is corrupt here*]

. . . one upon another, fighting
To bury the vast numbers of their dead.
Wearied with tears and sorrow they returned;
And many then took to their beds in grief.
1250 Nor could a man be found at such a time
Whom neither plague nor death nor grief had touched.

Moreover now the shepherd and the herdsman
And the strong steersman of the curving plough,
All, all were fainting. Deep within their huts
Their bodies huddled lay, consigned to death
1255 By poverty and by the foul disease.
And sometimes you might see the lifeless bodies
Of parents lying upon their lifeless children,
Or see in turn the children breathe their last
Upon the bodies of their mothers and fathers.

And this affliction to no small extent
Flowed to the city from the countryside;
1260 For crowds of country-folk struck by the plague
Thronging every quarter brought it in.
They filled the lanes and lodgings everywhere,
And crammed together within stifling walls
Death the destroyer piled them up in heaps.
And overcome by thirst bodies lay strewn
1265 Along the roadsides by the drinking fountains
Of multitudes from whom the breath of life
Had been cut off by water all too welcome.
And everywhere in streets and public places
You could see half-dead bodies, fainting limbs
Covered with rags and caked with filth and squalor,
1270 Dying, with naught but skin upon their bones,
Skin almost buried in foul sores and dirt.

And all the holy temples of the gods
Death filled with lifeless bodies, and everywhere
The shrines of the celestials, which the priests
Had filled with guests, stood loaded high with corpses.   1275
For reverence now and worship of the gods
Counted for little, present grief was all.
No longer too the ancient customs stood
Of burial, which the city was wont to use.
Confusion and fear were everywhere, and in sorrow   1280
Each buried his own as circumstance allowed.
And sudden need and poverty inspired them
To many actions horrible and shameful.
They placed their own kin on the funeral pyres
Of others, and with frenzied cries set light to them,
And often in the fighting that ensued   1285
They shed much blood rather than leave the bodies.

EXPLANATORY NOTES

Book One

1 *mother of the Roman race*: in mythology, Venus was the mother of Aeneas, the traditional ancestor of the Romans: the story of her encounter with his father Anchises on Mt Ida is told in the *Hymn to Aphrodite* ascribed to Homer, and the introduction to that hymn is recalled in the prologue at several points.

delight: pleasure was the central good of the Epicurean system: see Introduction.

2 *Venus*: the Roman equivalent of the Greek Aphrodite, goddess of love and sex. Her name in Latin means something like 'attractiveness', and her principal festival was on 1 April, the beginning of spring (cf. the opening of Chaucer's *Canterbury Tales*). The poem begins at dawn on the first day of spring (10 ff.), when navigation resumes again after the winter (3 ff.).

26 *Memmius*: C. Memmius, praetor in 58 BC and consular candidate in 54: see Introduction. Venus was used as an emblem on the coinage of the family of the *Memmii*.

33 *Mars' dominion*: Venus restraining the warlike impulse of her husband Mars was a frequent subject of ancient as of modern painting (see especially Botticelli's *Venus and Mars*). Their union was sometimes allegorized as bringing about harmony: they also look back to the two cosmic principles of 'Love' and 'Strife' of the fifth-century BC Greek poet Empedocles, who was one of Lucretius' major models (see Introduction).

44–8 *for perfect peace . . .* : these lines translate the first of Epicurus' 'Master Sayings': 'The blessed and deathless [i.e. the divine] is neither itself troubled nor provides trouble to others, and so it is not compassed either by gratitude or by anger; for all such is weakness.' Some scholars excise these lines (which are repeated at 2. 646 ff.) as at odds with the terms of the invocation to Venus and the run of thought: the lines are certainly shockingly abrupt about the real nature of divinity, but this is not necessarily without point.

56 *Nature creates, increases, nourishes*: Nature begins to take over the functions of 'Venus most bountiful' (2 ff.).

66 *a man of Greece*: Epicurus. The oblique reference is in oracular style: Empedocles so refers to Pythagoras (fr. B129), and later Virgil will refer to Lucretius with similar anonymity (*Georgics* 2. 490–2, 'Happy the man who knows the causes of things . . . '). Epicurus is depicted as a giant in revolt against heaven (cf. 5. 117 ff.), a hero defeating the monster religion as Apollo defeated Python. This passage was widely imitated in later poetry: see the introduction for Abraham Cowley's celebration of Francis Bacon's victory over 'Authority' in his Ode 'To the Royal Society'.

77 *deep-set boundary stone*: 76–7 are repeated at 1. 595–6, 5. 89–90, and 6. 65–6. It was a sacrilege to move a boundary stone (Latin *terminus*): there was even a deity 'Terminus' who oversaw them (cf. Livy 1. 55. 3). Epicurus' journey through the infinite universe ends in an expression of human finitude (for the image cf. also 2. 1087, 3. 1020).

84–101 *as once at Aulis . . .* : Iphigenia (here called Iphianassa as in Homer, though the latter does not have the story of her sacrifice) was sacrificed by her father Agamemnon at the instigation of the priest Calchas in order to appease Diana (Artemis) and provide a following wind for the expedition against Troy. There were several versions of the story: Lucretius uses those details which reflect worse on religion, especially those found in Aeschylus' play *Agamemnon* (228 ff.) and Euripides, *Iphigenia in Aulis*.

117 *Our own Ennius*: Q. Ennius (239–169 BC), the 'father' of Roman poetry. In the opening of his great historical epic the *Annales* he described a meeting with the shade of Homer in Pythagorean terms (frr. 3–11): the work survives only in fragments, but was clearly extensively used in the prologue to *On the Nature of the Universe*.

141 *sweet friendship*: friendship played an important role in Epicurean communities, but the term was also used for the relationship between clients and patrons in Rome.

148 *the face of nature and her laws*: lines 146–8 also conclude the opening sections of Books 2, 3, and 6. The dual reference to the outward appearance of the world and its inner workings reflects the Epicurean insistence on empiricism and reason (*physiologia*: see Introduction).

159 *if things came out of nothing*: see Epicurus' *Letter to Herodotus* 38, 'nothing comes to be out of what is not, for everything would then come to be out of everything, without needing a seed', a view described by Aristotle (*Metaphysics* 1. 983ᵇ) as the common belief of ancient natural philosophers. On the argument form used here, see Introduction.

174 *why do roses flourish in the spring*: the opening address to Venus is recalled, but now science replaces myth. The 'argument from design' based on the orderly procession of the seasons is here turned against belief in providence: similarly in 208–14 myths of a Golden Age when human beings did not need to work are debunked.

215 *The next great principle*: cf. Epicurus, *Letter to Herodotus* 38, 'and if what disappears was destroyed into what does not exist, all things would have perished, since that into which they were dissolved would not exist'.

250–61 *father ether . . .*: the 'hieros gamos' or wedding of earth and sky was a common literary and religious motif from the time of Homer's account of the union of Zeus and Hera (*Iliad* 14. 346–51): Lucretius' account here is close to that in Aeschylus' *Danaids* (fr. 44), just as his later version in Book 2 (991 ff.) is based on Euripides' *Chrysippus* (fr. 839). Lucretius sails close to the wind in perverting the commonplace to his own ends, and this is one of the passages that have led critics to see an underlying religious feeling belying Epicurean orthodoxy; the concluding lines, however, remind us that these are all natural processes.

280–9 *just as water . . .*: the behaviour of wind is compared to that of water in an extended comparison which is at once an Epicurean scientific analogy and an epic simile with multiple correspondences between tenor and vehicle.

330 *There is void in things*: cf. Epicurus, *Letter to Herodotus* 37. The Epicureans were one of the few philosophical schools to accept the notion of empty space within the universe.

402 *these small traces*: the hunting simile here develops a central metaphorical complex of *On the Nature of the Universe*, the pursuit of the truth by following up the 'traces' (the Latin word also means footprints) visible in the phenomenal world. The metaphors go back to Epicurus (e.g. *Letter to Pythocles* 96) and continue to underlie much scientific and other thinking.

419–20 *All nature . . . consists | Of two things*: cf. Epicurus, *Letter to Herodotus* 40.

445–8 *no third substance . . .*: cf. Epicurus, *Letter to Herodotus* 40, 'besides these nothing can even be thought of either by conception or on analogy with things that can be conceived, if considered as an independent entity rather than the accidents or properties of such an entity'.

449–50 *properties . . . | Or . . . accidents*: for the transition here see the passage from the *Letter to Herodotus* quoted in the previous note: Epicurus discusses the distinction in more detail later in the *Letter*, at 68–71.

459–63 *Time . . . does not exist by itself . . .*: cf. Epicurus, *Letter to Herodotus* 72–3.

464–82 *Helen's rape | And Troy's defeat . . .*: Lucretius simultaneously attacks rival semantic theories (the target is disputed, but it may be in part Stoic) and the epic tradition going back to Homer's *Iliad*: in contrast Epicurean semantics retain a firm grip on reality.

483–4 *Material objects are of two kinds*: cf. Epicurus, *Letter to Herodotus* 40 (immediately after the passage quoted on 445–8), 'among bodies, some are compounds, others those of which compounds are formed'.

485–6 *no force can ever quench*: cf. Epicurus, *Letter to Herodotus* 41, 'and these latter [i.e. atoms] are indivisible and unchangeable . . . being completely solid in nature'.

499 *In a few verses*: in fact, we get a series of eleven arguments, most of which are not found in the *Letter to Herodotus*. The plethora of proofs has an epic amplitude, and demonstrates how Lucretius has drawn 'bounteous draughts from springs o'erflowing' (412).

521 *The universe*: the first explicit mention of the universe as a whole since the prologue (74), preparing for the arguments in 951 ff. In contrast, the *Letter to Herodotus* mentions 'the all' from the beginning.

567 *air, water, earth, and fire*: the Epicureans accepted the notion of four elements, but denied that they were primary: see below 705 ff. attacking Empedocles.

596 *deep-set boundary stone*: these important lines (594–6) recur at 76 ff., 5. 89 ff., and 6. 65 ff. Epicureanism laid great stress on the fact that the clear boundaries between what is possible and what is not bring certainty to human life.

601–2 *the smallest | Thing that can possibly exist*: the Epicureans believed in a universe where there were minimal units of space and time. The smallest possible atom would be one minimal space unit in each dimension, but the dimensions of most atoms would be greater than this, since atoms varied in shape. Cf. Epicurus, *Letter to Herodotus* 56–9, in a discussion of primary qualities (treated by Lucretius in 2. 80 ff.).

635–920 Lucretius refutes in turn the views of three 'pre-Socratic' physical philosophers: Heraclitus (*c.*500 BC), who made fire the principle of his cosmology, Empedocles (*c.*492–392 BC), who had a system of four elements, and Anaxagoras (*c.*500–428 BC), who believed that there was an unlimited number of different stuffs. They represent three rival approaches to the substance of the physical world: monism, limited pluralism, and unlimited pluralism. Lists of the opinions of the various philosophers ('Doxography') existed in various forms in antiquity, and establishing one's own views through argument with rival approaches was a standard device of ancient as of modern philosophy: see especially Aristotle, *Metaphysics* 1. 983ᵃ. Epicurus' discussion of the pre-Socratics came in Books 14 and 15 of *On Nature* (see Introduction): the later Epicurean Diogenes of Oenoanda (fr. 6) tackles a superset of Lucretius' list. In each case the favoured approach is seen as the culmination of earlier efforts: similarly Lucretius (following in the footsteps of his master) comes immediately after the trio of earlier philosophers.

638 *Heraclitus, famed for his dark sayings*: Heraclitus of Ephesus expounded in riddling aphorisms a system in which fire was the underlying substance of the universe, constantly changing into other forms. He was later popular

with the Stoics, who also made a form of fire their primary substance, and hence a good initial target (as in Diogenes of Oenoanda). Lucretius puns on the second element of his name, which means 'renowned' in Greek, and also attacks Heraclitus' obscurity of language (in contrast to what he will claim for himself in 921 ff.) and military metaphors.

670 *things have limits fixed*: the principle that change is a form of death is used on several occasions in *On the Nature of the Universe* (cf. 1. 792–3, 2. 753–4, 3. 519–20): ironically it goes back to Heraclitus (fr. B6: cf. also Melissus (fifth century BC) fr. B7).

707 *air is the principle*: this was the view of Anaximenes (sixth century BC) and Diogenes of Apollonia (fifth century BC), while Thales (sixth century BC) was said to have made water his single principle: there was no major thinker who upheld the claims of earth.

716–17 *Empedocles | Of Acragas*: see Introduction. The description of Sicily (Acragas, modern Agrigento, is in the south of the island) suggests a possible genesis for the four elements of his theory in his native land, and demythologizes the stories associated with it.

722 *Charybdis*: a mythical whirlpool situated opposite Scylla (cf. *Odyssey* 12. 101 ff.) and later located in the Straits of Messina, which separate Sicily from Reggio di Calabria.

738–9 *more holy . . . | Than those the Delphic prophetess pronounced*: repeated in Book 5 (III ff.) of Lucretius himself. The priestess of Apollo at Delphi still in Lucretius' day gave notoriously ambiguous verse oracles, sitting on the tripod of the god and crowned with laurel, but the imagery of oracular inspiration was often appropriated by philosophers, including Epicureans. Cf. Epicurus, *Vatican Sayings* 29, Diogenes Laertius, *Lives of the Philosophers* 10. 12, Philodemus, *On Piety* 71. 2044–5, Cicero, *On the Nature of the Gods* 1. 66, *On Divination* 1. 23.

782 *these men*: Aristotle and the Peripatetics, and later the Stoics, believed in the interchangeability of the four elements.

824 *letters common to many words*: a famous comparison of the composition of the world to the composition of the text (cf. 1. 196 ff., 912 ff., 2. 688 ff., 1013 ff.). The analogy of atoms and letters goes back to the early atomists (cf. Aristotle, *Metaphysics* 1. 4. 985^b, *On Generation and Corruption* 315^b), but Lucretius considerably extends the scope of the comparison.

830–920 *Anaxagoras' | Homoeomeria . . .* : Anaxagoras believed the basic stuffs of the world were infinitely divisible, and that the things we see around us were mixtures of all these stuffs. Modern scholars doubt that the word *homoeomeria* (Greek for 'similar-partedness') was used by him, but it was widely seen as his term in antiquity: it probably derives from Aristotle's discussion (*Metaphysics* 1. 984^{a}11 ff.). As with the other pre-Socratic philosophers in this section, Anaxagoras' linguistics come under scrutiny as well as his physics. Anaxagoras was said to be the pre-Socratic philosopher most admired by Epicurus (Diogenes Laertius, *Lives of the Philosophers* 10. 12), perhaps because of his scientific explanations for natural phenomena (he was exiled from Athens for denying the divinity of the sun: cf. 5. 114 ff.): Democritus praised his formulation of the empiricist principle that visible phenomena can be evidence for the unseen (Sextus Empiricus, *Against the Professors* 7. 140).

919–20 *shake their sides and rock with laughter*: the argument is repeated at 2. 976 ff.

923 *holy wand*: the 'thyrsus' carried by Bacchants in their worship of Dionysus. The Bacchic trance was a symbol for inspiration from the time of Plato on (cf. *Ion* 553e ff.); Lucretius again flirts with religious language in turning to his own rationalist account of the world.

926 *A pathless country of the Pierides*: after describing and criticizing rival views, Lucretius uses the language of poetic initiation to describe his own mission. The details of the scene are common in poetry from the time of Hesiod (seventh century BC), who described in his *Theogony* a meeting with the Muses on Mt Helicon (in his home region of Boeotia) but who says that they were born further north in Pieria (near Mt Olympus: cf. *Theogony* 53, *Works and Days* 1). Lucretius perhaps pointedly dissociates his 'Pierian' inspiration (cf. 1. 946) from the commoner setting on Mt Helicon (cf. 1. 118, 3. 1037). The Hellenistic poet Callimachus (third century BC) dreamt of a meeting with the Muses on Helicon at the opening of his influential poem the *Aetia* and images such as those of the untrodden path and the untouched spring go back to his poetry and are associated with his aesthetic of small-scale precision. Lucretius appropriates this imagery (as had Ennius in the opening of his *Annals*, cf. 1. 117 ff.) but stresses that his revelation is 'of matters high' (931: cf. 5. 1 ff.): 'the pathless country' of poetic exclusivity is also the sublimely infinite universe of the Epicureans (cf. 1. 958 ff.).

933 *of things so dark in verse so clear*: clarity was the sole virtue of style for Epicurus (Diogenes Laertius, *Lives of the Philosophers* 10. 13), and Lucretius sets himself against the obscurities of philosophers such as Heraclitus (cf. 1. 639 ff.) as well as against poetical fancy. Language is, however, not simply transparent: it is also itself a source of illumination (cf. 941 ff., 1114 ff.).

938 *Sweet yellow honey on the goblet's rim*: the celebrated image of the 'honey round the cup': poetry sweetens the philosophical message. This does not tell the whole story of the role of poetry in *On the Nature of the Universe*, but it stresses how the verse both brings the reader to drink and holds the reader in its grip while the 'medicine' of philosophy does its work. The image goes back to Plato (*Laws* 2. 659e).

970   *and threw a flying lance*: the argument from stretching out a hand or a stick at the end of the universe goes back to the Pythagorean mathematician Archytas (fourth century BC, fr. A24), but Lucretius rephrases it in terms of the Roman practice of declaring war by a priest launching the 'fetial spear' into enemy territory (cf. Livy 1. 32).

1052–3   *the theory . . . | That all things press towards the centre of the universe*: versions of this view were held by both the Peripatetics (followers of Aristotle) and the Stoics.

1094–1101   There is an eight-line gap in the manuscripts at this point, caused by damage to an earlier copy.

1101–2   *the ramparts of the world | Would burst asunder*: for the image of the 'ramparts' or walls of the world, cf. 1. 73 (where Epicurus travels beyond them) and 2. 1144 ff. in another concluding description of cosmic destruction. Like all compounds, our world-system is held together by the interlacing of atoms (2. 99 ff.) and will one day decay. The image is not found in Epicurus, but he does remark that because of the fear of death all people live in a city without walls (*Vatican Sayings* 31). The analogy between the world and a city state sets civil order within a wider cosmic perspective, especially for a Roman for whom the walls of Rome were sacrosanct (cf. Virgil, *Aeneid* 1. 7). Book 1 ends with a counter-factual destruction of the world: Book 2 will end with its collapse in actuality.

1116   *Right to the heart of nature's mysteries*: after the preceding apocalypse, Book 1 ends with the reader promised in the language of the Greek mysteries a continuing revelation and passage from darkness to light (see 3. 1 ff. and nn.). The lines are a partial translation of Empedocles fr. B110.

Book Two

1–13   *A joy it is . . .* : like Book 1, Book 2 begins with pleasure: in the figure known to modern rhetoricians as the 'Priamel', the pleasures of watching others' distress on sea or land when safe oneself are capped by those of the wise, for whom, as Francis Bacon paraphrased in his essay *On Truth*, 'no pleasure is comparable to the standing upon the vantage ground of truth (a hill not to be commanded, and where the air is always clear and serene), and to see the errors, and wanderings, and mists, and tempests, in the vale below'. (Cf. George Eliot, *Felix Holt*, ch. 30, and the heading 'Lucretian Pleasure in a Hot Bath' in John Betjeman, *Summoned by Bells*, ch. 7.)

11   *The clash of intellects, the fight for honours*: Lucretius dramatizes the opposing slogans of the so-called 'new men' in Roman politics, who claimed to rise through talent, and the established 'nobles', whose claims were based on family distinction.

16-19 ... *Nature cries for this* ... : Lucretius encapsulates all four of the types of pleasure analysed by Epicurus, *katastematic* or 'steady-state' pleasure of the body (absence of pain) and the mind (absence of anxiety), and *kinetic* or 'motive' pleasure of the body (pleasure of the senses) and mind (reflection on sensual pleasure): see Introduction.

24 *golden statues of young men*: Lucretius echoes Homer, *Odyssey* 7. 100-2, describing the mythical luxury of Phaeacia. Moralizing interpretations of the Phaeacian episode in the *Odyssey* were common in antiquity, and Heraclitus 'the Allegorizer' (perhaps first century AD) calls Epicurus 'the Phaeacian philosopher' (79. 2). At *Odyssey* 9. 5 Odysseus (in a line much discussed by ancient moralists and echoed here in 23) tells his hosts that there is nothing more pleasing than when everyone has 'good cheer' (*euphrosyne*) at a banquet: Epicurus took over the word *euphrosyne* for bodily pleasure and certainly did not reject sensual pleasure (cf. e.g. fr. 67), but true Epicurean 'luxury' is much simpler, as Lucretius explains here.

31-3 ... *On the soft grass beside a flowing stream* ... : the description here is repeated in Book 5 (1392-6) (significantly dealing there with the simple life of early man), and places in a new Epicurean context the commonplaces of the so-called *locus amoenus* or pleasance, as seen canonically in Hesiod, *Works and Days* 588-96, and Plato, *Phaedrus* 230b.

55 *like children frightened of the dark*: 55-61 are repeated at the end of the prologues to Book 3 (87 ff.) and Book 6 (35 ff.), while 60-1 also conclude the prologue to Book 1 (see above on 148). The contrast of light and dark that runs through the prologue to Book 2 is the most obvious of the symbolic complexes that structure the poem: here and in Book 6 the light of reason is set against the darkness of ignorance, while in Book 3 the fear of death is the more prominent target, but the weapons of enlightenment remain the same.

62-323 *motions* ... : atoms for the Epicureans were constantly moving at the greatest possible speed (one minimal space-unit per minimal time-unit: cf. *Letter to Herodotus* 61-2). Compounds consist of more-or-less stable clusters of atoms whose movements interlock, and the properties of compounds are in part determined by the nature of these motions. As Lucretius explains at the end of Book 2 in connection with the human body and the cosmos, there is a constant interchange of atoms between compounds and their surrounding environment: some motions lead to the creation of new compounds and the replenishment of existing ones, others to decay and destruction (cf. 2. 569 ff.). A proper appreciation of this cycle of change has wider implications for Epicurean ethical theory: human beings have to see that they themselves are also part of this process (cf. 76 ff.). On the presentation of atomic motion before atomic shape, see below on 334 ff.

76-7 *mortals live* ... | *Some races increase*: although 'mortals' is general and 'races' includes the different species of animals, the language used here suggests human institutions such as families and whole peoples, and the common-places of the rise and fall of empires and polities (cf. e.g. Herodotus, *Histories* 1. 5. 4, Polybius, *Histories* 1. 2, Ovid, *Metamorphoses* 15. 420 ff.).

79 *the torch of life*: in the Latin 'vitai lampada', adopted as the title for the poem of Henry Newbolt whose refrain is 'Play up! Play up! and play the game!' The image (from Athenian torch races) goes back to Plato, *Laws* 6. 777b, in the context of marriage (torches were borne at both weddings and funerals in antiquity).

94 *I have shown*: in 1. 958 ff.

112 *An image and similitude of this*: the example of dust in a sunbeam (which goes back to Democritus fr. A28, and Epicurus fr. 293) is used in two ways by Lucretius: to give a conceptual picture of what atomic motion is like (112 ff.) and as an argument from observed phenomena to underlying atomic causa-tion (125 ff.: see Introduction). Although molecular movement is responsible for the 'Brownian motion' of particles in fluids and gases, the movement of dust in a beam of light is in fact due merely to air currents (as the Stoics held in antiquity: cf. Seneca, *Natural Questions* 5. 1). Through a paraphrase of Lucretius in the church father Lactantius (third–fourth century AD: *On Anger* 10. 9), the image enters Dante's *Paradiso* (14. 112 ff.).

153 *particles of heat*: something like the modern conception of 'molecules', but without the notion of fixed size and constitution. Atoms always move at the same speed, within and outside compounds, but the motion of a 'molecule' is the sum of all the motions of its constituent atoms (as in a swarm of insects moving *en masse*).

164 Although this is not noted in the manuscripts, there seems to be a substan-tial portion of text missing at this point.

175 *all things for men's sake*: although Lucretius' target in this section is generally all those who believe in divine providence, and Xenophon (fifth–fourth cen-tury BC) already has Socrates arguing that everything is ordered for man (*Memorabilia* 4. 3. 12), the Stoics were particularly renowned for believing that all was for the sake of man in this best of all possible worlds (cf. e.g. Cicero, *On Duties* 1. 22, *On the Nature of the Gods* 2. 133).

182 *I will make clear to you later*: 177–81 are repeated at 5. 195–9, where the argu-ment is pursued in more detail.

185–6 *no material thing can . . . | . . . travel upwards*: all atoms in Epicureanism have a natural motion 'downwards', even though the universe is infinite in space and time, and there has never been a time when all atoms were pur-suing this natural motion rather than moving as a result of collisions or the 'swerve'. This natural motion reasserts itself, so that an atom travelling 'hor-izontally' as a result of a collision will eventually return to a natural down-ward path. Epicurus seems to have introduced this notion of natural motion partly in response to criticisms of the earlier atomists made by Aristotle (cf. e.g. *On the Heavens* 3.2, 300^{b}8 ff.).

219 *swerve slightly from their course*: the famous 'swerve' of the atoms has been much discussed in ancient and modern times (Karl Marx devoted part of his doctoral dissertation to it) and remains controversial. Atoms 'jump tracks' (probably by one minimal space-unit, and without changing direction) at indeterminate moments: this not only provides a way in which atomic collisions might occur (though, as explained above, there has never been a time when collisions have not been occurring) but is somehow involved in 'free will' (256–7). The swerve is well attested in Epicurean sources, but is not mentioned in any extant passage of Epicurus himself: this may be just chance. Swerves were probably frequent occurrences, but usually had little effect in the relatively robust compounds of the world: if they took place, however, in the fine substance of the souls of people and animals (cf. 3. 177 ff.), and in particular in its nameless 'fourth part' (3. 273 ff.), a change might occur which at the level of consciousness would be an act of decision. Many details remain unclear, but the swerve paradoxically enabled Epicureans to stress individual agency and freedom from fate on a moral level (cf. 279 ff.).

254 *the bonds of fate*: 'fate' was especially the watchword of the Stoics, who were strict determinists, and believed in an unbroken chain of cause and effect.

276 *Until the will has reined limbs back*: Lucretius' continued use of the imagery of chariot-racing can be seen as an appropriation of Plato's image of the chariot of the soul in the *Phaedrus* (253d).

324 *in mimic war*: the mock battles of the prologue (5 ff., 40 ff.) return, suggesting an underlying ethical point to the physical observation. There is a place to stand where all the epic grandeur of human endeavour (Homer, *Iliad* 19. 357 ff. and other passages are recalled) is sound and fury, signifying nothing.

334–5 *shapes | And . . . figures*: the shape of the atoms determines how their motions interact, and the topic is treated by Epicurus before that of their motion in *Letter to Herodotus* 54–5, 55–6. Lucretius, however, proceeds from shape to primary and secondary qualities (treated separately in the *Letter to Herodotus* 68 ff.) in a movement 'upwards' from the atomic level to that of compounds which is part of the wider plot of the poem: see below on 2. 730 ff.

352 *in front of noble shrines of gods*: Lucretius insinuates a point against religion into his argument from the variety of things, but there is perhaps also a further anti-providentialist point: the Greek church father Nemesius (*c*.400 AD) argues that the ability of animals to recognize each other is providential (*On the Nature of Man* 41. 154 ff.) and in general the wondrous variety of the world is a common argument for divine activity (cf. e.g. Cicero, *On the Nature of the Gods* 2. 98 ff.).

416 *Cilician saffron*: before dramatic performances (cf. e.g. Ovid, *Art of Love* 1. 104) the stage was sprinkled with saffron, imported from Corycus in Cilicia (southern Turkey); cf. Pliny, *Natural Histories* 21. 31.

480 *atoms have a finite number of shapes*: cf. Epicurus, *Letter to Herodotus* 42, 55–6. Democritus seems to have been prepared to accept atoms even as big as a world-system (frr. A43, A47): Epicurus saw that, if the number of different shapes was infinite and there were minimal units of space, we should have to suppose that there were infinitely large atoms. Again, Epicurus seems to have been responding to Aristotle: cf. *On the Heavens* 303ª, *On Sensation* 442ᵇ.

485 *minimal parts*: see above 1. 601 ff.

501 *Meliboean purple*: Meliboea was a town in Thessaly, where purple dye was made from shellfish (like the more famous 'Tyrian purple').

524–5 *atoms which are made of similar shapes | Are infinite in number*: cf. Epicurus, *Letter to Herodotus* 42, 55–6.

532–40 *certain animals are rarer . . .* : The Epicureans used a principle of *isonomia* or 'equal distribution' (our only source for the term is Cicero, *On the Nature of the Gods* 1. 50. 109): if one set of things is rarer in a particular location than another, but there is no reason why there should be more in total of the one than the other, there must be a place somewhere (possibly in another world) where the proportions are reversed, and if things are destroyed in one part, they must be being created elsewhere.

538 *Of ivory, a rampart none can pass*: some traveller's tale must lie behind this 'wall of ivory', but there is no exact parallel in extant literature.

577 *the wailing of the infant child*: it has often been observed that Lucretius' opposition between the 'positive' cry of a child being born and the 'negative' cries of lamentation for death still tends towards a negative view of human life: cf. 5. 222 ff.

598 *Great Mother of the Gods*: Cybele the 'Great Mother', an Anatolian deity whose cult was brought to Rome in 204 BC. Her worship combined a continuing orientalism with a central role in Roman public cult through the festival of the Megalensia, aided by the Romans' belief in their Trojan origins (cf. 1. 1 ff.). Lucretius' description is of the public procession of her eunuch priests at the festival. Various allegorical interpretations of her attributes similar to those offered here are extant (Varro (first century BC) in St Augustine, *City of God* 7. 24, Cornutus (first century AD), *Theology of the Greeks* 6). The Epicureans rejected allegory as it was normally employed, to save a religious interpretation of an implausible myth, though Lucretius' own use of myth is more complicated (see Introduction). Lucretius associates her with the Cretan goddess Rhea (see below 632 ff.) and with 'Mother Earth': she joins Venus and Nature as another powerful female figure within the poem.

600 *Grecian poets*: we do not know who these poets were, but that this is more than a vague generalization is suggested by the parallel phrase at 6. 754, where there is a specific reference to the poet Callimachus (see below).

611 *Idaean Mother*: Cybele was associated with Mt Ida near Troy (in Phrygia, northern Turkey), but there was also a Mt Ida on Crete linked to the worship of Rhea.

614 *Eunuchs*: the priests of Cybele (known as *Galli*) were eunuchs (cf. Catullus 63).

633 *Curetes*: the Curetes were young men of Crete who made a noise with their shields to drown the cries of Rhea's son Jupiter in order to prevent his father Saturn (Cronos) eating him. Here (as elsewhere) they are identified with the worshippers of Cybele, the Corybantes.

646–51 *perfect peace . . .* : these lines translate the first of Epicurus' *Master Sayings* and are repeated from the prologue to Book 1 (44–9: see above).

655 *the sea Neptune | And corn Ceres*: cf. 2. 472, 6. 1076 (Neptune), 5. 742 (Ceres), 3. 221, 5. 743 (Bacchus), and compare the use of Venus for 'sex' at the end of Book 4 (1058 ff.). Lucretius does not say why one might want to use mythological figures in this way, and his own use of myth is more extensive: see Introduction.

689 *Many letters common to many words*: see above on 1. 823 ff.

708 *fixed seeds* cf. 1. 189 ff.

730–1022 *Now here's a matter . . .* : primary and secondary properties. Lucretius had objected to the rival philosophers in Book 1 that to endow primary substance with properties such as heat would make it impossible to account for the varied nature of the phenomenal world (cf. 1. 645 ff., 880 ff., 915 ff.), and here he emphasizes that his atoms do not possess colour (730–841) or other properties such as heat, sound, moisture, or smell (842–64), and in particular are in no way sentient or conscious (865–1022, preparing for the argument against the immortality of the soul in Book 3). Epicurus had dealt with secondary properties in *Letter to Herodotus* 68–9, in connection with the discussion of properties and accidents (see above 1. 449 ff.): Lucretius' position reflects the overall plot of *On the Nature of the Universe* (see above on 2. 344 ff.), and in particular the attention given to the lack of sentience amongst the atoms as leading up to Book 3. From the time of the first atomists, policing the boundary between the properties of the phenomenal world and those of its 'underlying' reality has been a perennial concern of science and philosophy: cf. Democritus fr. B9, B11, and e.g. John Locke, *An Essay concerning Human Understanding* 2. 7. 9 ff., 4. 3. 11 ff.

748 ff. At least one line has been lost here, and there may be further disruption to the text.

753 *fixed boundaries*: see above on 1. 670.

867–8 *Nor do things plainly known to us | And manifest refute this*: Lucretius' metaphors here reflect Epicurus' use of terms like *antimarturesis* 'witnessing against' (e.g. *Letter to Herodotus* 47) and *machesthai* 'fight against' (e.g. *Letter to Pythocles* 90) for the relation between visible phenomena and hypothesized underlying reality, but also the etymology of Roman words such as *manufestus* 'manifest', which was originally used of things that can be grasped with the hand (*manus* in Latin).

871–3 *living worms emerge*: cf. 3. 719. Belief in the spontaneous generation of organisms from rotting matter was almost universal until the development of microscopy: Louis Pasteur had a fierce debate on the subject with the biologists Pouchet and Bastion which was not resolved until the late nineteenth century.

944–62 *Consider this also . . .* : the examples look forward to the proofs of mortality in Book 3 (459 ff., 592 ff.).

976 *shake their sides and rock with laughter*: repeated from 1. 919–20.

991 *we are all sprung from heavenly seed*: a second appropriation of the *hieros gamos* or 'holy wedding' of earth and sky (see above 1. 250 ff.), this time based on a philosophizing passage of Euripides' lost play *Chrysippus* (fr. 839).

1013–18 *Moreover in my verse . . .* : see above on 1. 824.

1023 *A new thing now*: the Epicurean doctrine of an infinite number of worlds (cf. *Letter to Herodotus* 45, *Letter to Pythocles* 88 ff.) followed from their belief in the infinity of the universe and of matter and played an important part in their doctrines on possibility and necessity: if anything is possible, there is a world in which it is actual (see below on 5. 528). Lucretius also draws out the antiprovidential implications (1090 ff.). By contrast, most other schools posited a single world-system.

1030–9 *Take first the bright pure azure of the sky . . .* : Lucretius here perverts to his own ends a theist argument used by Aristotle in his lost dialogue *On Philosophy* (fr. 12, Cicero, *On the Nature of the Gods* 2. 37): if people living underground suddenly saw the sky for the first time, they would believe it the work of god.

1101 *Oft shatter his own temples*: see below on 6. 417.

1105 *Since the first natal hour of the world*: 1077–89 had introduced the idea that worlds are born and die, and 1090–1104 had then in a sense concluded the section on the infinite number of worlds, highlighting the problems the notion poses for a belief in divine providence. The book concludes by returning to the birth, growth, acme, decay, and death of worlds, in relation to the specific example of our world-system. The model is that of human growth and decay, and the passage also therefore again leads into the discussion of human mortality in Book 3. Plato in the *Timaeus* (33a, 81b, etc.) had rejected the implications of the biological analogy (especially in relation to matter coming in from outside) for the mortality of the world-system, presumably in opposition to the use of it by Democritus (cf. fr. A40): Lucretius' employment reflects elements of Plato's attack as well as atomist tradition.

1107 *added | In multitudes from outside*: Epicurus (*Letter to Pythocles* 89) talks of 'irrigations' of the world by atoms from outside. See below on 6. 483 ff.

1153 *No golden chain*: Zeus in Homer, *Iliad* 8. 19, says that he could not be pulled down from heaven even if all the gods pulled on a golden chain. This was allegorized in various ways by philosophers and commentators, though there is no close parallel to Lucretius' interpretation, which has more the air of parody.

1173 *all things . . . | . . . are moving towards their end*: the 'pessimistic' end to the book is paralleled by those to Books 3, 4, and 6, whereas 1 and 5 end more 'optimistically': in each case there is a reference to movement and change which is both closural and potentially suggestive of continuance. At the opening of Book 3 Epicurus will bring light into this darkness.

Book Three

1–30 *You, who from so great darkness could uplift | So clear a light . . .* : Book 3 begins with a 'hymn to Epicurus' which recalls the opening hymn to Venus: hence e.g. the repeated second-person address typical of hymns (cf. 9 ff.). There is a similar dispersal of darkness (cf. 1. 6 ff., 3. 16 ff.) and opening up of the world to joy and light, and Epicurus reveals the life of the gods in terms which recall 1. 44 ff. in the prologue to Book 1; he is the father (9 ff.) where she was the mother of things (1. 1 ff.).

3 *glory of the Greeks*: Epicurus is again referred to with an honorific periphrasis: cf. above on 1. 67 ff. 'man of Greece', and compare Venus' address as 'delight of men and gods' in 1. 1 ff.

4 *footprints*: see above on 1. 402 and 926 ff. Lucretius follows up the tracks of Epicurus, which are also the tracks through the wilderness which lead us to the truth.

14–15 *Starts to proclaim the nature of the world*: Epicurus' proclamation is phrased in terms which recall again the Eleusinian mysteries, at the climactic point of which the initiate was brought into a room filled with light and received a mystic announcement by the priest of the birth of a child and revelation of happiness after death (cf. e.g. Plutarch, *On the Soul* fr. 178, and, for the shout of the priest, Hippolytus, *Refutation of all Heresies* 5. 8. 40). Lucretius' revelation, on the other hand, is that there is no afterlife, and felicity must be sought and found in this world. Epicurus himself was said to have been initiated into the mysteries according to Lucretius' contemporary Philodemus (*On Piety* 20. 554 ff.).

16 *The walls of heaven open*: see above on 1. 1101 ff. In the mysteries, a shrine was opened at the moment of revelation (cf. Plutarch, *On Progress in Virtue* 81e).

18-22 *The gods appear now and their quiet abodes*: Lucretius translates a celebrated description of life on Mt Olympus in Homer, *Odyssey* 6. 42-6, appending to it another version of the first of Epicurus' *Master Sayings* (23 ff., cf. 1. 44 ff.). The easy and tranquil life of the Homeric gods is not only a model for that of the Epicurean gods, but also provides an example of how the individual Epicurean can and should live. The 'appearance' of the gods resembles a divine epiphany; they are not, however—and cannot be—physically present, but are perceptible only through contemplation. See below on 5. 148 ff.

28-9 *delight and joy | . . . and awe*: Lucretius reacts like an initiate before the revelation of nature's mysteries, or like someone receiving a divine epiphany (cf. the Annunciation: Luke 1: 28 ff.). But there is a sense in which what he sees is nothing: nature 'open and in every part displayed' is no more than atoms moving endlessly in infinite void. The secret of the universe is that there is no secret.

39 *suffusing all | With the blackness of death*: Lucretius' image for the soul, as a pool of water which is clear so long as the bottom is not stirred, but which for true salvation has to be cleaned out (cf. 4. 1133 ff.), anticipates Freudian views, although the precise nature of the 'unconscious' in Epicureanism is disputed, and in theory the cleansing of the soul for the Epicureans comes about through wholly rational means and leads to the complete elimination of the unconscious drive that is the fear of death.

41-93 *For when men say . . .* : Lucretius has two arguments against those who would say that there is no need to tackle the fear of death, as most people are not possessed of its terror (an accusation made by Cicero, *Tusculan Disputations* 1. 48). First, while this may be true in normal circumstances, any hardship shows that the fear has been there all the time (41-58), and, second, even in normal circumstances, the fear is operative as a root cause of human unhappiness (59-93).

43-4 *blood | . . . or even wind*: similar views were held by early philosophers (cf. Empedocles fr. B105 for blood, Anaximenes fr. A23 and Diogenes of Apollonia fr. A20 for air), but here are representatives of the careless imprecision of those who believe that they do not need Epicurean truth. The third-century BC Epicurean Polystratus (third head of the school) has a similar attack on those who think that they can do without scientific reason in his treatise *Against those who irrationally despise popular beliefs*.

48 *These men in exile*: a member of the Roman élite accused or condemned on a serious charge might go into exile to escape punishment, as, for instance, Memmius later did when prosecuted for electoral corruption in 52 BC (see Introduction).

52 *they slay black cattle*: black animals were sacrificed to underworld gods.

67 *lingering | Before the gates of death*: death is figured as a Roman man of power, on whom the living attend like dependent clients.

71 *murder upon murder | Piling in greed*: the reference is especially to the literal murders of the 'proscriptions' under Sulla in 82–1 BC, but the day-to-day political strife of the late republic was also often expressed in hyperbolically violent terms.

73 *A kinsman's board supplies both hate and fear*: there is an implied mythological model, that of Atreus serving up the children of his brother Thyestes: in the *Atreus* of Accius (170–86 BC) Atreus uttered the famous lines 'let them hate, so long as they fear' (frr. 203–4).

78 *Some die to get a statue and a name*: the desire for statues is listed amongst those desires which were neither necessary nor natural by an ancient commentator on Epicurus, *Master Sayings* 29 (see Introduction).

87–93 *For we, like children frightened of the dark . . .* : see above on 2. 55.

94–1094 *First I say*: 94–416 expound the nature of the soul, 417–829 argue for its mortality, and 830–1094 attack the fear of death directly.

99–100 *A sort of vital essence of the body, | Called harmony by the Greeks*: the view that consciousness is not located in a part of the body but is a state of the whole is espoused by Simmias and Echecrates (fifth–fourth century BC) in Plato's *Phaedo* (85e, 88d) and later by the Aristotelian philosophers Dicaearchus (fourth century BC, frr. 5–12) and Aristoxenus (fourth century BC, frr. 118–21). The latter is especially significant here as an important theorist of music (cf. Cicero, *Tusculan Disputations* 1. 19, 41). Another thinker who may have held similar views was the first-century BC medical philosopher Asclepiades of Bithynia, sometimes linked to Dicaearchus (Tertullian (second–third century AD), *On the Soul* 15. 3, who also mentions the third-century BC doctor Andreas) and active in Rome for part of his life. The 'harmony' or attunement theory was criticized in the *Phaedo* and by Aristotle in his lost dialogue *Eudemus* (fr. 7, cf. *On the Soul* 1. 4. 407^{b}27 ff.): Epicurus is said by John Philoponus (sixth century AD) in his commentary on this last passage to have criticized Plato's arguments, but we do not know the context.

134 *gave | The name to something till then nameless*: Lucretius suggests the technical language of rhetoric and the definition of *katachresis*, or 'necessary' metaphor.

136 *mind and spirit*: in the Latin, two words from the same root, *animus* 'mind' and *anima* 'soul', 'spirit': Lucretius exploits an existing distinction in the language where Epicurus had referred rather to the reasoning and non-rational parts of the souls (cf. the 'scholion' or ancient comment on *Letter to Herodotus* 67 preserved with the text).

138 *head and master as it were*: Lucretius ironically alludes to rival theories that placed the seat of intelligence in the head rather than the chest, and to the Greek (especially Stoic) term for the controlling intelligence often used in such accounts, *to hegemonikon* ('ruling element'). The Epicureans persisted in their view that sensations felt in the chest pointed to it as the location of thought as well as emotion despite the discovery of the nervous system by the Hellenistic doctors Herophilus and Erasistratus (fourth–third century BC): some other thinkers, following Plato (*Timaeus* 44d, 69d) separated the two functions, placing the immortal function of rational thought in the head but emotion in the heart. Ancient summaries of philosophical views (so-called *Placita Philosophorum*) offer a variety of different locations for the functions by various thinkers: cf. 'Aetius' 4. 5 (in H. Diels, *Doxographi Graeci* (Berlin 1879): see Bibliography).

154–6 *we sweat, grow pale, | Our speech is broken* . . . : Lucretius translates part of a famous passage of Sappho (seventh century BC), describing her feelings on seeing a man talking to a girl she loves: 'my tongue is paralysed, a subtle | flame has at once coursed beneath my skin, | with my eyes I see nothing, and my | ears are buzzing; | sweat pours down me, and trembling | seizes me all over, I am paler | than grass' (fr. 31, translated by G. Goold). Significantly Sappho continues with the words 'and I seem to be on the verge of dying'. The Sappho poem was also translated by Lucretius' contemporary Catullus (51): the Greek text is later quoted by the critic 'Longinus' in his treatise *On the Sublime* (perhaps first century AD), where he comments on Sappho's linking of mind and body and sees an element of fear as well as erotic passion in the original.

161–2 *mind and spirit | Are bodily*: cf. Epicurus, *Letter to Herodotus* 67.

179–80 *Most delicate . . . and formed | Of atoms most minute*: cf. Epicurus, *Letter to Herodotus* 63.

211 *As soon as death's calm quiet takes a man*: throughout this section Lucretius' exposition of the nature of the soul insinuates arguments also relevant to the later arguments for its mortality and assault on the fear of death.

231 *do not suppose that this nature is single*: for the parts of the soul, cf. Epicurus, *Letter to Herodotus* 63 (who, however, does not seem to distinguish between air and wind or breath: but a fourfold division similar to that of Lucretius is ascribed to Epicurus in fr. 315).

255 *through all the channels of the body*: the Epicureans (with many other theorists, including Empedocles and Asclepiades) believed in both visible and invisible passages or 'pores' within the body and leading to the outside. Matter both leaves and enters by these: see above 2. 1105 ff. Their role in death is also stressed in the treatise *On Death* by Lucretius' Epicurean contemporary Philodemus (4. 8. 18 ff., 37. 31 ff.).

260 *The poverty of our language*: cf. 1. 139 ff., 832 ff.

265 *a kind of single body*: the soul is a special mixture of its four components, in which their constituent atoms recombine to form a new compound substance, in which, however, the individual properties of the components may be more or less manifest.

273 *For deep deep down | This nature hidden lies*: the spatial terms here are not literal, but refer to the perceptibility of the properties of the fourth nameless component within the mixture.

288–9 *when anger | Boils*: 288–93 explain differences of mood, 294–306 differences of temperament between animal species, 307–22 the limits within which temperamental differences in human beings may be changed by belief. Lines 294–5, however, sound at first as if they are referring to humans. For the effect of the different constituents of the soul, cf. Epicurus fr. 314–15.

296 *Lions are most like this*: the three animals used as examples of temperament—lion, deer, and cow—are traditional: cf. e.g. Aristotle, *History of Animals* 488^{b}13 ff.

322 *lives . . . like those of gods*: cf. Epicurus, *Letter to Monoeceus* 135, 'you shall live as a god among men'. The happiness of the wise person is literally equivalent to that of the gods, since the only difference, that divine happiness is everlasting, is not significant for an Epicurean: see below on 5. 8.

325 *with common roots | They cling together*: theories which make the soul a part of the organism are open to the possibility of that part being separated and potentially living on after death: but for the Epicureans, sensation and consciousness are only possible when the soul is mingled with the body, and there is no possibility of its existing separately.

360 *mind looks out, as through a door*: this view is ascribed to Heraclitus (fr. A16, 'as it were through certain doors') and to the Aristotelian philosopher Strato (third century BC) and (?) the first-century BC sceptic Aenesidemus (Sextus Empiricus, *Against the Professors* 7. 350). Theaetetus holds that the soul rather than the sense organs perceive in Plato, *Theaetetus* 184b ff.: the Stoics held similar views, though allocating a greater role to the sense organs (cf. Cicero, *Tusculan Disputations* 1. 46).

371 *A view held by the great Democritus*: Democritus is said by Aristotle to have held that the soul was 'in the whole perceiving body' (Aristotle, *On the Soul* 409^{b}2), but this is the only testimony for the equality in number of soul and body atoms. The later Epicurean Diogenes of Oenoanda also argues that the number of soul-atoms is less than that of body-atoms, however (fr. 37).

396 *The mind more strongly holds the barriers | Of life*: Lucretius' language is similar to that of Epicurus, *Letter to Herodotus* 65, and especially Diogenes of Oenoanda fr. 37, though both of those passages deal rather with the relation of the soul as a whole to the body.

417–829 *Well now, that you may know that mind and spirit | Are born in living crea-
tures and are mortal* . . . : Lucretius now begins his great series of twenty-five
to thirty proofs for the mortality of the soul (the exact number depends on
whether some related points count as separate arguments). Although the
arguments are grouped into sections (e.g. arguments against survival
(417–669), arguments against pre-existence (670–783); proofs from non-
mortal afflictions (445–547)), the main effect is of a continuous stream of
arguments continually pressing the reader to admit mortality.

421 *apply both these names to one thing*: see above on 3. 136. Lucretius uses
whichever of the terms is most appropriate to the phenomenon being discussed.

440 *the body which is its vessel | As it were*: the vessel imagery suits opponents
(especially Platonists) for whom the body is just a temporary receptacle of
the soul (cf. Cicero, *Tusculan Disputations* 1. 52), but Lucretius perverts it to
his own ends with the image of the breaking of the pot. Epicurus similarly
talks of the body 'containing' the soul (*Letter to Herodotus* 64, 66); a fragment
close at several points to Lucretius of the late Platonist Iamblichus (second–third century AD, quoted in the *Eclogae* or 'Selections' of John Stobaeus
(fifth century AD), 1. 49. 43; Epicurus fr. 337) uses the image of air in a wine-
skin in summarizing atomist views.

453 *the intelligence | Limps, the tongue rambles, the mind gives way*: Lucretius imi-
tates the listing of symptoms in medical writing, cf. 6. 1145 ff., 1182 ff. Cf.
also 3. 169 ff., 478 ff.

456 *like smoke*: the disappearance of souls like smoke into the air goes back to
Homer (e.g. *Iliad* 23. 100, Patroclus' ghost leaving Achilles) and remains an
epic commonplace (cf. e.g. Virgil, *Aeneid* 5. 740), but was also used by
philosophers, including Epicurus (cf. Empedocles fr. B2, Epicurus fr. 337).

461 *we can see the mind to suffer also*: the argument was used by the eclectic Stoic
Panaetius (second century BC; see Cicero, *Tusculan Disputations* 1. 79).

468 *calling him back*: it was a Roman death-bed ritual to 'call back' the dying person by name (*conclamatio*, extended for several days after death).

478–81 *His legs give way* . . . : see above on 3. 169 ff., 453 ff. Epicurus discussed the
effects of wine in his lost *Symposium* (frr. 57–65).

487 *Now, take another case*: epilepsy, known in Greek as the 'sacred disease', was
much discussed by philosophers and medical writers: see especially the treatise ascribed to Hippocrates, *On the Sacred Disease* (fifth–fourth century BC).
Another Hippocratic work, *On Breaths* (fifth century BC), has several points
of contact with Lucretius' account.

509 *blown by strong winds*: Socrates in Plato, *Phaedo* 77d, had described as child-
ish the fear that the soul might be blown away by strong winds at death. Cf.
again Epicurus fr. 337.

519 *Its boundaries are fixed*: see above on 1. 670.

525 *a double refutation*: Lucretius uses a form of the figure known in Greek as the *dilemma* or 'double premiss' (cf. 3. 713 ff.), but his word for 'double' also suggests a two-bladed axe.

526 *how a man | Passes slowly away*: Lucretius polemically recalls Plato's hagiographical account of the death of Socrates in *Phaedo* 117e ff. but makes the process much more one of decay and decomposition, so that a clean escape of the soul from the body seems less plausible.

560 *Nor without body can the mind alone | Make living movements*: cf. Epicurus, *Letter to Herodotus* 66.

577 *body's clothing*: the clothing metaphor goes back to accounts of early Pythagoreanism (cf. Aristotle, *On the Soul* 407^{b}23) and was famously used by Socrates in Plato's *Phaedo* (87d).

583 *like smoke*: see above on 456, but here linked to the notion of death as like the burning of a house.

614 *like a snake*: the snake which sloughs off old age with its old skin was a common symbol for rejuvenation (perhaps already in Hesiod (seventh century BC), *Catalogue of Women* fr. 204. 138): Lucretius will use the snake model for his own very different purposes later in 657 ff.

629 *Painters and poets*: especially Polygnotus (fifth century BC) in a famous painting at Delphi (Pausanias (second century AD), 10. 28) and Homer with Odysseus' visit to the underworld in *Odyssey* 11.

632 *tongue*: cf. Cicero, *Tusculan Disputations* 1. 37.

642 *chariots bearing scythes*: famously used by Antiochus III at the battle of Magnesia (189 BC: cf. Livy 37. 41) and possibly described in Ennius' *Annals* (frr. 483–4, recalled in Lucretius 3. 654–6). Cf. 5. 1301 (which may also specifically suggest the battle of Magnesia).

646 *the blow's too sudden*: with the delay for the transmission of sensation to the mind, compare the reverse process in 2. 261 ff.

673 *Why can we not remember time that's past*: a problem recognized but not fully answered by Plato (cf. *Phaedo* 72e) and others, for whom 'Our birth is but a sleep and a forgetting' (Wordsworth, 'Ode. Intimations of Immortality', v: cf. Aristotle, *On the Soul* 430^{a}23 ff.).

679–80 *if the body is complete | Before the quickened mind can enter it*: cf. Ennius, *Annals* frr. 8–10 on birds' eggs, 'the soul itself by divine power comes later to the chicks'.

684 *a quiet hole*: the Platonic imagery of the body as a cage or prison is suggested: cf. Plato, *Phaedo* 82e.

696 *safe and unharmed*: the language is Platonic, see *Phaedrus* 250c1 ff.

707 *the channels of the body*: see above on 3. 255.

713 *here's another question*: another use of the figure of *dilemma*: see above on 3. 525.

719 *worms*: cf. 2. 871 ff.

741 *lions*: cf. 3. 269 ff.

749 *the behaviour | Of animals would be all mixed up*: the counterfactual confusion of nature (cf. e.g. 1. 161 ff.) recalls the poetic commonplace known as the *adunaton* or 'impossibility', where the impossibility of something happening is equated with a series of inversions of normal life: see e.g. Theocritus (third century BC), *Idylls* 1. 132 ff.

753 *Reason, in men | No more*: Aristotle (*On the Soul* 407ᵇ20, 414ᵃ22) particularly objected to interchange between human and animal species in metempsychosis, and it was an early target of ridicule (Xenophanes (sixth century BC) fr. B7).

756 *For that which changes is | Dissolved*: cf. above on 1. 670.

784 *A tree can't grow in the sky*: the 'impossibilities' (see above on 749) are the sort of natural perversion classified in Roman religion as omens or portents (cf. Livy 42. 2. 5, Juvenal 13. 65).

806–18 *Few things there are that last eternally . . .* : 806–18 are repeated at 5. 351–63.

820 *fortified against all forms of death . . .* : the reference is probably to the form of immortality enjoyed by the Epicurean gods in the spaces between the worlds, though the details are much disputed (cf. 5. 146, Cicero, *On the Nature of the Gods* 1. 18, Epicurus, *Letter to Menoeceus* 124, Philodemus, *On the Gods* 3. frr. 32a, 41, 77, Origen (second–third century AD), *Against Celsus* 4. 14).

829 *lethargy's black waters cover it*: the section of arguments for the mortality of the soul, like the book as a whole, ends gloomily: see above on 2. 1173 ff. But the message of 830 ff. is that this need not in any way impede our happiness.

830 *death nothing is to us*: the famous Epicurean catchphrase, from the second of the *Master Sayings*: 'death is nothing to us, because what has been dissolved is without sensation, and what is without sensation is nothing to us.' The final section of the book draws extensively on attacks on the fear of death from many non-Epicurean sources, especially those within the traditions of consolation and so-called 'diatribe' or practical philosophical exhortation. See B. P. Wallach, *Lucretius and the Diatribe against the Fear of Death* (Leiden, 1976), with many parallels.

833 *when the Phoenicians | Were coming in upon us*: Lucretius uses a version of the so-called 'symmetry' argument from our lack of concern for events before our birth. Our state before birth is the same as that after death: non-existence. If we are unconcerned about events which took place when we

were in the former state, we should also be unconcerned about the latter. This was a commonplace (cf. e.g. Euripides (fifth century BC), *Trojan Women* 636, the *Axiochus* (wrongly ascribed to Plato and of uncertain date) 365d, Bion (fourth–third century BC) fr. 67, Cicero, *Tusculan Disputations* I. 90): Lucretius uses the Roman example of the Second Punic War (218–201 BC), alluding to the treatment in Ennius' *Annals* (frr. 309–10). We know of the terrors of that war only through the vicarious experience of literature: like the future after our death, they are really 'nothing to us'.

848–9 *if time should after death | Collect our matter and bring it back*: cf. Epicurus fr. 283a, 307. The Stoics believed in the infinite repetition of a fixed sequence of events, the Epicureans that in infinite time individual local states of the universe would be infinitely repeated, but in no fixed sequence.

870 *when you see a man resent his fate*: philosophers united in rejecting the concern for the fate of the body after death common in literature and life (cf. e.g. *Axiochus* 365e ff., Bion fr. 70); the Stoic Chrysippus is said to have made a collection of burial practices amongst different nations (Cicero, *Tusculan Disputations* I. 108). Epicurus said that the wise person will not take thought of burial (Diogenes Laertius, *Lives of the Philosophers* 10. 118), and the argument is pursued at length in Philodemus' *On Death* (4. 31 ff.; cf. also Diogenes of Oenoanda fr. 73).

881–2 *he doesn't separate | Himself from the body lying there*: Lucretius alludes to a celebrated tragedy of the Roman dramatist Pacuvius (first century BC), the *Iliona*, in which the ghost of Deiphilus complained to his mother about his burial (frr. 197 ff., cf. Cicero, *Tusculan Disputations* I. 106). Similar examples from Greek tragedy are frequent (cf. e.g. the Cynic Teles (third century BC) 30. 1 ff.).

893 *Be crushed under a weight of earth*: cf. the formula on Roman tombs, 'let the earth be light for you'.

912 *Men lie at table*: 912–18 have been transposed. Lucretius' picture ironically reflects popular views of the Epicurean life (cf. e.g. the *Copa* or *Innkeeper* ascribed to Virgil 29 ff., Horace, *Odes* I. 11, Petronius, *Satyricon* 34; Cicero, *On Ends* 5. 3).

894–6 *No longer now a happy home will greet you . . .* : famously translated by Thomas Gray in the *Elegy Written in a Country Churchyard* as 'For them no more the blazing hearth shall burn, | Or busy housewife ply her evening care: | No children run to lisp their sire's return, | Or climb his knees the envied kiss to share'. Lucretius' lines echo laments on tombs but are more satirical, and the simultaneous presence of pathos and sarcasm has a didactic point: the reader needs to feel the pull of conventional emotion to be able fully to reject it. There is more straightforward mockery in the treatise *On Grief* by Lucian (second century AD), 13–14, 16.

904 *the sleep of death*: a commonplace of consolation, found often on tombstones, but here taken more seriously in Epicurean terms (920 ff.).

931–2 *suppose that nature suddenly* | *. . . upbraided one of us*: Lucretius uses the figure of thought known as *prosopopoeia* or personification. Figures with a claim on the emotions such as one's native country were commonly summoned up by speakers (e.g. Cicero, *Against Catiline* 1. 18, Demetrius (date uncertain), *On Style* 265: Plato in the *Crito*, 50a, imagined Socrates addressed by the laws of Athens). Lucretius' use of the more general (and Epicurean) figure of Nature especially recalls a celebrated personification of poverty by the Cynic Bion (fr. 17), but with much greater force.

936 *through a broken jar*: an allusion to the story of the Danaids or water-carriers in Hades (cf. 3. 1003 ff.), especially as interpreted by Plato in *Gorgias* 493a–d. Cf. also 6. 20 ff.

938 *dined* | *Full well on life*: the image of life as a banquet is common: cf. e.g. Epicurus fr. 499, Bion fr. 68, Cicero, *Tusculan Disputations* 5. 118.

945 *everything's the same*: a pointed application of the physical principle outlined at 2. 294 ff., that there is no real change in the universe.

966 *black Tartarus*: cf. the description of Tartarus in *Iliad* 8. 13 ff., 'where the deepest pit lies under the earth'.

967 *Matter is needed*: cf. 1. 262 ff.

971 *life none have in freehold, all as tenants*: the image of life as a loan is common, both in literary tradition (cf. e.g. Euripides, *Suppliant Women* 534, *Axiochus* 367b, Bion fr. 68, Cicero, *Tusculan Disputations* 1. 93, the *Consolation to Apollonius* ascribed to Plutarch 116a ff.) and on tombstones.

975 *the mirror nature holds for us*: see above on the 'symmetry' argument (833 ff.), but here the paragraph leads into the absence of mythological terrors in the afterlife.

978–1023 *all those things . . . which fables tell*: attacks on belief in the terrors of the underworld are called an 'Epicurean refrain' by Seneca (*Letters to Lucilius* 24. 18): cf. especially Diogenes of Oenoanda fr. 73, 'I have no fear on account of the Tityoses and Tantaluses whom you describe in Hades'. Tityos (Tityrus), Tantalus, and Sisyphus are the three canonical sinners from the time of Homer (*Odyssey* 11. 576–600) on: cf. especially Plato, *Gorgias* 525d ff. (where the late commentator Olympiodorus (sixth century AD) offers an allegorical interpretation similar in part to that of Lucretius). Lucretius' account is not exactly allegorical: the punishments exist 'for us in this our life'.

980 *Tantalus*: two versions of Tantalus' punishment (usually for serving up his son Pelops to the gods) were current: either he was perpetually thirsty and hungry but 'tantalized' by water and fruit about him, or as here he was threatened by a hanging rock (cf. Pindar (sixth–fifth century BC), *Olympian*

1. 57, *Isthmian* 8. 10). The latter punishment suits Lucretius' imagery for the fear of the gods (cf. 1. 62 ff.).

984 *Tityos*: Tityos was a son of earth punished for trying to rape the goddess Leto.

992 *lying in love*: cf. the picture in 4. 1177 ff. of the archetypal Roman unhappy lover.

995 *Sisyphus*: Sisyphus was punished for trying to cheat death (cf. Homer, *Odyssey* 11. 593 ff.).

996 *the Lictor's rods and axes*: consuls and praetors were attended by lictors carrying axes and rods (the *fasces* or bundles appropriated by Mussolini for his Fascists).

1001 *the plain below*: significantly, Roman elections took place on the 'Plain of Mars' (Campus Martius).

1003 *The Danaids*: The Danaids (daughters of Danaus) were punished for killing their husbands on their wedding night: it is not known how far the identification of them with the mythical water-carriers in Hades (first explicit in *Axiochus* 371e) goes back. Compare Plato's use of the image of the 'leaky jar' in *Gorgias* 493a–d (see above 936).

1010 *Cerberus*: the monstrous dog who guarded the entrance to Hades.

1016 *dread hurling from the rock*: the Tarpeian Rock on the Capitol, from which murderers and traitors were flung.

1025 *good Ancus*: Ancus Marcius, the fourth king of Rome. The line is a quotation from Ennius, *Annals* 137.

1026 *A better man than you*: an echo of Homer, *Iliad* 21. 109, 'Patroclus also died, a man much better than you' (Achilles to the suppliant Lycaon).

1027 *many kings and powers*: lists of the illustrious dead, as later in the *ubi sunt* or 'where are now . . . ?' commonplace of medieval poetry (e.g. Dunbar, 'I that in heill was . . . ', Villon, *Ballade des Dames du Temps Jadis*), are frequent in diatribe and consolation: cf. e.g. the *Consolation to Apollonius* ascribed to Plutarch 100d, Marcus Aurelius (second century AD) 3. 3, 6. 7.

1029 *he who laid a highway through the sea*: the Persian king Xerxes, who bridged the Hellespont in his unsuccessful attack on Greece during the Persian Wars (480 BC: cf. Herodotus (fifth century BC) 7. 35 ff.). He was later murdered in 465 BC.

1034 *Great Scipio*: more than one Scipio was great and terrified Carthage: the reference could be to either Scipio Africanus the elder, who defeated Hannibal at the battle of Zama, not far from Carthage, in 202 BC, or Scipio Aemilianus Africanus the younger, who razed Carthage to the ground in 146 BC.

the thunderbolt of war: probably echoing a phrase of Ennius, playing on the etymology of the name Scipio, as if from the Greek *skeptos*, a thunderbolt: cf. Cicero, *For Balbus* 34.

1041 *Offered his head right willingly to death*: cf. Diogenes Laertius (third century AD), *Lives of the Philosophers* 9. 43.

1042 *Epicurus himself*: the only time Epicurus is named in the poem.

1045 *will you doubt and feel aggrieved to die*: again echoing Achilles' words to Lycaon in the *Iliad* 21 106 (see above 1026).

1060 *A man leaves his great house*: the vignette from everyday life is in the style of Roman satire: see Introduction.

1071 *Leave everything*: the exhortation to abandon trivial concerns and concentrate on the important matters in life is a commonplace of the philosophical 'protreptic' or conversion discourse: cf. e.g. Aristotle, *Protreptic* fr. 52, Horace, *Epistles* 1. 3. 28 ff. The images offered of the unphilosophical life all belong to the first, diagnostic, stage of philosophic conversion: in a sense, the second half of *On the Nature of the Universe* provides the cure for the gloomy prognosis offered at the end of Book 3.

1077 *lust of life*: philosophers frequently criticized excessive fondness for life: cf. e.g. Philodemus, *On Death* 4. 39. 6, Seneca, *Consolation to Polybius* 10. 5.

Book Four

1–25 *A pathless country . . .* : the second half of *On the Nature of the Universe* begins with a repetition of 1. 926–50, with some small changes. In their new position, the lines function as a 'proem in the middle', introducing the second half of the poem: similar central prologues are found in a number of other works (e.g. Virgil, *Eclogues*, *Georgics*, *Aeneid*). For the structure, see Introduction.

25 *Its value and its usefulness to men*: slightly altered from Book 1, with 'usefulness' replacing a concern with the shape of things, perhaps signalling a move in the second half of the poem more towards the applications of the first principles.

26 *And since I have shown . . .* : 26–215 outline the Epicurean theory of 'images' (Latin *simulacra*, Greek *eidola*), thin films of atoms continually cast off from bodies and responsible for perception. 216–721 then deal with the various senses (216–521 sight, with a long section on optical illusions and related phenomena (324–521), 522–614 hearing, 615–72 taste, and 673–705 smell, with 706–21 as a general conclusion and transition to the following section: see below) and 722–822 with thought. 823–57 then argue against the notion that the sense organs were created to perform their functions. 858–906 explain the role of images in hunger and thirst (858–77) and locomotion (878–906). 907 ff. then expound the nature of sleep (907–61) leading to the discussion of dreams (962–1057) and the final attack on the delusions of love (1058–1287). Throughout, the focus is on mental process, and the role of images within it.

35 *strange shapes and phantoms of the dead*: Lucretius takes pains to relate the subject matter of Book 4 to that of the preceding book: cf. 1. 132 ff.

41 *I say therefore*: as the manuscript text stands, we seem to have more than one version of the summary of the opening section of Book 4. Some believe we have traces of alternative beginnings for the book, one dating from a time when Book 4 followed on directly from Book 2, others that the text has been corrupted in transmission. The translation excises lines 45–50, and transposes line 44 after 53. Epicurus deals with the basic theory of images in *Letter to Herodotus* 46: cf. also frr. 317, 320. They were the principal subject of Book 2 of his major work *On Nature*.

76 *Spread over a great theatre*: temporary wooden theatres had been common at Rome from early days, and a particularly elaborate one had been erected in 58 BC by M. Aemilius Scaurus when aedile (Pliny (first century BC), *Natural Histories* 36. 114), but the first readers of *On the Nature of the Universe* would have been able to experience Rome's first stone theatre, built by Pompey in 55 BC. The sun awnings were spread from large masts, holes for which can still be seen in extant Roman theatres, and there was considerable competition amongst politicians to provide the most impressive arrangements (cf. Pliny, *Natural Histories* 19. 23).

98 *In mirrors*: the phenomena of reflection were of constant interest to ancient scientists, mathematicians, and philosophers: cf. 150 ff., 269 ff. below, and especially Diogenes of Oenoanda fr. 9. 1. 4–12.

126 There are clearly some lines missing at this point in the manuscripts, although it is uncertain how many, and what they dealt with.

131 *of their own accord | Come into being*: the mingling of images in the air to produce new forms (cf. Epicurus, *Letter to Herodotus* 46, 48) explains how we can think of non-existent objects such as Centaurs, as Lucretius later explains (724 ff.). The figures seen in clouds are a similar chance phenomenon: Lucretius also uses the comparison to suggest the airy unreality of mythological stories such as the battle of giants and gods.

143 *how easily and swiftly | These images arise*: cf. Epicurus, *Letter to Herodotus* 48.

173 *black face of fear*: cf. 1. 64 ff. 170–3 are repeated at 6. 251–4.

176 *how fast these images move*: again, cf. *Letter to Herodotus* 48.

181 *Better the swan's brief song*: Lucretius translates part of an epigram by the Hellenistic poet Antipater of Sidon (second century BC: *Greek Anthology* 7. 7. 13), drawing again on the imagery of small-scale precision associated with the aesthetics of the poet Callimachus (see above on 1. 926—the lines repeated at the beginning of this book).

217 *the bodies which strike our eyes*: there may be further textual disruption at this point, with more lines lost.

230 *a shape that is handled in the dark*: there was considerable debate in antiquity about the notion of what Aristotle called the 'common sensibles', things like shape perceived by more than one sense: cf. e.g. Aristotle, *On the Soul* 418ᵃ6 ff., 425ᵃ15 ff.

297 *a mask | Of plaster*: theatrical masks were made of linen and plaster.

332 *People with jaundice see everything yellow*: the effect of disease on perception was one of the arguments used by sceptics against the reliability of the senses (cf. Sextus Empiricus (second century AD), *Outlines of Pyrrhonism* I. 101, the fourth 'trope' of the sceptic Aenesidemus (first century BC): see below on 469). Lucretius' focus in this section on miscellaneous problems of vision is increasingly on the problems raised by sceptical attacks.

338 *black air of darkness*: the Epicurean conception of darkness as a sort of thick, black air that is cleaned out by light is relevant to Lucretius' extensive imagery of light and dark.

353 *square towers of a city*: a famous Epicurean example, much discussed (cf. e.g. Diogenes or Oenoanda fr. 69, Petronius (first century AD) fr. 29, Sextus Empiricus, *Against the Professors* 7. 208, Plutarch (first–second century AD), *Against Colotes* 25 1121a).

386 *Do not then blame the eyes for this fault of the mind*: the Epicureans famously held that 'all sensations were true' (fr. 247): the precise sense of this is disputed, but they made a clear distinction between the presentation offered by the senses and our judgement of the presentation. Error was always in 'the addition of opinion' (*Letter to Herodotus* 50, cf. below 462 ff.): we should 'wait' until we can get a 'clear' perception before dogmatizing about the nature of an object (cf. *Master Sayings* 24).

387 *A ship we sail in moves*: a stock example of optical illusion, cf. Cicero, *Academica* 2. 81, *On Ends* 2. 58. There are parallels in sceptical writings to many of Lucretius' examples here: see J. Annas and J. Barnes, *The Modes of Scepticism* (Cambridge, 1985).

453 *sleep*: significantly, Lucretius' last example of illusion deals with dreaming, a major concern of Book 4.

465 *notions of the mind | Which we ourselves bring to them*: translating Epicurus, *Letter to Herodotus* 50; see above on 386.

469 *if someone thinks | That nothing is known*: although sceptical arguments appear in earlier philosophers such as Protagoras (fifth century BC) and Democritus (who was criticized on these grounds by Epicureans), the first thoroughgoing sceptic was Pyrrho (fourth–third century BC). Arcesilaus (fourth–third century BC), the fourth head of the Platonic Academy, turned it towards scepticism: in the first century BC it returned to holding positive doctrines, while Aenesidemus revived Pyrrhonism. Our major source of sceptic doctrine is the writings of the later sceptic Sextus Empiricus (second

century AD). Not all sceptics accepted that nothing could be known: some suspended judgement even about that proposition. Epicurean arguments against scepticism are criticized especially in Plutarch's treatise *Against Colotes* (Colotes (third–fourth century BC) was a disciple of Epicurus who wrote a work *That it is not possible even to live according to the doctrines of the other philosophers*).

472 ff. *Who has put his head where his feet ought to be*: Lucretius actualizes Greek terms for self-refuting argument such as *peritrope* or 'turning upside-down' (cf. Epicurus fr. 34. 28. 1 ff. Arrighetti).

508 *Life itself also would at once collapse*: the 'inactivity' argument that sceptics cannot live their scepticism, used for example by Colotes (see above on 469 ff.: cf. e.g. Cicero, *Academica* 2. 37 ff.).

513 *if the ruler is crooked*: Lucretius alludes to the Greek term *kanon*, literally a straight-edged rule but used for the criterion of truth by Epicurus (a lost work of whom was called *Kanon*) and other philosophers. Lucretius elaborates the metaphor into one of a building being constructed on secure foundations, which brings it into contact with a broader metaphorical field within *On the Nature of the Universe*: Epicurean security is contrasted with disorder and destruction.

524 *every sound and voice is heard*: cf. Epicurus, *Letter to Herodotus* 52–3, frr. 321–3.

529 *Roughens the windpipe*: Lucretius plays on the Greek technical term for the windpipe, *tracheia arteria* (*trachea* in modern anatomical Latin): *tracheia* means 'rough' in Greek.

537 *a speech that lasts from the first gleam of dawn*: the reference is especially to political speeches in the Senate, where sessions lasted from dawn to dusk and there was no time limit under the Republic.

564 *a cryer*: 'cryers' (*praecones*) were used on several different occasions at Rome, but the language here suggests especially the opening of a public meeting (*comitia*).

580 *Nymphs and goat-footed satyrs*: the description follows a familiar Lucretian pattern, with a poetic evocation of the sort of rural piety often associated with early humanity (cf. 5. 1379 ff.) capped by the cynical observation of 594 'mankind | Is greedy aye for things that please the ear' (i.e. eager to have an audience).

615 *taste*: Epicurus does not deal with taste in the corresponding section of the *Letter to Herodotus*, since (like touch) it is not accomplished through images. Lucretius, however, includes it, since it provided sceptics with a series of important arguments against the veracity of the senses (cf. Sextus Empiricus, *Outlines of Pyrrhonism* 1. 52–8, 101 etc.; Plutarch, *Against Colotes* 1109b ff.).

638 *the snake*: cf. Aristotle, *History of Animals* 607ª29 ff., Pliny, *Natural Histories* 7. 2. 15.

672 *A thing which I have explained to you before*: cf. 2. 398 ff., 3. 191 ff.

673 *smell*: cf. Epicurus, *Letter to Herodotus* 53.

683 *that saved Rome's citadel*: the sacred geese on the Capitol were said to have revealed a night attack by Gauls in 387 BC (cf. Livy 5. 47).

706 *Nor yet is this confined to smells and tastes*: i.e. variability between different perceivers, as in 633 ff. (taste) and 677 ff. (smell).

712 *Before him ravening lions cannot stand*: cf. Sextus Empiricus, *Outlines of Pyrrhonism* 1. 58. Democritus was one of those who were said (perhaps falsely) to have described the supposed phenomenon.

722 *what things move the mind*: thought for the Epicureans was explained in almost exactly the same way as perception (cf. Epicurus fr. 317): the mind is continuously bombarded by images flying around, though it 'sees' only those on which it chooses to focus. Cf. Epicurus, *Letter to Herodotus* 49–51, Diogenes of Oenoanda frr. 9–10.

726 *meet in the air*: cf. 131 ff. above.

740 *no such animal did ever exist*: cf. 5. 878 ff.

746 *As I showed before*: in 726, unless the reference is back to 131 ff.

757 *When sleep has laid out the limbs*: cf. Diogenes of Oenoanda fr. 9.

773 *The former seems to have changed its attitude*: as has often been noted, Lucretius anticipates the principle of cinematography.

795 *one instant of time that we perceive*: the Epicureans believed in minimal units of time and space (see above on 1. 601–2), far below the level of perception. In each perceptible time-unit, therefore, there are countless numbers of minimal time-units that can be apprehended only by reason. Cf. Epicurus, *Letter to Herodotus* 47.

816 *from small signs we draw great inferences*: the process of 'addition of opinion' to sensory or mental perception: see above on 4. 386.

825–6 *Do not suppose that the clear light of the eyes | Was made that we might see*: 'teleological' explanation of parts of the body in terms of their purpose or end (in Greek *telos*) is found in Greek thought from early on: it is parodied in Aristophanes' comedy *Women at the Thesmophoria* (411 BC: 14–18), and Xenophon puts a striking example into the mouth of Socrates in his *Memorabilia* (1. 4. 5). Plato also has a notable example in the *Timaeus* (44d ff.). This sort of explanation was associated with Aristotle and his notion of 'final cause' (see especially the treatise *On Parts of Animals*) but found also amongst Stoics, particularly in connection with the notion of divine providence, and enthusiastically taken up by Christian writers, for whom the body of man was a wonder of divine creation (cf. e.g. Cicero, *On the Nature of the Gods* 2. 133 ff., Nemesius (*c*.400 AD), *On the Nature of Man*). Even today, apparently teleological statements are often used as shorthand for the process of natural selection or random mutation in evolution.

848 *to give the wearied body rest*: Lucretius anticipates the account of human development to be given in Book 5, and insinuates a moral point: in the beginning man got by without soft beds (cf. 2. 29 ff.).

859 *Every animal seeks food*: the emphasis is on the desire for food as a mental process with a bodily explanation.

877–8 *how it is that we walk* | *... when we wish*: Lucretius explains here not how we come to wish to walk (cf. 2. 251 ff.), but how the wish is transformed into action.

883 *Hence follows will*: images are all the while striking the mind, but until we decide to concentrate on a particular set they are not present to consciousness. The interpretation of this passage is controversial, but the act of will seems to be identified with his act of concentration, which sets in train the process of movement.

907 *sleep*: sleep is a puzzling phenomenon, much discussed by ancient (and modern) scientists and philosophers: see especially the treatise *On Sleep and Waking* included in the so-called 'Parva Naturalia' of Aristotle (453^b ff.). For the Epicurean view, compare the comment preserved in *Letter to Herodotus* 66 (fr. 311), and fr. 325, with Diogenes of Oenoanda fr. 9.

909 *verses sweet though few*: see above 180 ff.

962–3 *those pursuits which most we love to follow*: the connection between the manifest content of dreams and preceding waking action was a commonplace of ancient as of modern thought, even when they were thought also to foretell the future (cf. e.g. Aristotle, *On Prophecy in Sleep* 463^a, Accius (second–first century BC), *Brutus* frr. 29–31, Fronto (second century AD), *On the Holidays at Alsium* 3. 13). Belief in divination through dreams was widespread (cf. e.g. the *Dream Book* of Artemidorus, second century AD) and provided with a theoretical underpinning by Stoic theories of the universal 'sympathy' of the universe (cf. especially Cicero's dialogue *On Divination*). Epicureans were naturally opposed (cf. Epicurus frr. 326–8, Diogenes of Oenoanda frr. 9–10, Petronius fr. 30), though they did believe that dreamers could see visions of the gods (5. 1169 ff.).

1029 *Babylonian coverlets*: cf. 1123.

1030–1 *when the seed first penetrates* | *The racing tides of youth*: the production of semen in adult males and at puberty was another phenomenon of considerable interest to ancient doctors and philosophers. Epicurus believed that seed was produced by both men and women, and that its substance came from the whole body: cf. 'Aetius' 5. 3–5 (Epicurus frr. 329–30, following on from the discussion of dreams as in Epicurus fr. 311).

1053–4 *Whether a boy . . . | Or a woman*: the addressee of the poem remains male: as normal in antiquity, it is taken for granted that male sexual desire may be for either a younger male or a female.

1056 *the fluid*: at several points in this passage Lucretius plays on the resemblance between the Latin words *umor* 'fluid' and *amor* 'love'.

1058 *the name of love*: probably a play on the Latin word for desire ('yearning' in 1057) *cupido*, personified as Cupid, the companion of Venus. As in the opening lines of the poem, Venus is equated with pleasure ('bliss' in 1057): sex is opposed to love (cf. 1073 ff.). The Epicureans classified the desire for sex as a desire for sensual pleasure that was natural but not necessary: sexual pleasure was real in that it consisted in 'variation' of the sense organ of touch, and hence the desire for it could be satisfied, but it was not necessary for human life in the way that food, drink, and heat were. Love, on the other hand, was seen as a desire that was neither natural nor necessary: it was classified as a fetishistic desire for a particular type of sex (with a particular person) and thus as unsatisfiable, because lovers cannot attain the union they desire and therefore there can be no physical reality corresponding to the mental passion. We need food in general, it is natural to like nice-tasting food, but it is irrational and debilitating to be able to eat only a particular brand of chocolate; similarly, to insist on sex with a particular person only was wrong for the Epicureans (cf. frr. 456, 483, and see Introduction). The second poem in Horace's first book of *Satires* expands on the theme; later Propertius and the Roman love-elegists were masochistically to embrace the servility and degradation of love that Lucretius attacks. Throughout the passage Lucretius draws on and perverts the familiar imagery of Graeco-Roman love-poetry, especially epigram.

1061 *images*: the theory of *simulacra* (see above on 4. 26 ff.) is used throughout the account of love: cf. especially 1095 ff.

1075 *a purer pleasure*: the language is Epicurean: cf. *Master Sayings* 12. Epicureans can concentrate on the pleasure of the moment during sex because they are not distracted by insatiable desires for possession of the unattainable.

1122 *Obeying another's whim*: the 'slavery of love' later celebrated by Propertius and the other love elegists (though Lucretius does not explicitly use the metaphor).

1123 *Wealth vanishes*: young men in Roman comedy are frequently seen squandering their family's wealth on women, as was the Caelius defended by Cicero in his speech *Pro Caelio* (56 BC).

Babylonian coverlets: recalling 1029, the coverlets drenched with urine by the boys. 'Babylonians' were expensive textiles (cf. Pliny, *Natural Histories* 8 196): elaborately coloured or embroidered cloth as the embodiment of luxury is an unfamiliar idea in the modern world, but it remained a potent symbol of wealth down to the development of aniline dyes. (The text may be corrupt here, and the reference in fact to Babylonian perfume.)

1125 *slippers from Sicyon*: an expensive type of women's shoes, also mocked by the satirist Lucilius (second century BC, fr. 1161).

1130 *A gown of silk from Elis or from Ceos*: both geographical epithets are textually uncertain, but the reference is clearly to expensive clothing. Elis is a region of mainland Greece (north-west Peloponnese), Ceos an island in the Cyclades. The most famous silk came from the suspiciously similar sound-ing island of Cos in the Sporades.

1153–4 *attributing to them | Virtues with which in truth they are not endowed*: a famous list of 'hypocorisms' or euphemistic terms of endearment. Plato has a similar list in *Republic* 5. 474d (of boys), and the hellenistic 'love manual' ascribed to Philaenis seems to have begun with advising the lover to use them (*Oxyrrynchus Papyri* 2891, cf. Ovid, *Art of Love* 2. 657 ff. (imitating Lucretius), reversed in *Remedies for Love* 323 ff.). Theocritus (third century BC), *Idyll* 10. 24 ff. is another model: Lucretius is also imitated by Horace (*Satires* 1. 3. 38 ff., fathers of their children) and Juvenal 8. 30 ff. Sextus Empiricus, *Outlines of Pyrrhonism* 1. 108, gives the deception of men about their mistresses' beauty as an example of the fourth sceptical trope (cf. Plato, *Phaedrus* 233b). Most of Lucretius' terms are Greek words current in Rome, and some are the sort of terms used as professional names by prostitutes: for the use of Greek by lovers, cf. Martial (first century AD) 10. 68. 5 ff., Juvenal (second century AD) 6. 187 ff.

1168 *Ceres | Suckling Iacchus*: gods of the Eleusinian mysteries (Ceres = Demeter: Iacchus was sometimes identified with Dionysus/Bacchus). Lucretius clearly alludes to an artistic representation, though there is no obvious type extant.

1175 *She fumigates herself*: the reference is disputed, and possibly ambiguous: it may be to literal medical 'fumigations' for gynaecological complaints (cf. e.g. Celsus (first century AD), *On Medicine* 4. 27. 1), or to foul-smelling cosmetics (Ovid, *Art of Love* 3. 213, *Remedies for Love* 355 ff., Lucian, *Loves* 39), but it is phrased to suggest more widely traditional male disgust at 'female smells in rooms' (T. S. Eliot, 'The Lovesong of Alfred J. Prufrock').

1177 *The lover, shut out*: the 'excluded lover' was a familiar figure in Roman com-edy and especially love-elegy.

1183 *placing her above all mortal women*: again, love poets typically see their beloveds as 'divine': cf. e.g. Catullus 68. 70.

1192 *Not always is a woman feigning love*: female sexual pleasure seems to have been connected by the Epicureans with the notion of female ejaculation (see above on 1030–1 and cf. Aristotle, *Generation of Animals* 727^{b}33 ff.).

1211 *From the mother's seed then children like the mother | Are born*: from antiquity down to the experiments of Mendel (published 1866, but little noticed until the beginning of the twentieth century) there was much speculation about the workings and mechanism of genetic inheritance, and in particular the respective contributions of male and female (cf. the summaries of views in 'Aetius' 5. 3 ff.). For Aristotle (*Generation of Animals* 726ᵃ28 ff.) the female contributed matter, the male form, but he also used the principle of 'prevalence' (*epikrateia*) of one influence over another (767ᵇ20 ff.). The Epicureans believed that both parties provided seed, and both had an influence on the nature of the child: the seed derived from the whole body of each parent ('pangenesis', a view still held by Darwin in *On the Origin of Species* (1859)), and the characteristics fought it out at the time of conception.

1233 *And it is not the power of gods that blocks | The generating seed in any man*: an emphatic anti-theological motivation for a traditional topic, again much discussed by both doctors (e.g. the third book of the Hippocratic *Gynaecia*, fifth–fourth century BC) and philosophers (e.g. Aristotle, *Generation of Animals* 746ᵇ12 ff.). Offerings for infertility were a common form of votive dedication in temples.

1268 *Wives have no need at all of wanton movements*: a famously depressing view into Roman marital life; note, however, the context of a concern with fertility, and contrast 1192 ff. on female sexual pleasure.

1277 *And not from power divine or Venus' shafts | It sometimes happens that a wench is loved*: so Diogenes Laertius, *Lives of the Philosophers* 10. 118, remarks that, according to Epicurus, 'love is not sent from god' (contrast e.g. Plato, *Phaedrus* 242d, *Symposium* 206c).

1281 *gentle pleasing ways*: an allusion to the promise made by a Roman bride to be complaisant to her husband.

1286 *a drop of water | By constant dripping wears away a stone*: cf. the end of Book 2, with a similar emphasis on gradual decay.

Book Five

4 *the man who left us such great treasures*: Epicurus. He is named only at 3. 1042. Cf. 6. 5 ff.

8 *He was a god, a god indeed*: the Epicureans liked to shock by playing with the exaggerated language of praise used for rulers and other supposed benefactors (which sometimes passed over into real cult); so, for instance, the young Epicurean Colotes is said to have prostrated himself before Epicurus (Plutarch, *Against Colotes* 1117b–c). This was justified for them by the magnitude of Epicurus' blessings for mankind, but it was also true that the Epicurean wise person was literally as happy as the gods (see above on 3.

322). Virgil imitates the line in *Eclogue* 1. 6 referring to the young Octavian (the future Augustus).

13 *and earned the name divine*: an influential 'euhemerist' theory, put forward first by Prodicus (fifth century BC) and later by Hecataeus of Abdera and most famously Euhemerus of Messene (both fourth–third century BC), held that the gods were originally human beings deified for their achievements. Prodicus used the examples of Dionysus (Bacchus) and Demeter (Ceres) as here (fr. B5, cf. Euripides, *Bacchants* 274 ff.): Euhemerus was translated into Latin by Ennius (third–second century BC).

20 *through mighty nations spread*: gods, culture heroes, and great conquerors like Alexander all spread their gifts by global travel (cf. Diodorus Siculus (first century BC), *Library of History* 6. 1 ff.), but they must yield place to the spread of Epicureanism through the master's words.

22 *Hercules*: 'paradoxical' criticism of generally accepted heroes or praise of bad things or people was an established rhetorical exercise, and Lucretius' assault on Hercules is paralleled in a speech of Euripides, *Heracles* (c.414 BC, 148 ff.) which shares some details. Hercules was allegorized as an ideal model by Stoics and Cynics (cf. e.g. Heraclitus 'the Allegorizer' (perhaps first century AD) 33, Cicero, *On Ends* 2. 118). And he is a particularly pointed target here as a man who became a god through his labours (cf. Theocritus (third century BC), *Idylls* 17, 13 ff., Cicero, *Tusculan Disputations* 1. 28). In general, cf. G. K. Galinsky, *The Hercules Theme* (Oxford, 1972).

24–7 *Nemean lion . . . Arcadian boar* | *. . . Cretan bull . . . Lerna's pest* | *The Hydra*: Lucretius mentions eight of the canonical twelve labours of Hercules (first attested in the sculptures of the temple of Zeus at Olympia, c.460 BC), concentrating on those that involve the slaying or capture of wild beasts (and stressing their geographic remoteness). The killing of the lion that terrorized Nemea (mainland Greece) regularly came first: it provided him with his lion skin. Nemea and Lerna are in central Greece (Argolid).

28 *Geryon*: a monstrous three-bodied herdsman killed by Hercules in Spain.

29 *Stymphalus' horrid birds*: man-eating birds that infested Lake Stymphalus (Arcadia) and were shot by Hercules with his arrows.

30 *Diomed's Thracian horses*: man-eating mares owned by Diomedes of Thrace (north Greece), to which his guests were fed. Bistony and Ismara are in eastern Thrace.

32 *The golden apples of the Hesperides*: in the far west (the 'wild Atlantic shore'), taken by Hercules after killing their guardian snake.

64 *the order of my theme*: in 64–75 Lucretius outlines the subject matter of 91–109 and 235–415 (65–6), 416–508 (67–8), 771–924 (69–70), 1028–90 (71–2), and 1161–1240 (73–5). He then returns to the subject matter of 509–770, the workings of the heavenly bodies (76–81). In the order of the book, this

comes as a digression after the account of the creation of the earth, since the workings of the system are bound up with its origins, but Lucretius singles it out here to provide a firmly anti-theological conclusion to his summary.

82–90 *For men who have been well taught about the gods . . .* : repeated at 6. 58–66.

83 *may wonder still*: a primary aim of Lucretius in both Book 5 and Book 6 is to remove any sense of wonder at phenomena of the world which might lead to religious belief. Such attacks on wonder go back to Democritus (fr. A169, B4).

87 *cruel masters*: contrast 2. 1091.

90 *deep-set boundary stone*: see above on 1. 77.

95 *One day will give to destruction*: Aristotle had held that the world was uncreated and everlasting, but both Stoics and Epicureans believed in its destruction, though for the Stoics it was then reborn to repeat the same cycle of events. Cf. 2. 1105 ff.

100 *some unaccustomed thing*: Lucretius once more perverts to his own ends a religious statement: these lines translate a fragment of Empedocles (B133) dealing with the difficulty of apprehending god.

110 *oracles*: cf. 1. 738 ff. (of Empedocles).

117 *Men should, like giants, suffer punishment*: see above on 1. 67 for the imagery of the battle of gods and giants: after their defeat, the giants were imprisoned in various ways by Zeus. Both Plato (*Sophist* 246a) and Aristotle (*On Philosophy* fr. 18) had cast the early atomists as giants, because they were materialists grasping things with their hands and threatening with their reason the stability of the world.

128–41 *There can be no trees in the sky*: 128–41 repeat 3. 784–97, with small changes. There the lines were part of the argument against the survival of the soul outside the body: throughout this passage the similarities and differences between the world-system and the human body play an important role.

148 *the nature of the gods*: the exact nature of the Epicurean gods is controversial amongst scholars, but what Lucretius says here about their 'dwelling places' (cf. 3. 18 ff.) fits what we are told elsewhere about their living in the so-called *metakosmia* or *intermundia*, Tennyson's 'lucid interspace of world and world' (*Lucretius*: cf. Epicurus, *Letter to Pythocles* 89, fr. 359, Cicero, *On Ends* 1. 75, *On the Nature of the Gods* 1. 18). Philodemus' fragmentary treatise *On the Gods* goes into more detail about their lives. At any rate it is clear that the gods are far from being able to be concerned with our world.

155 *later at some length*: not in the extant *On the Nature of the Universe*, but vague forward references like this are not uncommon as devices for bringing a subject to a close: cf. e.g. Plato, *Timaeus* 50c6–7, Velleius Paterculus (first century AD), *Roman History* 2. 96. 3, Seneca, *Natural Questions* 2. 7. 2.

156 *for the sake of men*: see above on 2. 174 ff., and especially Diogenes of Oenoanda fr. 20.

168 *what new thing*: if the gods are perfectly happy, there is no reason for them to want to change their previous life by creating the world. The problems for the divine decision to create the world generated by the principle of sufficient reason (why at one time rather than another if there was no change) were well known to Christian theologians, who faced them by moving their god outside time: cf. Augustine, *Confessions* 11. 13.

182 *concept of mankind*: to be able to speak or act, we need a concept (Greek *prolepsis*, Latin *notities*) of what we intend to say or do, but there is nowhere where the gods could have obtained such a concept (cf. 5. 1046 ff., arguing against human invention of language).

195–9 *But even if I had no knowledge of atoms* . . . : 195–9 repeat 2. 177–81 and then develop the argument with further examples.

204 *Nearly two thirds*: on the commonest version of the theory of the 'zones' of the world (*zone* in Greek means 'belt': see especially Aristotle, *Meteorologica* 362^{b}5 ff., Eratosthenes (third–second century BC), *Hermes* fr. 15, Virgil, *Georgics* 1. 231–9), there were two temperate zones surrounding an uninhabitable equatorial torrid zone and surrounded by two frozen zones at the extremes. Cf. Diogenes of Oenoanda fr. 21.

218 *the wild beasts' fearsome breed*: cf. Cicero, *Academica* 2. 120.

222–34 *the child, like sailor cast ashore* . . . : famously translated by Dryden and imitated by Wordsworth, *To* ——, *Upon the Birth of her First-Born Child*. Cf. e.g. the *Axiochus* attributed to Plato 366d, Cicero, *On the Republic* 3. 1, Seneca, *Letters* 102. 26.

226 *fills the place with cries*: Epicurus used the crying of babies at birth as part of the 'cradle' argument that humans naturally flee pain, explaining it as a reaction to cold air (cf. Sextus Empiricus, *Against the Professors* 11. 96, Epicurus fr. 398). Other philosophers offered different explanations: the issue was connected with that of when the baby became alive (cf. e.g. Plutarch, *On Stoic Contradictions* 1052, Tertullian (second–third century AD), *On the Soul* 25. 2). Epicurus perverts to his own purpose Empedocles fr. B118, 'I wept and wailed on seeing an unfamiliar place': Lucretius restores the tone of the original, adding the image of the shore of life (from Empedocles fr. B20. 5).

259 *The mother of all*: see above on 2. 598 ff.

308 *the shrines and images | Of gods*: as usual, Lucretius insinuates an explicit point against religion.

318–19 *that which* . . . | *Holds the whole earth in its embrace*: i.e. the sky. Lucretius imitates a philosophical fragment (86 ff.) of the tragedy *Chryses* by Pacuvius (first century BC: see above on 3. 881 ff.).

326 *Before the Theban war and doom of Troy*: cf. Horace, *Odes* 4. 9. 25, 'many brave men lived before Agamemnon . . .'. The Theban story of the Seven against Thebes was first told in a lost epic *Thebais* (perhaps seventh century BC): for the Trojan war as the limit of human knowledge, see e.g. Diodorus Siculus 1. 5. 1 ff.

330 *the world is young and new*: contrast 2. 1150 ff.

337 *the very first*: not strictly true—Cicero refers to two Latin (prose?) Epicurean writers, C. Amafinius (*Tusculan Disputations* 4. 6–7) and T. Catius (*Letters to his Friends* 15. 16), who were probably earlier than Lucretius.

339 *perished in burning fire*: theories of periodic cataclysmic destruction were used by Plato (*Timaeus* 22c—with the same three types of catastrophe, *Statesman* 269c) and Aristotle (*Meteorologica* 352ᵃ, *Politics* 1269ᵃ5) to explain the apparent youth of human culture despite the eternity of the world, while the Stoics believed in a deterministic cycle of destruction and rebirth.

351–63 *Few things there are that last eternally . . .* : see above on 3.806–10.

381 *In most unrighteous war*: the metaphorical complex of the war of the elements is an old one (cf. e.g. Heraclitus fr. B80, Empedocles fr. B115) but was particularly congenial to the Epicureans, since it reinforced their view of the instability of the world. Lucretius uses it frequently of the atoms.

397 *Phaethon*: the story of Phaethon disastrously attempting to drive the chariot of his father the sun, already allegorized by Plato (*Timaeus* 22c), was later interpreted in terms of the Stoic periodic destruction by fire (in Greek *ekpyrosis*), although not certainly before Lucretius: cf. Manilius, *Astronomica* (first century BC–first century AD) 1. 735 ff., 4. 831 ff., Dio Chrysostom (first century AD), *Speeches* 36. 48.

412 *so legend tells*: the story of the flood, from which only Deucalion and his wife Pyrrha survived to begin again the human race.

419 *not by design or intelligence*: 5. 419–23 are repeated from 1. 1021–5.

436 *strange storm and surging mighty mass*: for the creation of the world from the atomic storm or whirl, cf. Epicurus, *Letter to Pythocles* 88 ff., 'Aetius' 1. 4. 1 ff., Epicurus fr. 308.

487 *salt sweat*: the sea as the 'sweat' of the earth is Empedoclean (fr. B. 55, cf. Aristotle, *Meteorologica* 353ᵇ).

507 *Pontus*: the Black Sea (Pontus) was believed to flow in one direction only, into the sea of Marmara (Propontis), which joined it to the Aegean: cf. e.g. Seneca, *Natural Questions* 4. 2. 29.

509 *The causes of the motions of the stars*: Lucretius deals with the motions of the heavenly bodies in the context of their first emergence, because the nature of the explanations offered for these motions is connected with how they first came about.

528 *In various worlds created in various ways*: while for the basic principles of Epicureanism only one account is possible, for many of the phenomena described in Books 5 and 6 the Epicureans accepted the possibility of alternative explanations (the so-called *pleonachos tropos*, 'mode of multiple explanations': cf. 6. 703 ff., Epicurus, *Letter to Herodotus* 79–80, *Epistle to Pythocles* 86–7, Diogenes of Oenoanda fr. 13). Since everything possible was held to be substantiated somewhere in the infinite universe, although only one explanation of a phenomenon might be true for our world, the other explanations would be valid for other worlds. Cf. 2. 1023 ff.

554 *By common roots united*: cf. 3. 325 ff. of the union of soul and body.

564 *The sun's heat and its size*: the Epicureans notoriously held that the sun was no larger than it appeared: cf. e.g. Epicurus, *Letter to Pythocles* 91 (and cf. Cicero, *On Ends* 1. 20 etc.).

575 *whether it shines with borrowed light*: see below on 705.

616 *Sinks down to Capricorn in winter*: the arc that the sun appears to describe through the sky is nearest the horizon in winter and furthest from it in summer. Its highest points each day are all situated on a great circle through the celestial sphere known as the ecliptic. The belt of the sky 8 degrees either side of the ecliptic was divided into twelve regions (the zodiac), named from the principal constellations visible in them at night. The zodiac belt rotates around the earth, and within one year the sun appears to move at its highest point through all the constellations in turn. At the winter solstice, when the sun is moving nearest to the horizon, it moves through Capricorn, at the summer solstice it moves through Cancer. Lucretius attempts to offer possible explanations for the complexities caused by the fact that the sun and the zodiacal belt (and the moon) are moving at different rates. Cf. Epicurus, *Letter to Pythocles* 93.

622 *Democritus*: cf. fr. A39.

656 *Matuta*: a Roman dawn goddess, linked to the Greek Leucothea (cf. Cicero, *Tusculan Disputations* 1. 28, *On the Nature of the Gods* 3. 48). She had a temple in the Forum Boarium at Rome.

663 *from Ida's mountain peaks*: for the story that the apparent creation of a new sun each day can be observed from Mt Ida in Phrygia (Turkey), see Diodorus Siculus, *Library of History* (first century BC) 17. 7. 5 ff., Pomponius Mela (first century AD) 1. 18. 94 ff., Euripides, *Troades* (415 BC) 1066 ff.

669 *At a fixed time*: the stress on the regularity and certainty of natural phenomena also has an anti-theological and ethical point. Far from being an argument for divine intervention in the world (the argument from design), it removes any necessity for divine action.

687–8 *the two knotted circles of the year*: the 'knot of the year' is the point at which the sun's daily course when it intersects the ecliptic is in line with the celestial equator (cf. Aratus (third century BC), *Phainomena* 245, Manilius 3. 622). The sun passes through this knot twice a year, at the spring and autumn equinoxes.

705 *the moon*: that the moon reflected light from the sun was an early discovery of Greek philosophy (cf. especially Plato, *Cratylus* 409a, Anaxagoras fr. B 18, etc.), but the Epicureans again preferred to suspend judgement (cf. Epicurus, *Letter to Pythocles* 94 ff.). For the various theories, see 'Aetius' 2. 28.

727 *the Babylonian Chaldees*: the doctrine is ascribed to the Babylonian priest Berosus, who wrote a *Babylonian History* dedicated to Antiochus I (ruled 281–261): cf. 'Aetius' 2. 28, Vitruvius (first century BC) 9. 2. It is unlikely that Epicurus himself mentioned Berosus' doctrines.

737 *Spring comes*: Lucretius' picture here is one of the sources for Botticelli's *Allegoria della Primavera*.

739 *Zephyrs steps*: the divinity of the West Wind.

Flora: an Italian goddess with temples on the Quirinal hill and near the Circus Maximus: cf. Ovid, *Fasti* 5. 159 ff.

742 *Aquilo*: the North Wind.

745 *Volturnus*: the East-South-East Wind.

Auster: the South Wind.

751 *The sun's eclipses and the moon's retreats*: a much discussed topic in ancient astronomy: cf. Epicurus, *Letter to Pythocles* 96 and in general 'Aetius' 2. 24, 2. 29.

783 *In the beginning*: Lucretius' account of the development of life and civilization on earth occupies the rest of the book. Its most important characteristic is its resolute materialism and avoidance of any suggestion of divine providence: and to explain the various phenomena, he uses extensively what has been termed 'diachronic analogy', that is, conjecture about early developments through analogy with phenomena that can be observed today. The many different accounts of the beginning of life and emergence of human civilization current in antiquity are conveniently collected in A. O. Lovejoy and G. Boas, *Primitivism and Related Concepts in Antiquity* (Baltimore, 1935): Democritus was an important early source.

793 *fallen from the sky*: see above on 2. 1153 ff.

795 *The name of mother*: see above on 2. 598 ff.

797 *come up from earth*: see above on 2. 871 ff.

808 *Wombs would grow*: cf. Diodorus Siculus, *Library of History* 1. 7. 3–4 (possibly from Democritus), Epicurus fr. 333, Diogenes of Oenoanda fr. 11.

827 *like a woman worn out by old age*: cf. 2. 1150, and contrast 5. 330.

837 *many monsters in those days*: Lucretius has the notion of random mutation and
survival of the fittest, but only in extreme terms: organisms either die or live
within one generation, rather than mutations having a small cumulative effect
on genetic success over many generations. Cf. Empedocles fr. B61 (though
Lucretius rejects some of the mutant forms there as impossible), Aristotle,
Physics 198ᵇ24 ff., and for the hermaphrodites Plato, *Symposium* 189d ff.

862–3 *Courage has kept the savage lion safe*: cf. Plato, *Protagoras* 230e, Cicero, *On
the Nature of the Gods* 2. 127, in contexts of divine providence.

878 *Centaurs never existed*: cf. 4. 732 ff.

893 *Scyllas*: figures like the mythical monster of the *Odyssey* (12. 85 ff., 245 ff.),
later in art, as here, girded with dogs who were kennelled in her womb.

905 *Chimaera*: cf. Homer, *Iliad* 6. 179–82 (905 translates 181–2), Plato, *Phaedrus*
229d, *Republic* 588c.

911 *rivers ran with gold*: Lucretius constantly sets his own realistic 'hard primitivism' against notions of early life as a 'Golden Age', though it was rivers of
milk, honey, wine, etc. that were normal features of such descriptions (cf.
e.g. Ovid, *Metamorphoses* 1. 111), and the discovery of gold typically marked
the end of any Golden Age (cf. 1113 ff. below). There is also an allusion to
the legends associated with the gold-bearing rivers Pactolus in Lydia
(Turkey: cf. Strabo (first century BC–first century AD), *Geography* 13. 4. 5) and
Tagus in Spain (cf. Lucan (first century AD), *Civil War* 7. 755).

925 *the men that roamed the earth*: Lucretius now turns to the account of human
development which is the most celebrated part of Book 5, and perhaps of
the whole poem. With Plato, *Protagoras* 320c ff., Diodorus Siculus 1. 8 ff.,
and Seneca, *Letter* 90 (based on the views of the second–first-century BC
Stoic Posidonius), Lucretius' account is the most extensive to have come
down to us, but the topic was handled by many thinkers and became a
poetic commonplace also (cf. e.g. Ovid, *Metamorphoses* 1. 76 ff.). Although
individual elements are common between accounts, several different models can be distinguished. 'Primitivist' models idealize early life, either as a
Golden Age (so-called 'soft primitivism', common in poetic accounts, e.g.
Hesiod (*c.*700 BC), *Works and Days* 109 ff., Aratus (third century BC),
Phainomena 96 ff.), or as harsh but simple and bracing, as in the accounts
of the 'Cynic' philosophers (e.g. Maximus of Tyre (second century AD),
Oration 36). 'First discoverer' or 'heurematist' models originally stressed the
providential role of the gods in introducing developments (cf. e.g. *Homeric
Hymn to Demeter* (seventh century BC) 470 ff.), but were later secularized
with humans as the first discoverers (see above on 5. 13). 'Teleological' models see human development as one of the perfection of innate capacities,
either by natural process (cf. Aristotle, *Politics* 1252ᵇ ff.) or by divine intervention in a form of the argument from design (cf. Plato, *Timaeus* 44d ff.,
Cicero, *On the Nature of the Gods* 2. 87 ff., Virgil, *Georgics* 1. 121 ff.). In

contrast to all of these, the materialist account followed by Lucretius, many details of which may go back to Democritus, concentrates on technological developments as mainly communal responses over long periods of time to practical needs, and opposes any element of divine intervention. For the details of the accounts, see the work of Lovejoy and Boas mentioned above (on 783 ff.), and T. Cole, *Democritus and the Sources of Greek Anthropology* (2nd edn., Cleveland, 1990), though the latter may exaggerate Democritus' contribution to the later accounts. Epicurus dealt with the origin and development of civilization in Book 12 of his *On Nature*, though we have very few fragments.

932 *like wild beasts*: the notion of the 'beast-like life' was common in accounts of early man (cf. e.g. Euripides, *Suppliants* (*c.*442 BC) 201 ff., Euripides or Critias, *Sisyphus* (Critias fr. B25), Moschion (third century BC) fr. 6; Hobbes, *Leviathan* 1. 13). Three elements are normally stressed: rule by superior force, the helplessness of the human race, and the harshness of the living conditions. Lucretius, however, avoids extreme elements such as cannibalism (cf. Moschion fr. 6, Horace, *Art of Poetry* 391–2).

938 *a gift enough to bring content*: in 938–57 the three natural and necessary desires in Epicureanism (cf. *Vatican Sayings* 33: see Introduction, and note on 2. 17 ff.), for food, drink, and warmth, are all satisfied.

955 *caves*: another regular element in accounts of early human beings, cf. e.g. Aeschylus (fifth century BC), *Prometheus Bound* 452–3, *Homeric Hymn to Hephaestus* (*c.*400 BC) 4, Diodorus Siculus 1. 8. 7.

963 *Mutual desire*: cf. 4. 1193 ff.

967 *the beasts that roamed the woods and plains*: the danger from wild animals is frequently mentioned: it sometimes plays a part in the development of social organization (cf. Plato, *Protagoras* 332b, Hermarchus (fourth–third century BC) fr. 34 = LS 22 m–n, Diodorus Siculus, *Library of History* 1. 8. 2).

973 *wandering frightened in the shades of night*: contrast Manilius, *Astronomica* (first century BC–first century AD) 1. 66 ff., Statius, *Thebaid* 4. 282–4. The Stoics held that the fear of the dark was a natural fear, because it reminded one of one's death: cf. Seneca, *Letters* 82. 15, Hierocles (second century AD), *Elements of Ethics* 7. 5 ff.

993 *a living tomb*: a common notion, first extant in Aeschylus, *Seven against Thebes* (467 BC) 1020–1.

996 *Orcus*: a mysterious figure, common in poetry for the god of the underworld or the underworld itself.

1006 *The wicked art of seamanship*: the first boat (in myth the Argo) was often made a decisive moment in the fall of man from Golden Age simplicity and happiness: cf. e.g. Hesiod, *Works and Days* 236 ff., Aratus, *Phainomena* 110 ff., Virgil, *Eclogue* 4. 31 ff.

1014 *Then first the human race began to soften*: contrast the hardiness of humans when first born from the earth, 925 ff. Lucretius suggests that a number of factors are responsible for the 'softening' of human beings, and that the process takes place gradually: cf. 1101 ff., 1368 ff.: other accounts make for example change of diet decisive (cf. Hippocrates, *On Ancient Medicine* 3. 26, Moschion fr. 6, Virgil, *Georgics* 1. 147). Epicurus seems to have envisaged two stages in human development, one of direct response to nature, the second involving human reasoning and experimentation (*Letter to Herodotus* 75–6). Lucretius' account seems to be loosely structured around these two stages, with 1011–1104 describing the 'natural' phase, 1105–1457 developments based on active human reasoning. Both phases include social and techno-logical developments. Many developments discussed in the second phase also involved at an earlier stage nature's compulsion or prompting, and the need to establish a sense of an overall plot of continuous progress means that Lucretius cannot be rigid about the distinction between phases.

1017–18 *children . . . | With winning smiles*: Epicurus notoriously denied that par-ents instinctively loved their offspring (fr. 525–9), and, although in Lucretius the stress on the pleasure that the parents take is in accordance with ortho-dox Epicureanism, a closer emotional bond is perhaps suggested.

1020 *Wishing to do no ill nor suffer harm*: according to the Epicureans, justice existed because of a social contract neither to harm nor be harmed (*Master Sayings* 33, cf. 31–2). Lucretius has an initial contract here in the 'natural' phase, and then introduces a more developed system of laws as a response to social breakdown in the second phase (1143 ff.). Contractarian theories seem to have been for-mulated first in the fifth century BC in the context of the so-called 'Sophistic' movement (cf. famously Glaucon in Plato, *Republic* 358a ff.), and it is likely that Democritus' approach was contractarian: in turn Lucretius' account was influential in the development of social-contract theory in the modern period by Hobbes, Locke, Pufendorf, and especially Rousseau.

1028 *the various sounds of speech*: cf. Epicurus, *Letter to Herodotus* 75–6, Diodorus Siculus 1. 8. 3 ff. In this passage Lucretius covers only Epicurus' first natural phase (see above on 1014).

1041 *allotted | Names to things*: Diogenes of Oenoanda fr. 12 mocks the idea of early human beings being taught language by the god Hermes. The issue of the natural or conventional origin of language was raised especially by Plato in the *Cratylus* (e.g. 388e ff.).

1047 *the concept of this usefulness*: cf. 5. 182 for the necessity to have a conception of something before being able to think or speak about it.

1063 *Molossian hounds*: a breed of dog from west Greece, famous as hunting dogs and frequently mentioned in literature.

1092 *Fire was first brought to earth for mortal men*: Lucretius alludes to the myth of Prometheus bringing fire to men (cf. e.g. Hesiod (*c.*700 BC), *Works and Days*

42 ff., *Theogony* 561 ff.), but replaces Prometheus with the random activity of lightning.

1105 *as the days passed*: at this point we move to the second stage, where there is a limited role for first discoverers (1108). Kings arise and create cities for their own protection (1109); they distribute property on the basis of beauty and strength (1110–11) until wealth becomes more important (1113–16). As a result of men's desire for power and fame (1120–2), the kings are then overthrown and a state of anarchy results (1141–2). Eventually magistrates and laws are introduced because mankind is tired of living in violence (1145).

1117 ff. *greatest riches are a frugal life*: cf. Epicurus, *Master Sayings* 15, 'the wealth demanded by nature is both limited and easily got; that demanded by empty opinion extends to infinity'.

1120 *men . . . sought after fame and power*: translating the first part of Epicurus, *Master Sayings* 7. Although Lucretius is giving a historical account, the reference to contemporary Roman society is clear: note especially the imperatives of 1131 ff.

1130 *To live a life of quiet*: an allusion to the famous Epicurean maxim 'Live unknown': cf. Epicurus frr. 551, 548, 554. Plutarch wrote a treatise 'On whether the Epicurean maxim "Live Unknown" was well said'.

1137 *The ancient majesty of thrones and sceptres proud*: Lucretius' language recalls the names of the fifth and last kings of Rome, Tarquinius Priscus ('the ancient') and Tarquinius Superbus ('the proud'). Throughout this passage he combines a general account of the development of law based on Epicurean theory with specific allusions to Roman institutions.

1156 *Though he should keep it hid from gods and men*: cf. Epicurus, *Master Sayings* 35 (where, as here, the stress is on the inability of the guilty man to be confident that he will escape detection, not on the actual chances of being caught), 17, 34, *Vatican Sayings* 7, fr. 532.

1161–2 *reverence for gods | Has spread*: Lucretius again uses the language of discoveries spreading throughout the world (see above on 5. 20), but ascribes the initial impulse to a cause, not a person. Two reasons are given for the origin of religious belief: visions of the gods, especially in dreams (1169–82) and ignorance of the causes of natural phenomena (1183–93). The first reason is justified, in that the Epicureans did believe that it was possible to have visions of the gods, and indeed that the true Epicurean would have better visions, as more tranquil and able to receive them without disturbance: cf. 6. 78 ff., Epicurus, *Letter to Menoeceus* 123, fr. 353, Diogenes of Oenoanda fr. 15. Not all the inferences that men make about the gods from their visions, however, are necessarily correct. The second reason for belief in divinity, from contemplation of the heavens, was often appealed to by theists (cf. e.g. Aristotle, *On Philosophy* fr. 12, see above on 2. 1030 ff., Diodorus Siculus,

Library of History 1. 11. 1, Sextus Empiricus, *Against the Professors* 9. 26 ff.), but for the Epicureans was wholly wrong (cf. Epicurus, *Letter to Herodotus* 76 ff., Democritus fr. A75). In general on the gods in Epicureanism, see Cicero, *On the Nature of the Gods* 1. 18 ff., and the fragmentary treatises of Philodemus, *On the Gods* and *On Piety*. The origin of belief in the gods was treated in Book 12 of Epicurus' *On Nature* (cf. Philodemus, *On Piety* 8. 225 ff.).

1191 *night-wandering torches of heaven*: theists tended to distinguish between regular and irregular phenomena of the heavens as causes of divine belief (cf. Cicero, *On the Nature of the Gods* 2. 13 ff., the fourth and third reasons for belief offered by the Stoic Cleanthes (fourth–third century BC)), but for Lucretius there is no difference: neither should lead to belief in the gods.

1228 *elephants*: although the use of elephants was especially associated with the Carthaginians (cf. 5. 1303), the Romans also used them, for example, at the battle of Cynoscephalae (197 BC, cf. Livy 33. 8. 3).

1241 *metals first were found*: cf. e.g. Seneca, *Letters* 90. 12 (arguing against Posidonius). In traditional accounts of the Golden Age, there were no metals (cf. Ovid, *Amores* 3. 8. 35 ff.): Lucretius has none of this idealization of the past, but he does not refrain from moralizing comment (1259, 1273 ff.).

1283 *ancient weapons*: the discovery of iron leads to an account of developments in warfare, and the intensification of the moralizing criticism of the uses to which technological developments were put. Lucretius rationalizes mythical accounts of the decline from the Bronze to the Iron Age (cf. Hesiod, *Works and Days* 176 ff.).

1289 *with bronze they tilled the soil*: a close imitation of Hesiod, *Works and Days* 150–1.

1303 *men of Carthage*: the Carthaginians used elephants in both the First and Second Punic Wars, most famously when Hannibal crossed the Alps in 218 BC.

1308 *Bulls too were pressed into the service of war*: a famous passage, sometimes used to substantiate allegations of madness against Lucretius. But although there is no close parallel, there is no reason to doubt that the practice of using wild animals was attested in some lost source, and the notion that if this did not happen in our world, it will have done so in another is straightforward Epicurean doctrine about possibility (see above on 5. 528). The main focus is on the moral implications of the perverted ingenuity displayed.

1350 *The plaited garment*: cf. Diogenes of Oenoanda fr. 12.

1354 *men's work*: for Herodotus (fifth century BC), one of the reversals of normal custom seen in Egypt was that the men did the weaving (2. 35, cf. Sophocles, *Oedipus at Colonus* (404 BC), 337). Lucretius' observation that men are 'more clever' is not without some irony: his other use of the word translated as 'clever' is in 1010, 'today with greater skill they poison others'.

1367 *cherished plots*: the description of the gardens of early man suggests the 'Garden' of Epicurus (cf. also *Catalepton* (ascribed to Virgil) 5. 8–10, 8. 11 ff.): a fragment of Diogenes of Oenoanda (56) says that, when everyone becomes an Epicurean, '[we ourselves shall plough] and dig and tend [the plants] and [divert rivers and watch over the crops]'.

1383 *First taught the country-folk to blow through pipes*: Lucretius' picture is in the spirit of pastoral (and was in fact influential on later pastoral, from Virgil, *Eclogue* 1. 1 ff. on).

1391 *When they had had their fill of food*: cf. Democritus fr. B144: 'Music . . . is one of the younger arts . . . [because] necessity did not decree it, but it arose only when there already existed a superfluity.'

1392–6 *So often, lying in company together . . .* : repeated from 2. 29–33.

1436–8 *sun and moon . . . | Have taught men well*: the reference is perhaps to the discovery of philosophy from the observation of the motions of the heavenly bodies: cf. Plato, *Timaeus* 47a. Contrast 1183 ff. on belief in the gods.

1440 *fenced in with strong towers*: cf. Thucydides (fifth century BC), *Histories* 1. 8–10.

1447 *Except where reason may point out the traces*: Lucretius self-reflexively draws attention to the very procedure that he has been adopting in Book 5. See above on 1. 402.

1450 *all the delights of life*: i.e. all the things that it is natural to desire but not necessary to have: see above on 1391.

1456 *brighten in their minds*: the imagery of light and dark recalls the end of Book 1.

Book Six

1–2 *Athens of glorious name*: Book 6 opens with another 'Priamel' or focusing device (see above on 2. 1 ff.) in which the achievements of Athens are capped by its production of Epicurus. The book thus opens with a celebration of the greatness of Athenian civilization, and closes with the account of the plague there in 430–426 BC and of that civilization brought low (see below on 1138 ff.). Athens, as one of the most praised cities in antiquity (cf. e.g. Pindar, *Pythian* 7 (486 BC) 1 ff., Isocrates, *Panegyricus* (380 BC) 47), is a representative of the 'peak' of civilization that humanity was said to have reached at the end of Book 5, but all of this achievement cannot bring human happiness without the Epicurean message.

First brought corn-bearing crops: an allusion to the myth of Triptolemus, who was said to have been taught agriculture by Demeter and then to have carried the gift throughout the world (see above on 5. 20) in a winged chariot. The story was told for example in Sophocles' lost play *Triptolemus* (468 BC): cf. Dionysus of Halicarnassus (first century BC), *Roman Antiquities* 1. 12. 2.

8 *exalted to the skies*: cf. the victory over religion on 1. 79. The language is used in Homer of the fame of the 'good king' (*Odyssey* 19. 108, cf. 8. 74).

9–10 *nearly all those things | Which need demands*: for the Epicureans, human needs were easily satisfied by simple means: cf. Epicurus, *Letter to Menoeceus* 130, *Master Sayings* 15, 18, 21, Diogenes of Oenoanda fr. 2, and see above on 2. 17 ff.

14 *deep in every home*: cf. 5. 43 ff.

17 *He understood*: Epicurus in this passage acts like a doctor, noting the symptoms (9–16), understanding their cause (17–23), and providing a two-stage cure, removing what is diseased (24–5) and providing a positive regimen for the future (26–34).

the vessel itself | Produced the flaw: a Platonic analogy (cf. *Gorgias* 493a ff.), but one which links to a complex of imagery within the poem: see above on 3. 936, 1003, and cf. Epicurus fr. 396.

22 *tainted everything that entered it*: the image comes from the Cynic Diogenes, cf. Maximus the Confessor, *Commonplaces* 44c.

24 *purged men's hearts*: philosophical imagery of 'purgation' goes back to Plato (cf. e.g. *Cratylus* 396e, 405a, *Sophist* 227c) and is part of the general conception of the philosopher as a doctor or a religious healer. In Epicureanism, pleasure is 'pure' when uncontaminated by pain or the fear of pain: see above on 4. 1075. The essentials of the philosophy are simple, and based on nature: much of its effort is directed towards cleaning out false ideas that spoil happiness.

26 *that highest good*: in the Latin *bonum summum*, the philosophers' term for the good to which all other goods are referred. In Epicureanism, this is pleasure, which we all instinctively pursue, but which has been obscured by false opinions: Epicurus brings us consciously to pursue this natural goal.

27 *the strait and narrow path*: cf. 1. 81, 406, 1116; 1. 926 = 4. 1, 2. 10 ff., etc. The metaphor of the path in life is another common philosophical image: Epicurus is 'the way, the truth, and the life' (John 14: 6). Seneca reports Epicurus as dividing Epicureans into three groups: the first 'makes its own way', the others follow eagerly or reluctantly (*Letters* 52. 3–4, 11. 8–9): Epicurus and his close associates were known as the 'leaders'; for Lucretius as a 'follower', cf. 3. 3 ff., 5. 55 ff. With the straitness of the way, contrast the wanderings of the unphilosophic at 2. 10 ff.: it is a narrow or small path because little is needed for happiness (and cf. 1. 926).

31 *by natural chance*: although there was indeterminacy at the atomic level in the Epicurean universe because of the 'swerve' (see above on 2. 219 ff.), this

was probably not usually with effect outside the human soul, and chance events were those not predicted by a particular causal chain, rather than in any sense uncaused (cf. Epicurus, *Letter to Menoeceus* 133 ff., *Master Sayings* 16, fr. 489, Diogenes of Oenoanda fr. 71–2).

38 *like children frightened of the dark*: see above on 2. 55 ff.

58–66 *For men who have been well taught about the gods . . .* : 58–66 are repeated from 5. 82–90: see notes there.

73 *in their untroubled peace*: cf. Edwin Muir, 'The Labyrinth', 'But they, the gods, as large and bright as clouds, | Conversed across the sounds in tranquil voices | High in the sky, above the untroubled sea, | And their eternal dialogue was peace.'

75 *To come before their shrines with quiet mind*: cf. 5. 1161 ff.

86 *the sky | Divided into parts*: in Etruscan augury (see below on 6. 381), it was significant from which part of the sky lightning came, and to which part it went (it not being known that the return path was identical to the path of arrival). The heavens were accordingly divided into sixteen regions (cf. Cicero, *On Divination* 2. 42–5, Seneca, *Natural Questions* 41–2).

94 *Calliope*: the roles of the muses were still fluid in Lucretius' day, although set functions had begun to be assigned to them. Calliope was usually the muse of epic poetry, but she had famously been invoked by Empedocles (fr. B131) and also had links with philosophy (cf. Plato, *Phaedrus* 259d): she was the mother and teacher of Orpheus.

Solace of men, delight of gods: recalling the opening address to Venus in 1.1 ff.

96 *First, thunder shakes the blue expanse of sky*: Lucretius deals first with thunder, lightning, and thunderbolts (96–422), the phenomena of the sky most associated with fears of divine action. He then deals with waterspouts (423–50), clouds (451–94), rain (495–523), rainbows (524–6), and miscellaneous phenomena of weather (527–34); earthquakes (535–607), the constancy of the sea (608–38), and Etna (639–702), followed by an excursus on multiple causation (703–11); the Nile (712–37), Avernian sites (738–839), wells and springs (840–905), and the magnet (906–1089); and finally the aetiology of disease (1090–1137) followed by the plague at Athens (1138–1286). All of these topics were frequent subjects of discussion amongst scientists and philosophers: see especially Aristotle's *Meteorologica* ('meteorologia' in Greek has a wider semantic range than the English equivalent) and Seneca's *Natural Questions*. Aristotle's follower Theophrastus (fourth–third century BC) wrote an influential *Meteorology* (known through Syriac and Arabic translations: see Bibliography), and many of these topics were also discussed in his treatise *Opinions of the Physicists*, which was the foundation for the later 'doxographic' tradition (see above on 1. 635–920) seen in 'Aetius' (first century AD). The extant *Letter to Pythocles*, which may not be completely by

Epicurus himself, deals with a number of these topics: for thunder and lightning, see 100–4. Lucretius offers ten possible explanations for thunder (seven are given in Theophrastus, *Meteorology* 1) and four each for lightning and thunderbolts: cf. in general 'Aetius' 3. 3, who deals in the same order with thunder, lightning, thunderbolts, waterspouts, and whirlwinds.

96–107 *clouds . . . | Are dashed together*: explanations of thunder by means of cloud collisions were widespread: cf. e.g. Democritus A93, Aristophanes, *Clouds* 383 ff., Theophrastus, *Meteorology* 1. 3–5, Epicurus, *Letter to Pythocles* 100–1, Cicero, *On Divination* 2. 44.

99 *no sound comes from a clear sky*: cf. 247 ff.

109 *awnings*: see above on 4. 76.

130 *a small bladder*: the analogy is already parodied in Aristophanes' *Clouds* (404 ff.): cf. Theophrastus, *Meteorology* 1. 17, Seneca, *Natural Questions* 2. 27. 3.

148–9 *As red-hot iron . . . | Hisses*: for the comparison cf. Archelaus fr. A16, Theophrastus, *Meteorology* 1. 10–11, Pliny, *Natural Histories* 2. 112. The theory was widespread amongst the pre-Socratic philosophers (Empedocles fr. A63, Archelaus fr. A16, Diogenes of Apollonia fr. A16) but is not in the *Letter to Pythocles*.

154 *Phoebus' Delphic laurel*: the laurel or bay was sacred to Apollo, and was burnt by the priestess in his oracle at Delphi.

161–2 *as stone | Strikes stone or iron*: for the analogy, cf. Pliny, *Natural Histories* 2. 113.

164 *Our ears receive the sound of thunder later*: cf. Epicurus, *Letter to Pythocles* 102–3, Democritus fr. A126a, Aristotle, *Meteorologica* 369b, Theophrastus, *Meteorology* 5, Seneca, *Natural Questions* 2. 12. 1. Epicurus' account was close to that of Theophrastus, giving two possible explanations: first, that lightning actually occurred before thunder, and, second, that they occurred simultaneously but the lightning moved faster. The woodcutter example is in Theophrastus (5. 5): cf. also Sextus Empiricus, *Against the Professors* 5. 69.

178–9 *leaden bullets | Melt*: for the notion that sling bullets can travel so fast that they melt, cf. 306 ff. below, Aristotle, *De Caelo* 289a, Theophrastus, *Meteorology* 6. 20–1, Virgil, *Aeneid* 8. 588, Ovid, *Metamorphoses* 2. 726–9, 14. 825–6, Lucan, *Civil War* 7. 513, Seneca, *Natural Questions* 2. 57. 2, Statius, *Thebaid* 10. 533–4.

197 *They vent their indignation with a roar*: Lucretius takes over and demythologizes the traditional imagery of the winds controlled in a cave by the god Aeolus (cf. e.g. Homer, *Odyssey* 10. 47 ff.). Epicurus talks of the clouds as like 'vessels' (*Letter to Pythocles* 100).

209 *from the sun's light*: cf. Epicurus, *Letter to Pythocles* 101, Empedocles fr. A. 63, Seneca, *Natural Questions* 2. 12. 3.

219–20 *thunderbolts*: ancient scientists distinguished between lightning flashes (*fulgura* in Latin) and thunderbolts (*fulmina*: cf. Seneca, *Natural Questions* 2. 12. 1 ff.). Like Theophrastus (*Meteorology* 6. 3 ff.), Lucretius emphasizes that thunderbolts are fiery and have a penetrating power.

221 *sulphur*: in fact the smell is due to ozone from the electrical discharge, but the belief that it was due to sulphur was widespread from the time of Homer (e.g. *Iliad* 8. 133), although this passage is the first explicit extant statement of the belief in scientific literature (cf. the *Problems* ascribed to Aristotle 937^{b}25, Seneca, *Natural Questions* 2. 21. 2).

229 *As sounds and voices do*: cf. 1. 489 ff.

231 *wine inside a vessel*: cf. e.g. Pliny, *Natural Histories* 2. 137.

247–8 *they never strike | From a clear sky*: cf. 99. Later Horace will ascribe a conversion from Epicureanism to thunder from a clear sky (*Odes* 1. 34). See below 400 ff.

251–4 *so that we think . . .* : 251–4 are repeated from 4. 170–3.

257 *like pitch*: cf. Homer, *Iliad* 4. 275 ff. The reference to people seeking shelter is a typical feature of epic similes.

278 *in the hot furnace*: the imagery of the forge (see above on 148–9, and below 681 ff.) suggests the myth of the Cyclopes toiling underground to make the thunderbolts of Zeus.

287 *A violent tremor now assails the earth*: cf. 358. Belief in 'underground thunder' was widespread and often ascribed to supernatural sources (cf. e.g. Aeschylus, *Prometheus Bound* 993, Sophocles, *Oedipus at Colonus* 1606, Euripides, *Hippolytus* 1201).

292 *the universal Flood*: cf. 5. 412. We are reminded again of the fact that our world will one day be destroyed: we move from the everyday experience of thunder and lightning to future destruction on a cosmic scale.

306 *a leaden bullet*: see above on 178–9.

329 *catapults*: cf. Virgil, *Aeneid* 12. 921–3.

335 *all weights naturally possess | A downward momentum*: cf. 2. 203 ff.

349 *the pores*: the theory of small pores in compounds is used several times in the following accounts, e.g. 492, 776 ff., 979 ff., 1129; cf. 4. 344 ff., 949 ff., 976 ff.

352 *It readily dissolves bronze*: cf. Aristotle, *Meteorology* 352^b, Seneca, *Natural Questions* 2. 31. 1, Pliny, *Natural History* 2. 137.

357 *In autumn thunder shakes the house of heaven*: spring and autumn are usually seen as the main seasons for thunder (cf. Theophrastus, *Meteorology* 6. 68 ff., Horace, *Odes* 1. 4. 7 ff.), but Epicurus is said by one source to have claimed that it was more frequent in summer (John Lydus (fifth–sixth century AD, *On Portents* 21. 5, cf. Seneca, *Natural Questions* 2. 57. 2). For the imagery of

the war of the elements, cf. 5. 381 ff.: as ever, the implication is that the world is not providentially ordered, and that, if the war got out of hand, the world could be destroyed.

381 *scrolls of Tuscan charms*: augury was especially associated with and practised by the Etruscans (cf. Cicero, *On Divination* 1. 72, Seneca, *Natural Questions* 2. 41 ff., Pliny, *Natural Histories* 2. 138, John Lydus, *On Portents*).

383–5 *And ask them whence the flying fire has come* . . . : 383–5 are repeated from 87–9: see notes.

386 *what harm*: i.e. in terms of religious pollution. A place struck by lightning was known as a *bidental* (perhaps from the sacrifice of sheep and goats, *bidentes*), and was enclosed as a sacred place: cf. Lucan, *Civil War* 1. 606–8, 8. 864, John Lydus, *On Portents* 47–52.

390–1 *Why do they not arrange that when a man | Is guilty of some abominable crime | He's struck*: cf. 2. 1101 ff. For the arguments here against divination, cf. Aristophanes, *Clouds* 397 ff., Epicurus fr. 370, Cicero, *On Divination* 2. 44–5, Seneca, *Natural Questions* 2. 42 ff.

400 *Never when the sky is cloudless*: see above on 247 ff.

417 *why does he wreck the holy shrines of gods*: cf. 2. 1101–2, Aristophanes, *Clouds* 401, Cicero, *On Divination* 1. 19, Seneca, *Natural Questions* 2. 42.

424 *Those whirlwinds which the Greeks name from their nature | Presters*: Lucretius uses the Greek word *prester*, which has connections with words for 'burn' and 'blow' and covers both fiery and watery whirlwinds: hence the connection with thunderbolts (cf. Hesiod, *Theogony* 846), though Lucretius concentrates on waterspouts. Cf. Epicurus, *Letter to Pythocles* 104 ff., Aristotle, *Meteorology* 369ª, Seneca, *Natural Questions* 5. 13. 3, Pliny, *Natural Histories* 2. 131 ff.

426 *a kind of column*: cf. Epicurus, *Letter to Pythocles* 104.

434 *as though a fist thrust by an arm*: Lucretius mocks the implicit anthropomorphism of religious explanations.

451 *Clouds form*: cf. Epicurus, *Letter to Pythocles* 99, Theophrastus, *Meteorology* 7, Vitruvius (first century BC), *On Architecture* 8. 1 ff. The connection between clouds and religious belief goes back to the beginnings of Indo-European culture: already in Homer, Zeus is termed the 'cloud-gatherer'. Cf. 4. 131 ff. on the shapes of clouds as suggesting mythical monsters.

470 *from the surface of the sea*: the (roughly) correct origin of clouds in water vapour goes back to the pre-Socratic philosophers, cf. Xenophanes (sixth century BC) fr. B26, A46, Anaximander A11.

471–2 *clothes . . . hung out on the shore*: Lucretius uses the analogy several times: cf. 1. 305 and in this book 6. 114, 504, 617 ff.

483 *come into our sky from outside*: cf. 2. 1105 ff., 5. 366 ff., 6. 665 ff. and 954.

492-3 *channels of the ether | . . . breathing-holes*: like all compounds, the world has a protective outer membrane, which is, however, permeable with the outside and permits interchange of atomic matter with the environment (cf. 2. 1105 ff., 'Aetius' 2. 7. 2, and see below on 6. 954).

495-6 *rainy moisture*: cf. Epicurus, *Letter to Pythocles* 99-100.

526 *the rainbow*: cf. Epicurus, *Letter to Pythocles* 109 ff.

527 *all those other things*: Lucretius abbreviates his treatment of the remaining meteorological phenomena such as snow (cf. Epicurus, *Letter to Pythocles* 109-10, Diogenes of Oenoanda fr. 99): they have fewer theological implications. He also omits any systematic discussion of the causes of wind (cf. e.g. Aristotle, *Meteorology* 365ªff., immediately before the discussion of earthquakes).

535 *earthquakes*: Epicurus' treatment of earthquakes comes after whirlwinds but before other atmospheric phenomena: Lucretius' order of treatment marks a clearer break between phenomena of the sky and of the earth. Lucretius details three causes (535-51 subsidence, 552-6 earth falling into pools, 557-607 circulation of underground winds). Epicurus has the third and first of these (in that order): Theophrastus, *Meteorology* 15, adds fire to provide an explanation in terms of each of the four elements. Aristotle, *Meterology* 365ᵇff., makes winds the major cause. Cf. Epicurus, *Letter to Herodotus* 105 ff., fr. 350-1, Diogenes of Oenoanda fr. 98, Seneca, *Natural Questions* bk. 6, Pliny, *Natural Histories* 2. 191 ff., 'Aetius' 3. 14. Both Greece and Italy were (and are) major centres of seismic activity, and the mysterious phenomena associated with earthquakes were long a source of religious awe, in Greece linked to Poseidon (Neptune), the sea-god. At Rome, earthquakes were seen as portents (cf. Livy 3. 10. 6 etc.), and, like thunderbolts, the subject of the 'Etruscan discipline' (see above on 6. 381).

545 *age and time*: the personification of time and the stress on the role of decay are distinctively Lucretian: cf. e.g. 1. 225, 325 ff., 2. 69 ff.

565 *men fear to believe*: cf. 5. 235 ff.

585-6 *Sidon in Syria | And Aegeum in the Peloponnese*: sometime towards the end of the fifth century BC (cf. Strabo, *Geography* 158c, Seneca, *Natural Questions* 6. 24. 6), and in 373-372 BC respectively.

590 *sunk down to the bottom of the sea*: as well as Helice and Buris in the Aegeum earthquake (cf. Ovid, *Metamorphoses* 15. 293 ff.), compare the story of the mythical Atlantis in Plato, *Timaeus* 23e.

608-9 *nature does not cause | The sea to increase in size*: already for Aristotle an old puzzle (*Meteorology* 355ᵇ, cf. e.g. Ovid, *Metamorphoses* 8. 835 ff.), and treated by Lucretius as one of a series of wonders (*mirabilia*) which must be given a rational explanation to avoid the temptation to lapse back into religion. The position of Lucretius' treatment, between earthquakes and volcanoes, has often seemed strange, but all three are phenomena on a massive scale which need to be put in their place. For all the schools, the wise person is not affected by wonder at unusual phenomena: cf. Diogenes Laertius, *Lives of the Philosophers* 7. 123, Horace, *Epistles* 1. 6. 1 ff. Collections of these phenomena (the so-called 'paradoxographic' literature) began to be made from the third century BC.

617 *clothes dripping with water*: see above on 471–2.

639 *Mount Etna's throat*: the proverbial volcano for both Greeks (e.g. Pindar, *Pythian* 1, alluding to the eruption of 475 BC) and Romans (e.g. Seneca, *Letters* 79): the last eruption (presumably referred to in 641 ff.) had been in 122 BC (cf. Cicero, *On the Nature of the Gods* 2. 96). A later one around the time of Caesar's death was treated as a portent (Virgil, *Georgics* 1. 471 ff.). Vesuvius at this date appeared extinct. 'Longinus' in his treatise *On the Sublime* (35. 4, date uncertain) remarks on our wonder at 'the craters of Etna in eruption, hurling up rocks and whole hills from their depths and sometimes shooting forth rivers of that earth-born, spontaneous fire': there is a poem devoted to the subject amongst the works in the 'Appendix Vergiliana' ascribed to Virgil. Volcanoes were often discussed along with earthquakes and other 'meteorological' phenomena (e.g. Aristotle, *Meteorology* 367ᵃ, Strabo, *Geography* 1. 3. 16 (based on Posidonius)) but also in a more general context of marvels (e.g. Pliny 2. 236 ff.). They do not seem to be discussed in the *Letter to Pythocles*, but there may be a missing section.

660 *The fiery rash*: erysipelas, see below on 1167.

670 *the realms of heaven | Are set on fire*: possibly just a reference to the glow of the sky from the lava, but the ancients were aware that lightning sometimes accompanies eruptions because of electrical discharges from the clouds above the crater: cf. Seneca, *Natural Questions* 2. 30. 1.

681 *Etna's mighty furnaces*: recalling Hephaestus' forge in mythology (see e.g. Aeschylus, *Prometheus Bound* 363 ff.), but the role of a combination of wind and fire is similar to that in a blacksmith's forge (cf. Aristotle, *Meteorology* 366ᵃ).

687 *heated in fury*: the description recalls the myths of the Titan Typhoeus and the giant Enceladus, said to be imprisoned under Etna: see e.g. Pindar, *Pythian* 1. 15 ff.

694–5 *the sea | Breaks on the mountain's roots*: the Mediterranean volcanoes are all on the coast, and the sea frequently figured in explanations of both volcanoes and earthquakes. Aristotle (*Meteorology* 366ᵃ) comments that in Sicily the sea is thought to run in channels beneath the earth, and to drive violent winds back into it, while Posidonius also associated volcanic activity with movements of the sea (cf. Strabo 6. 2. 11, Seneca, *Natural Questions* 2. 26. 4–7).

700 *great clouds of sand*: volcanic ash was often termed 'sand' in antiquity: cf
Seneca, *Natural Questions* 2. 30. 1.

701 *mixing bowls*: in Greek *krater* originally meant a bowl for mixing wine and
water.

703 *It is not enough to state one cause*: the Epicurean doctrine of 'multiple explanations': see above on 5. 528.

705 *The lifeless body of some man*: argument over the causes of death to be deduced
from the appearance of a corpse also figured in rhetorical training: see for
instance the contemporary *Rhetoric to Herennius* ascribed to Cicero, 2. 8.

712 *The Nile, the river of all Egypt*: the annual inundation of the Nile was a topic
of wonder and intense scientific interest throughout antiquity: the pre-
Socratic philosophers Thales, Anaxagoras, and Democritus (sixth and fifth
century BC) already speculated about it, Herodotus has a long excursus on
the subject (2. 19 ff.), Aristotle wrote a treatise *On the Flooding of the Nile*, of
which a Latin version survives, and Seneca devoted a book of the *Natural
Questions* to it ('IVa' in modern numeration). The cause (rains in Ethiopia)
was known in antiquity (cf. with 729 ff. Aristotle fr. 248, Theophrastus, *On
Waters* fr. 211B), although the sources of the Nile were not fully explored
until the nineteenth century, notably by Sir Henry Morton Stanley: there is
a detailed discussion of the ancient theories in D. Bonneau, *Le Cru du Nil*
(Paris, 1963). The river was also a typical example of the literary sublime: cf
[Longinus], *On the Sublime* 35. 4.

716 *Etesian*: in Greek *etesios* means 'annual'.

738 *the lakes | And other places that are called Avernian*: as Lucretius explains,
'avernus', from the Greek *aornos*, means 'without birds'. Lake Avernus at
Cumae (near Naples) was regarded as the entrance to the Underworld (cf
most famously Book 6 of Virgil's *Aeneid*): hence the term came to mean
'infernal', but does not seem to have been used in Latin in the general sense
Lucretius gives it here (though *aornos* is used generally in Greek). The
strange properties of various locations, especially rivers and springs, were a
standard subject in the so-called 'paradoxographical' literature dealing with
natural wonders: so, for instance, Antigonus of Carystus (third century BC)
in his *Collection of Paradoxical Stories* (12, 122), as well as mentioning
Lucretius' example of the Athenian acropolis, reported that no bird could
fly over the temple of Achilles in Leuce.

750 *Tritonian Pallas*: the goddess Athena, whose temple, the Parthenon, stands
on the acropolis at Athens. Of the various explanations current in antiquity
for her epithet 'Tritonian', the most popular connected her with Lake
Tritonis in Libya.

754 *the anger | Of Pallas*: echoing a phrase from the *Hecale* of the hellenistic
Greek poet Callimachus (third century BC, fr. 260). In mythology, Athena

became angry at the daughters of the Athenian king Cecrops for opening a chest containing the boy Ericthonius: their action had been reported to her by a crow, and in consequence she banned crows from the air over the acropolis.

756 *In Syria also*: the reference is uncertain: one possible contender is a 'Plutonium' near Laodicea described by the first-century BC/first-century AD geographer Strabo (13. 4. 14).

761 *The gates of Hell*: a large number of places in the ancient world were thought to be entrances to or openings from the Underworld (in Greek *Charoneia*, from Charon, the infernal ferryman): Lucretius' contemporary Varro collected all the Italian examples (cf. Servius on Virgil, *Aeneid* 7. 563). They naturally figured in paradoxographical writing (see e.g. Antigonus of Carystus 123, Pliny, *Natural Histories* 2. 208, and cf. Ennius, *Annals* fr. 222, Virgil, *Aeneid* 7. 568). The Stoics, like the Epicureans, were emphatic that the wise person would have no fear of such places (Diogenes Laertius, *Lives of the Philosophers* 7. 123).

765 *light-footed stags*: for deer enticing snakes out of holes, cf. Pliny, *Natural Histories* 8. 118, 28. 149, Martial (first–second century AD) 11. 29. 5, Aelian (second–third century AD), *On the Nature of Animals* 2. 9, Oppian (third century AD), *On Hunting* 2. 233–41.

783 *trees | . . . so dangerous*: cf. Virgil, *Eclogues* 10. 76 (juniper), Pliny, *Natural Histories* 16. 70, 17. 89 (box and walnut), but the phenomenon is connected with the poetic mountain of Helicon only by Lucretius, perhaps polemically.

810 *Scaptensula*: a town in Thrace fames for its mines (its name *Skapte Hule* in Greek means 'dug-out wood'). Ancient writers often commented on the appalling conditions in mines, often within a moralizing framework which criticized the whole enterprise: cf. Posidonius (first century BC) fr. 240 Kidd; J. F. Healy, *Mining and Metallurgy in the Greek and Roman World* (London, 1978), 133–8.

840 *Water in wells grows colder in the summer*: cf. Cicero, *On the Nature of the Gods* 2. 25, Diodorus Siculus 1. 141, Seneca, *Natural Questions* 4. 2. 26, 6. 13. 2. Pliny, *Natural Histories* 2. 227–35, has a long discussion of the properties of springs and wells: cf. also Antigonus of Carystus 133–65.

848 *shrine of Ammon*: Ammon or Hammon (Amun) was an Egyptian god identified with Jupiter. The spring at his shrine in the oasis of Siwa in the Libyan desert was described by Herodotus 4. 181 (and cf. e.g. Pliny, *Natural Histories* 2. 228).

879 *a cold spring*: at another prophetic site, that of Zeus at Dodona in north-west Greece, also described by Herodotus 2. 55–7, and Pliny, *Natural Histories* 2. 228.

890 *spring at Aradus*: Aradus (Awad) was an island off the coast of Phoenicia: for its freshwater spring, cf. Pliny, *Natural Histories* 2. 227, Strabo 16. 2. 13.

907–8 *that stone | Which the Greeks call magnet, naming it from its home*: the 'magnet' (lodestone, magnetite, magnetic iron ore) seems to have taken its name from Magnesia in Asia Minor. It had no practical use in the ancient world (the magnetic compass was first used in the West in the thirteenth century AD) but was another frequent source of wonder and speculation. Thales (fr. A22) thought the magnet was alive in some way: Empedocles (fr. A89) introduced explanation in terms of emanations and pores, and this was developed by the atomists, making use of their concept of the void (Democritus fr. A165). Epicurus thought that all attraction takes place by means of the rebounds and entanglements of atoms (fr. 293 Usener). Lucretius' account gives an important role to the void, but otherwise comes closer to that of Plato, who denies the notion of attraction, and explains the phenomenon in terms of the dislodgement and movement of air (*Timaeus* 80c, cf. Plutarch, *Platonic Questions* 7); this prepares for the role to be played by diseased air in the account of the plague. Lucretius' contemporary Asclepiades of Bithynia seems to have held similar views to Plato and Lucretius (cf. Epicurus fr. 293). Cf. also in general Plato, *Ion* 535d–e, Theophrastus, *On Stones* 29, Pliny, *Natural Histories* 34. 147, 36. 126 ff.

911 *A chain of little rings*: the description recalls Plato, *Ion* 535d–e; cf. Pliny, *Natural Histories* 34. 147.

917 *unless first | Much is established*: the recapitulation of the Epicurean theory of emanations and pores is also useful for the coming account of the plague; 923–35 are repeated from 4. 217–29 with minor changes.

946 *Food is diffused all through the veins*: cf. Epicurus fr. 293, which also makes an analogy between digestion and magnetic attraction: cf. 3. 703, and 6. 1129–30, 1167 in the plague section.

1033 *as wind drives sails and ship*: cf. 4. 897.

1044 *Samothracian irons*: iron amulets from the island of Samothrace in the Aegean (the home of the Cabeirian mysteries, whose initiates wore iron rings): cf. Isidore (seventh century AD), *Etymologies* 18. 32. 5, Pliny, *Natural Histories* 33. 23.

1058–61 *Gold . . . | Wood*: the same examples of non-magnetic substances occur in Plato (cf. Plutarch, *Platonic Questions* 7).

1065 *These properties are not so different | From others*: Philodemus in his treatise *On Signs* (8, 16) deals with problems raised by the apparent uniqueness of the magnet.

1069 *Bulls' glue*: cf. Aristotle, *History of Animals* 517^{b}29 ff., Pliny, *Natural Histories* 28. 236.

1078 *gold to gold one thing alone can bond*: a substance known as *chrysocolla* ('gold-glue'), possibly a flux or solder.

1084 *mutually opposing textures*: the interaction of substances here will again be recalled in the account of the plague, where the affinity proves lethal (cf. 1232 with 1016). The Jewish Greek philosopher Philo explicitly compares contagion and magnetism (*On Providence* 2. 90).

1087 *hooks and rings*: cf. Epicurus fr. 293 Usener.

1090 *the nature of diseases*: Book 6 and the work as a whole concludes with a general account of the causes of diseases (1090–1137), and a description of a specific example, the plague at Athens in 430–426 BC (1138–1286). The atomist explanation in terms of destructive particles connects the subject with the preceding wonders of nature which have been explained in similar terms, but the subject obviously has much greater significance. Like the Lisbon earthquake in Voltaire's *Candide*, the horrors of the plague are the ultimate demonstration that the world is not providentially ordered, but they also offer a test to the reader. An Epicurean should be able to cope even with this. The aetiology of disease was naturally much discussed by medical writers in the ancient world, but also received considerable attention from philosophers: amongst the pre-Socratic philosophers, Alcmaeon of Croton (fifth century BC) paid particular attention to the subject, and there is a famous treatment by Plato in the *Timaeus* (81e–87b), who was probably reacting to Democritean theorizing (cf. Plutarch, *Convivial Questions* 8. 9). The Lucretian account draws on the treatise *Airs, Waters, Plates* (fifth century BC) ascribed to Hippocrates, which stressed the role of environmental factors, but adds the twist that it is the corrupt air which here travels rather than human beings moving into an unaccustomed area.

1099 *from without*: i.e. from outside the world-system: cf. 6. 483–94, 954–5. Democritus held that, when worlds broke up, matter from them could enter other worlds and cause plagues and new diseases: theories of extraterrestrial causation have occasionally been revived in modern times (as most recently by the astronomer Fred Hoyle).

1101 *From the earth itself*: the commonest explanation for diseased air; cf. Hippocrates, *Airs, Waters, Plates* 10, [Aristotle], *Problems* 862ª, Diodorus Siculus 12. 58. 3, Galen, *On the differences in fevers* 1. 6. 7.

1107 *where the world's great pole | Leans sideways*: i.e. the earth's axis is inclined.

1108 *Pontus*: the area of Asia minor in the Black Sea (modern Turkey), representing the east, as Cadiz represents the west, Britain the north, and Egypt the south (cf. Juvenal, *Satires* 10. 1 ff.). Rome had fought a long war with Mithradates of Pontus, who died in 63 BC, less than a decade before the publication of *On the Nature of the Universe*.

1114 *the elephant disease*: i.e. elephantiasis, though some forms of leprosy also seem to have been included under the term. Lucretius' contemporary Asclepiades of Bithynia is said to have been the first to describe the disease (Plutarch, *Convivial Questions* 8. 9), but other sources say that it was mentioned by Erasistratus (fourth–third century BC) and Strato (third century BC). It is usually caused by parasitic worms.

1138 *the realms of Cecrops*: i.e. Athens, from the name of a mythical early king. He appears in encomia of Athens celebrating the fact that the Athenians were 'autochthonous' or born of the land: ironically here, while they do not move, the plague is an unwelcome immigrant. Lucretius' account of the epidemic at Athens in 430–426 BC is based closely on that given by the fifth-century BC historian Thucydides in his *History of the Peloponnesian War* (2. 47–52), with the addition of some details from medical writings. What the 'plague' actually was remains controversial: the agent responsible may no longer be extant or may have mutated. Lucretius' tactic of using the horrors of the disease to offset the glories of the opening celebration of Athenian civilization picks up a similar contrast in Thucydides with Pericles' famous Funeral Speech in praise of the city, which immediately precedes the description of the epidemic (2. 35–46). In turn, Lucretius' account was much imitated: cf. Virgil, *Georgics* 3. 478–566, Ovid, *Metamorphoses* 7. 523–613, Seneca, *Oedipus* 110–201.

1139 *Laid waste the fields*: the plague is figured as an invading army (like that of the Spartans), pillaging the countryside, cutting communications with the city, and then besieging and sacking it. By contrast, in Thucydides the epidemic begins in the harbour of the Piraeus (2. 48. 2).

1142 *traversing a wide expanse of air*: while Thucydides also has an Egyptian origin for the epidemic, he lays stress on its transmission by human beings (2. 47. 1, 58. 2), whereas Lucretius emphasizes an airborne miasma.

1143 *all the people of Pandion*: Pandion was another early king of Athens: there is a play on the first part of his name, which means 'all'.

1154 *a noisome stench*: the human body has become a place of evil-smelling exhalations, as earlier the earth had been (810 ff.).

1166 *as if burnt into it*: an allusion to the torture of slaves, cf. 3. 1017.

1167 *The accursed fire*: *sacer ignis*, or erysipelas, a streptococcal skin infection: cf. 660.

1169 *as in a furnace*: a recurring image in Book 6: cf. 146 ff., 199 ff., 278, 281.

1174 *hurled themselves headlong into wells*: cf. Daniel Defoe, *Journal of the Plague Year*: 'some broke out into the streets, perhaps naked, and would run directly down to the river if they were not stopped by the watchman or other officers, and plunge themselves into the water wherever they found it' (Penguin edn., p. 99).

1182–98 *many signs of death*: this section has no counterpart in Thucydides, but recalls lists of symptoms enumerated in short phrases without syntactical connection found in the Hippocratic corpus (especially Hippocrates' *Prognostica*, a work on which the Epicurean Demetrius Lacon is said to have written a commentary).

1186 *either panting fast or deep and laboured*: similar alternatives are mentioned in Hippocrates, *Prognostica* 5.

1193 *Nostrils were pinched*: the following lines are based on a famous description of the human face at the time of death in Hippocrates, *Prognostica* 2.

1222 *man's faithful friends the dogs*: in Thucydides, dogs are seen as carrion-eating animals, whereas in Lucretius they die at their posts as faithful servants of the house.

1233 *Losing all heart*: cf. Defoe, *Journal of the Plague Year*, 183–4: 'in the plague, it came at last to such violence that the people sat still looking at one another, and seemed quite abandoned to despair.'

1236 *contagion*: the word *contagium* (literally 'contact') developed the sense 'contagion' from its use of the sheep disease scabies.

1239 *Men shunned the sick-beds*: the added twist that even those who tried to avoid nursing their relatives and friends died is Lucretian: Thucydides (2. 51. 5) mentions only the patients dying for lack of care.

1247–51 *one upon another . . .* : these lines are clearly out of place in the manuscripts: the parallel account in Thucydides (2. 52. 4) suggests that they come after 1286, and they are probably the original concluding lines to the whole poem, with 1251–2 'Nor could a man be found at such a time | Whom neither plague nor death nor grief had touched', a generalizing epigrammatic conclusion. Like the *Iliad*, *On the Nature of the Universe* ends with a funeral, but with one which lacks all sense of resolution and reintegration of the mourners.

1252–8 *Moreover now the shepherd . . .* : these lines have no counterpart in Thucydides, and the stress on the pathetic deaths of the rural poor is perhaps a Roman element (later accentuated in Virgil's plague episode at the end of *Georgics* Book 3). Cf. 2. 1164 ff., 5. 1386 ff.

1274 *The shrines of the celestials*: the uselessness of religion is emphasized by the contrast between the 'celestial' nature of the gods and the corpses of the men they could not help.

1277 *present grief was all*: the epiphany of pain has ironically routed the gods of religion: instead of the presence of the god, we have only grief.

1278 *the ancient customs . . . | Of burial*: Athens was renowned for its public funerals of the dead killed in war, such as inspired Pericles' 'Funeral Speech' in Thucydides.

1284 *with frenzied cries*: the shouts of the brawling mourners are a parody of the normal *conclamatio* or 'calling' to the dead man: see above on 3. 468.

A SELECTION OF OXFORD WORLD'S CLASSICS

American Literature

British and Irish Literature

Children's Literature

Classics and Ancient Literature

Colonial Literature

Eastern Literature

European Literature

History

Medieval Literature

Oxford English Drama

Poetry

Philosophy

Politics

Religion

The Oxford Shakespeare

A complete list of Oxford Paperbacks, including Oxford World's Classics, OPUS, Past Masters, Oxford Authors, Oxford Shakespeare, Oxford Drama, and Oxford Paperback Reference, is available in the UK from the Academic Division Publicity Department, Oxford University Press, Great Clarendon Street, Oxford OX2 6DP.

In the USA, complete lists are available from the Paperbacks Marketing Manager, Oxford University Press, 198 Madison Avenue, New York, NY 10016.

Oxford Paperbacks are available from all good bookshops. In case of difficulty, customers in the UK can order direct from Oxford University Press Bookshop, Freepost, 116 High Street, Oxford OX1 4BR, enclosing full payment. Please add 10 per cent of published price for postage and packing.